ELEPHANT TREES, COPALES, AND CUAJIOTES

Elephant Trees,
Copales, and Cuajiotes

A NATURAL HISTORY OF BURSERA

JUDITH BECERRA AND DAVID YETMAN

Foreword by Exequiel Ezcurra

THE UNIVERSITY OF
ARIZONA PRESS

TUCSON

The University of Arizona Press
www.uapress.arizona.edu

We respectfully acknowledge the University of Arizona is on the land and territories of Indigenous peoples. Today, Arizona is home to twenty-two federally recognized tribes, with Tucson being home to the O'odham and the Yaqui. Committed to diversity and inclusion, the University strives to build sustainable relationships with sovereign Native Nations and Indigenous communities through education offerings, partnerships, and community service.

ISBN-13: 978-0-8165-5194-1 (paperback)
ISBN-13: 978-0-8165-5195-8 (ebook)

Cover design by Leigh McDonald
Cover photographs: flycatcher photo by P. Percal, copal offering photo by César Rodríguez, all others by J. Becerra and L. Venable
Designed and typeset by Sara Thaxton in 10.5/15 Warnock Pro with Bulmer MT Std. All images in this book are licensed under CC BY-SA 2.0 unless otherwise indicated.

Library of Congress Cataloging-in-Publication Data
Names: Becerra, Judith, 1961– author. | Yetman, David, 1941– author.
Title: Elephant trees, copales, and cuajiotes : a natural history of Bursera / Judith Becerra and
    David Yetman ; foreword by Exequiel Ezcurra.
Description: Tucson : University of Arizona Press, 2024. | Includes bibliographical references
    and index.
Identifiers: LCCN 2023016728 (print) | LCCN 2023016729 (ebook) | ISBN 9780816551941
    (paperback) | ISBN 9780816551958 (ebook)
Subjects: LCSH: Bursera. | Bursera—Ecology. | Bursera—Geographical distribution.
Classification: LCC QK495.B8 B43 2024 (print) | LCC QK495.B8 (ebook) | DDC 583/.75—dc23/
    eng/20230722
LC record available at https://lccn.loc.gov/2023016728
LC ebook record available at https://lccn.loc.gov/2023016729

Printed in the United States of America
♾ This paper meets the requirements of ANSI/NISO Z39.48-1992 (Permanence of Paper).

Jerzy Rzedowski and Graciela Calderón de Rzedowski in their laboratory. Photo taken in 2018 by A. Barbosa.

This book is dedicated to the late Jerzy Rzedowski and Graciela Calderón de Rzedowski, not only for their devotion to the study of *Bursera* but also for their kindness and generosity of spirit. The authors also want to dedicate the book to Judith's family, Larry and Gabriela.

I, the singer, entered into the house strewn with flowers, where stood upright the emerald drum, where awaiting the Giver of Life the nobles strewed flowers around, the place where the head is bowed for lustration, the house of corrupt odors, where the burning fragrant copal incense spreads and penetrates, intoxicating our souls in the presence of the Cause of All.

—A song of Aztec festivals

CONTENTS

FOREWORD

Exequiel Ezcurra

If something is common to the great religions of the world, it is the use of aromatic resins for spiritual contemplation and prayer. As early as 2600 BCE, myrrh was being used in the Old Kingdoms of Egypt for embalming and purification. Buddhism, Judaism, Christianity, Hinduism, and Islam have all used different forms of incense for offerings, purification, and cleansing. Completely separated from the Old World by two large oceans, the inhabitants of Mesoamerica developed strikingly convergent practices, using a neotropical resin called copal for aromatic smoking, medicinal uses, and especially for religious offerings. But if different isolated civilizations, a world apart, gave these aromatic resins such surprisingly similar spiritual uses, the fact becomes even more remarkable when we realize that all these resins are extracted from trees in a single botanical family, the Burseraceae, whose species are distributed in all continents along the tropical dry forests and hot drylands of the Northern Hemisphere. To perhaps oversimplify their complex natural history, balsamic resins from the Burseraceae are classified into three large groups: Frankincense is extracted from trees in the genus *Boswellia*, growing mostly in the Arabian Peninsula, India, and the Horn of Africa. Myrrh is extracted from trees in the genus *Commiphora*, common in African dry woodlands and present in the dry forests of Asia and the Caribbean. And, finally, copal is extracted from trees in the genus *Bursera*, a lineage that has evolved and diversified into myriad species in the dry tropical valleys of Mesoamerica.

Despite the immense importance of the Burseraceae in the evolution of human spirituality and ethnomedicine, it is surprising how little is known about these extraordinary trees. Ask any Bible scholar what is myrrh, that miraculous product that the wise men of the Orient offered to the baby Jesus and was considered as valuable as gold, and in most cases, you will get an ambiguous reply. The Burseraceae have

accompanied human spiritual evolution for millennia, they have guided our medi-
tations and our thoughts, they have helped us reflect on the meaning of compassion
and on existence itself, and yet they are largely unknown to the general population.

Although there are many highly technical research papers on the chemistry,
ecology, taxonomy, and ethnobotany of the genus *Bursera* (many from Judith Becerra, the first author of this volume), there are no books synthesizing the natural
history of these remarkable trees. Becerra and David Yetman's book is a very welcome effort to put together the taxonomic and ethnobotanical knowledge on the
copales of Mesoamerica. This is the reason why I find this book so interesting and
so necessary: very few persons, including many field botanists, seem to know much
about these fascinating plants that have been so critically important in the evolution of traditional knowledge and natural resource use in the deserts and drylands
of North America.

And the authors carry out their task with remarkable success: the text is written
in an entertaining, nonspecialized language that makes it easy to read and very
interesting to reflect upon. For example, throughout the book Becerra and Yetman
discuss how the Mexican burseras superficially resemble many trees in the sister
family Anacardiaceae, the sumac family. But despite the superficial similarity, they
show us, the difference is critical. While the Burseraceae carry fragrant terpenes
in their resin ducts, many Anacardiaceae carry a highly allergenic substance called
urushiol that can cause painful rashes. Reading Becerra and Yetman's engaging text,
I suddenly realized what excellent botanists the Mesoamerican people were (and still
are). Many Mexican trees in the Anacardiaceae have Nahuatl names starting with
the prefix "copal-" to indicate their morphological similarity with the true burseras,
like *Copalcuahuitl*, the "green bud that looks like copal" (*Schinus molle*); *Copalxo-
cotl*, the "copal-resembling wild plum" (*Cyrtocarpa procera*); or *Copalquín*, the "false
copal" (*Cyrtocarpa edulis*). Indeed, reading this book will give any person interested
in the natural history and ethnobotany of Aridamerica and the Mesoamerican dry
tropics an inspirational deluge of ideas on the evolution of our drylands and the long
and fascinating human interaction with their unique flora. With a balanced mixture
of natural history, taxonomy, ecology, chemistry, and ethnobotany, the authors have
produced a fascinating synthesis.

ACKNOWLEDGMENTS

Judith Becerra wishes to acknowledge the generous assistance and support of Larry Venable; Joaquín Ruiz, Biosphere 2, University of Arizona; the Alfred P. Sloan Foundation; the Beckman Foundation; the National Science Foundation; and the National Geographic Society.

ELEPHANT TREES, COPALES, AND CUAJIOTES

Introduction

If you go hiking on the south-facing slopes of South Mountain Municipal Park in Phoenix, Arizona, you may come upon a strange, small tree not much larger than a shrub that resembles an overgrown bonsai, growing from what appears to be bare rock. It sports a swollen trunk—sometimes grotesquely so—and thick branches that often curl and dance around each other. The bark of the trunk and of the thicker branches is of a nondescript sandy hue with hints of green, but the smaller branches are often reddish. Look more closely and you will notice that the bark is papery and will pull off in semitransparent little sheets. The branches may sport a few fruits the size of currants—greenish when fresh; brownish, tough-skinned when dried. If they are fresh, wiggle one off and it will moisten your fingers. Taste it and you will find a pleasant, sour sensation. It will not harm you. It might even help whatever ails you.

Unless rains have failed to materialize for several months, the branch tips will support tiny greenish leaves. Crush them between your fingers and resin will cover your fingertips and give off a fresh scent somewhere between turpentine and pine incense. It is a plant like none other in the region and with good reason is called the elephant tree. Carve into the bark with a fingernail and a seemingly clear liquid will ooze out. It has the same pleasant smell, but do not let this liquid touch your clothes, unless you wish the garment to receive a permanent reddish stain.

This is the Southwest's lone member of *Bursera*, a genus made of 114 species that extends from here to northern South America.[1] In the United States, the elephant tree occurs only on hyperarid hills and mountainsides in the hot southwest lowlands of Arizona and in a few boulder-strewn lowland sites in southeastern Cali-

---

1. At least five records of *B. fagaroides*, a related species, were collected in Fresnal Canyon in the Baboquivari Mountains south of Tucson in the early twentieth century. Many are those who have since searched in vain for that small tree(s).

FIGURE I.1 *Bursera microphylla* in La Paz, Baja California (photo by L. Venable).

fornia like Anza-Borrego Desert State Park, where a trail is named after it. Scarce in the United States, it is common across the border in northwestern Sonora, Mexico, and in much of Baja California. In Mexico, the trees may reach 10 meters in height and resemble a more normal tree, but in the United States 3 meters is their common limit, and their trunks' branches are usually contorted, often assuming outrageous postures.

The elephant tree (*Bursera microphylla*; microphylla = tiny leaf) is the Southwest's ambassador of the genus *Bursera*, a collection of species that offers a spectrum of tree sizes, bark colors and textures, and aromatics unlike any other plant genus. A different species, *Bursera simaruba*, frequents the Everglades swamp system in southwestern Florida, flourishing on small islands of limestone that rise ever so slightly above water level. There it is called gumbo-limbo and is usually recognized by its attractive dark, shiny-green bark that peels away in reddish sheets that may cause the trunk to appear red. In Mexico, the gumbo-limbo reaches nearly 30 meters in height and sports a spreading crown.

Throughout its range, including southern Florida, residents plant gumbo-limbos to line streets and exhibit their green/red trunks. In tropical Mexico and Central America, farmers and ranchers lop off 2-meter-long branches and stick them in

FIGURE I.2 *Bursera simaruba* in southern Florida.

the ground. They soon take root and become living fence posts, often engulfing the barbed wire stapled to them. The trees lack the strong aromatic property that makes many other *Bursera* species notable.

These two species comprise the U.S. representation of the Burseraceae, the Torchwood family. Travel 2,000 kilometers south into Mexico and you may find 50 *Bursera* species in one drainage basin, a profusion of evolution so complex that only experts can distinguish among the species. Elephant trees range over more than 1,000 kilometers. Some *Bursera* species in the southern regions are limited to a radius of less than 50 kilometers.

Place our two species side by side and the differences are startling: the gumbo-limbo is tall, with a slender trunk and thick branches rising smoothly, its bark shiny, colorful, and flaking, larger trees with a spreading crown of large and lustrous leaves. The elephant trees from the southwestern United States are rather short, their bark duller. Their branches often grow more horizontally than vertically—out rather than up. The light-brown color of their trunks often matches the bare rock from which they grow. They may have no leaves at all. Neither plant offers much in the way of notable flowers, for they are small or even tiny, appearing for only short annual bursts and then for only a few days. These small flowers are characteristic of the genus. Fruits are seldom larger than peas. From their habitats, we know that neither species will tolerate freezing temperatures well, though the elephant tree seems to survive a few, brief degrees of frost, often at the cost of branch dieback that results in distorted tree shapes. In addition, *B. microphylla* is a desert plant. It prefers rocky soils, survives temperatures well over 45°C, and can persist for many months without rainfall, while *B. simaruba* must have deeper soils and abundant rainfall.

The two species mark the ends of the spectrum in the family. Between these extremes of distribution, size, and shape grow a bewildering diversity of species, most readily distinguished by their leaves, their bark, and their growth habits. Where these two outliers are found is also significant, for each flourishes in a habitat not characteristic of the *Bursera* genus as a whole. The elephant tree is supremely adapted to survival in deserts, where a year may pass with little or no rain, while the gumbo-limbo is completely at home at the margins of swamps or in a lushly tropical rainforest. It must have reliable rain, preferably a lot of it.

Across the border in Mexico, the elephant tree goes by *torote*, a name shared in the region by other burseras and by swollen-stemmed plants from other families as well.[2] Within a hundred miles of the border, additional burseras appear, with names like *torote de agua*, *torote amarillo*, *torote copal*, *torote prieto*, and *torote*

---

2. A superficially similar tree in Baja California also goes by the English common name, elephant tree, but is a different species, *Pachycormus discolor*, from a different family, Anacardiaceae. Its most widespread Spanish name is *copalquín*.

puntagruesa. Another is called *palo mulato*. Arizona and California share one species of *Bursera*. Sonora, the Mexican state adjacent to the south, has 9—some say 10. Some grow to be large trees. *Bursera* species extend south to the north of Brazil and Peru and in the West Indies, but Mexico must be considered *Bursera* heartland. It is home to the overwhelming bulk of species, is where the genus originated, and is home to the current evolutionary hotspots. After Mexico, the region of second-highest diversity and endemism for *Bursera* is the Greater Antilles and the Bahamas archipelago, where about 16 species occur, 14 of them endemic to the region.

Species of *Bursera* are most comfortable in tropical deciduous forests (also known as tropical dry forests), habitats of seasonally deciduous trees. A wide strip of this forest grows on mountainous slopes of western Mexico near the Gulf of California or the Pacific Ocean from Sonora in the north to the Isthmus of Tehuantepec in the south. *Bursera* grows farther south: South America has about 5. But Mexico has at least 90 species. And nearly all are plants of tropical deciduous forests, which makes the 2 U.S. species a bit nonconforming.

Mexican plant enthusiasts, with some justification, consider the genus a symbol of Mexico: it is extraordinarily diverse, and mostly tropical or semitropical. Wherever burseras abound, they are intimately incorporated into the local culture and form a part of indigenous industry, pharmacopeia, and art.

The greatest proliferation of species occurs precisely in the areas of the greatest national violence: the Balsas Basin, shared by the states of Guerrero and Michoacán in the southern part of Mexico. Furthermore, studies of the evolution of this genus reveal increasingly sophisticated defense against forces that attack the plants, mainly herbivorous insects. Drug wars among rival cartels and government forces have escalated over the years in the Balsas Basin, but in that *Bursera*-rich region, pitched battles have been taking place for millions of years between the multitude of *Bursera* species and creatures that would eat and damage them, primarily insects, at least in recent millennia. The story of that battle makes for one of nature's most intriguing struggles. The wide variety of aromatic oils that burseras produce is indicative of the plants' ongoing arsenal of weapons against herbivores of any stripe. One tree-sized species, *B. penicillata*, found as far north as central Sonora, produces an aroma so potent that the human nose can detect the tree's presence from afar.

Plant taxonomists (which include many informally trained resident field botanists) nonchalantly call these plants burseras, an informality that we follow here. In Mexico they divide them into two groups, both with names from Náhuatl, the language of the Aztecs: *copales*, trees with non-exfoliating bark; and *cuajiotes*, trees with colorful trunks, usually with exfoliating bark. Copales have mostly grayish bark, and several species are widely praised for the fragrant resin they produce, called *copal*. It serves as pungent incense that is collected and widely marketed. Alas, this

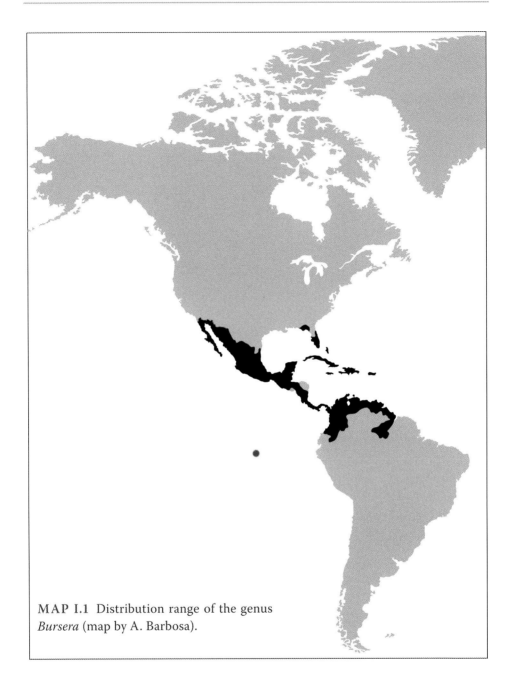

MAP I.1 Distribution range of the genus *Bursera* (map by A. Barbosa).

division does not always work in other places, such as the Caribbean. A group of burseras, all of them close relatives to *Bursera simaruba* (except for *B. graveolens*), have claimed these islands, and a good number do not seem to follow the rule that as cuajiotes they should have exfoliating bark. Instead, they present themselves with a dull, uniformly grayish exterior.

FIGURE I.3 Chemical defense in *Bursera schlechtendalii*. In *Bursera* the terpene-containing resin is stored in canals that travel along the cortex of the stems and along the leaf veins. In some species this resin is highly volatile and under pressure. When a leaf or a part of a leaf is injured, a syringe-like spray of resin is released. This squirt can travel as far as 2 m and last for several seconds. These resins are toxic, become sticky, and can deter or entrap defoliators (photo by L. Venable).

Vendors in nearly every public market in southern Mexico offer the resinous incense copal, widely burned by sprinkling it on burning charcoal in homes and shrines, at fiestas, and in religious ceremonies. Some traditional markets offer several varieties of copal, each with its distinct aroma and derived from a different copal species.[3] The incense-producing property of burseras is not surprising, for the frankincense and myrrh of old are derived from close Arabian relatives.

The trunks and lower branches of many *Bursera* species are thickly muscular, others less so. The bark of some species changes color from one season to the next. Among exfoliating species, the sheets often differ in color from the trunk, and scratching the bark surface may reveal a color beneath that is dramatically different from the outer layer. Part of the burseras' mystique lies in the rainbow of colors of their bark and, in some cases, their flowers and fruits—small, fleeting, but viewed up close, intriguing.

3. In some highland localities in Mexico and Central America, the sap of pine trees is also called copal, and it is collected and distributed to regional markets.

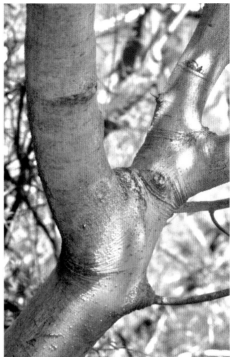

FIGURE I.4 *Bursera* species exhibit 2 main bark types: (A) colorful and exfoliating; (B) grayish and non-exfoliating and often smooth (photos by J. Becerra and L. Venable).

Most burseras shed their leaves at the advent of the dry season and leaf out around the onset of the rainy season, a characteristic typical of trees of the dry tropical forests. Many flower when leafless, immediately prior to the expected rainy season. Plant taxonomists, when classifying plants, prefer samples with leaves along with flowers for identification purposes. Burseras make this task difficult. Leaves are often the only recourse.

The wide diversity of species also makes for a wide variety of woods, many of them quite fragrant. Several species yield wood ideal for producing arts and crafts—masks, carved figures, aboriginal musical instruments, boxes, and bowls. The popularity of these woods often works to the great detriment of large populations of the more accessible trees. Olinalá, Guerrero, and San Martín Tilcajete, Oaxaca, have become centers of artisan production of crafts incorporating the wood of a *Bursera* and employing much of the community. Their consumption of that wood has exhausted most of the easily available sources of the lumber and forced carvers to resort to wood (usually inferior) of different species and forced suppliers to extend the range of wood cutting. The resulting deforestation is subtle and seldom attracts attention but has dire consequences. In both cases, communities have undertaken reforestation projects. Their limited scope and the slow growth rate of the preferred species, however, dampen the prospects for timely replacement of harvested trees.

In this book, we present the genus *Bursera*. The species are sometimes fiendishly difficult to distinguish from each other. Aesthetically, they top the list of attractive trees, even if their flowers and fruits are less than spectacular and the shade they produce less than all-encompassing. From a scientific standpoint, study of the burseras and their evolution is intimately related to the evolution of the Mexican landscape, inseparable from the work of tectonic forces that produced modern Mexico and the convulsions that shook the earth over the ages. We address the puzzling and impressive distribution of the genus and pursue the question of why so many species are crowded into a relatively small region. We follow the ecological intricacies of speciation and specialization in the genus, and the dynamics of *Bursera*'s evolution. We describe the peculiar biochemistry that has evolved in some members of the genus to produce the dazzling array of defenses and offenses, and, in the process, we describe how some insects may coevolve with the burseras' defenses. Finally, we examine briefly the economic importance of burseras and consider their future evolution and adaptation.

This book will show you why we consider the genus *Bursera* the most interesting in the world of plants.

CHAPTER 1

The Physical Setting

Mexico's Mountain Ranges and Climate

Mexico's topography has shaped the evolution of the tree-rich genus *Bursera* like none other and helps explain the complexities of burseras' distribution. Four major mountain chains figure prominently in Mexico's climate and hydrology. Two mountain ranges border the eastern and western portions of Mexico's north, which is largely a plateau: the Sierra Madre Oriental that parallels the coast of the Gulf of Mexico on the east, and the Sierra Madre Occidental that parallels the Gulf of California and the Pacific Ocean on the west. The ranges also parallel each other, plunging northwest-southeast until they intersect a third mountain range, the Trans-Mexican Volcanic Belt (TMVB), also known as the Neovolcanic Axis, which runs east-west at about latitude 19° N. When framed by the U.S. border on the north and the Trans-Mexican Volcanic Belt on the south, the ranges complete the sides of a parallelogram.

The interior enclosed by these ranges is the mostly arid to semiarid Mexican Plateau, which slopes from well over 2,000 m in elevation in the south to about 1,000 m in the north. The lengthy sierras intercept oceanic moisture—the Sierra Madre Oriental from the Gulf of Mexico, the Sierra Madre Occidental from the Gulf of California and the Pacific Ocean. That trapping, wringing action has left the vast interior starved for rain, except in the vicinity of the TMVB at the southern end, and where interior mountains are high enough to trap remaining moisture for themselves.

The Sierra Madre Occidental is about 1,200 km in length and reaches nearly into the United States, or slightly into it, depending on one's geological viewpoint. The highest peaks reach 3,300 m (nearly 10,800 feet), and the range presents a thick and convoluted mass so dissected and irregular that until the mid-twentieth century, no paved road crossed the range. The country rock is primarily volcanic, derived from enormous outpourings of lava and depositions of welded tuff and ignimbrites from

MAP 1.1 Mexico is the center of diversification of *Bursera*, where there are at least 90 species, most of them concentrated in the basin of the Balsas River in the south of the country. Mountain ranges, in particular the Sierra Madre Occidental and the Trans-Mexican Volcanic Belt, have allowed these tropical plants to thrive by protecting them from freezing Artic winds (map by P. Mirocha).

volcanic explosions ranging from the late Cretaceous (about 70 million years ago) well into the Miocene (about 20 million years ago). The western scarp of the range is replete with canyons that provide an endless variety of habitats. The lower reaches of this landscape, especially the foothills, are protected from frigid arctic air masses by intervening mountains to the north and are mostly frost-free from central Sonora south. This topographical barrier provides protection considerably farther north than frost-free zones on the eastern slopes of the Sierra Madre Oriental, accommodating tropical deciduous forests on the western slopes.

The Sierra Madre Oriental is primarily composed of limestone and other sedimentary rocks of the Mesozoic age. The chain extends roughly from the Big Bend in Texas to its intersection with the TMVB in the state of Veracruz, about 1,100 km. While in general the chain is not as dissected as its western counterpart, peaks reach 3,700 m (12,000 feet) elevation. The uplift of the range began about 20 million years ago.

The east-west Trans-Mexican Volcanic Belt, a string of volcanoes roughly 1,000 km in length, is a third physiographic factor in Mexican climates and habitats. At the eastern end is the towering but dormant Citlaltépetl (also called Pico de Orizaba), whose summit reaches 5,636 m in elevation (18,491 feet), the highest peak in North America south of Alaska, and the second most prominent volcanic peak in the world after Africa's Mount Kilimanjaro. At the western end is Nevado de Colima (Zapotépetl), another inactive volcano at 4,260 m (13,976 feet) in elevation. The Neovolcanic Axis is also the source of rivers that drain south into the Balsas Basin. Parícutin Volcano, which erupted from a cornfield in 1943, lies in the forested highlands toward the western end of the Axis.

Finally, the Sierra Madre del Sur completes the series of mountain chains that affect the bulk of the Mexican mainland. It runs for roughly 1,000 km along southern Mexico's Pacific Coast, slightly northwest to southeast, roughly parallel to the Neovolcanic Axis. Although its highest peaks are more than 3,700 m (12,000 feet) in elevation, it is the most tropical of the ranges. Its slopes feature coniferous forests at the highest elevation, moist tropical cloud forests at intermediate altitudes, and tropical deciduous forests at the lower elevation along the coast.

The four mountain ranges exert a powerful influence on Mexico's climate. In general, the country experiences moist summers and relatively dry winters. The rainy season extends from May through September in the south and west, somewhat shorter in the north. The extreme east, the Gulf of Mexico coast, often experiences more rain in the fall and winter months. The coastal areas of Veracruz, southern Tamaulipas, and Tabasco are remarkably wetter than the remainder of the country and receive year-round rainfall, often in copious amounts.

Hurricanes often affect the country, especially the southern portions. They may originate in the Atlantic Ocean or Gulf of Mexico and affect the Yucatán Peninsula as well as the remainder of the eastern seaboard. These sometimes powerful storms usually occur in mid-summer. In the Pacific Ocean, hurricanes originate south in the Gulf of Tehuantepec, at times beginning in June, and may exert a profound effect on coastal areas up to the south of Baja California, sometimes causing extensive flooding and landslides. For the most part, however, the climate of *Bursera* country in Mexico is predictable: a long dry season beginning in September and continuing through May or June, and a wet season of often daily rains, ranging from May through September. The regular pattern of rainfall has been an important variable in *Bursera* evolution.

CHAPTER 2

American Tropical Deciduous Forests

Tropical deciduous forests consist of dense communities dominated by low- to medium-sized trees that lose their leaves during the dry season. For about six months, often more, the forest presents a desolate and brownish-gray aspect, a mass of almost undifferentiated, bare tree trunks, dried vines, and withered ground-story shrubs and herbs. Howard Scott Gentry, one of the first plant explorers to provide a detailed description of the tropical deciduous forest (he referred to it as the *short tree forest*), captures it well:

> During the fall the air moves in sporadic gusts, which seem to have no other direction than that of the colored autumnal leaves they disturb and carry downward from the trees. They suddenly startle the great infinity of forest silence into local multitudinous rustle of descending leaves, of flapping paper-like copal bark, of rubbing branches, only to drop as suddenly back again into a pervasive silence.
>
> Out of the sea in the spring come the westerlies, which blow over the coastal valleys and the thorn forest. They are hardly felt over the short-tree forest, for the outer ranges buffet the winds aloft and they gain little purchase against the canyon sides and bottoms. On the plains the forest stands withering under the clear sun, until nearly all but the riparian plants are stayed into a spring dormancy. The arid breath of the westerlies aggravates the dry season and increases the transpiration of the plants, and during its continuation many of the deciduous trees shed the last of their leaves. (1942, 129)

Gentry described from personal experience the bleakness of the dry forest in the dry season:

In the long spring dry season the forest is a dreary scene: a naked infinite host of trunks and branches, spreading interminably over the volcanic hills and mesas, bared to the fiery sun, under which the last leaf seems to have withered and died. He who walks this land in the month of May walks with a parched throat. The plants are waiting for the rains and their union with the soil. (1942, 134)

The bleakness of the dry season landscape makes a remarkable contrast with the profuse greenness of the forest during the rainy season, for most species leaf out within a few days of the onset of rains or even with the arrival of higher humidity that precedes the first rains. Before long the forest becomes almost impenetrable, an unending tangle of newly sprouted leaves, branches, vines, and fast-growing ground plants, a mosaic of what seems to be an infinite expanse of shades of green. With the explosion of leaves of hundreds of plant species come hordes of insect herbivores

FIGURE 2.1 Landscape seasonal changes in the tropical deciduous forest around Chamela, Jalisco: (A) dry season; (B) rainy season (photos by A. Verduzco).

eager to feast on the fast-developing cornucopia of greenery. Some smaller insects welcome the arrival of humans as well.

This vegetation is characteristic of the west and the south of Mexico. It follows the Pacific slopes of Mexico, covering vast expanses from southern Sonora and extreme southwestern Chihuahua to the southern state of Chiapas. In northern Mexico, it develops mostly on the western slopes of the Sierra Madre Occidental at altitudes from 0 to 1,900 m elevation. In the south, it runs along the coast of Nayarit and Colima and then penetrates deeply inland along the Río Santiago and Río Balsas and their tributaries. From there it reaches eastward to the Valley of Tehuacán in Puebla and the Valley of Cuicatlán in Oaxaca, both of which lie in the drainage of the Gulf of Mexico.

Tropical deciduous forests form ragged patches that continue from Mexico into Costa Rica and Panama. They follow the coast of Ecuador and reach the north of Venezuela and Colombia at the east and eastern slopes of the Andes, often blanketing the transition zone between Andean montane forest and the *llanos* or plains below. In Cuba, Hispaniola, and Jamaica, tropical deciduous forests cover extensive areas. Farther south, the drylands of the Gran Chaco in Paraguay and the sertão—the Atlantic dry forest in northeastern Brazil—are the major extensions of this vegetation in South America. Alas, *Bursera* does not make it there.

MAP 2.1 Distribution range of tropical deciduous forest vegetation in Mexico. These forests have been severely reduced by deforestation, farming, and ranching. It is calculated that less than 20 percent of its former extent remains (map adapted from Rzedowski 1978).

The variation in leafing out and flowering of trees in tropical deciduous forests is a remarkable manifestation of plant diversification and adaptation. Although 95 percent of the trees of most tropical dry forest habitats drop their leaves, each species has its own schedule, some doing so at the first hint of the end of the rains, others persisting until well into the dry season, while some put out several successive cohorts of leaves during each rainy season. Some species drop their leaves quickly, others gradually, others over a period of weeks. As the rainless weeks pass, even the most persistent leaves gradually wither. The leaves of diehard species exhibit a nearly desiccated green condition. Leaves of some species turn colorful. Those of *Sebastiania pavoniana* (Euphorbiaceae) turn a bright red, leading many observers initially to mistake them for flowers. Leaves of *Bursera penicillata* turn bright yellow and are persistent, keeping a cheerful hue within the gathering loss of color about them. Leaves of other species melt into drab-brown insignificance.

Though most species in tropical deciduous forests flower shortly before or shortly after the onset of the rains, flowering periods are also highly diverse. A notable example of the species-specific schedule of leaf dropping and flowering is *Conzattia multiflora* (Fabaceae), usually the tallest tree in the forest. It has highly visible yellow flowers that appear long into the dry season, and its bronze-colored seed pods persist for many weeks, easily being mistaken for reddish flowers. *Conzattia* is late in leafing out, seemingly reluctant to make a bold move as it awaits the first rains. And at the slightest hint of hot, dry weather toward the end of the rainy period, it drops its leaves, seemingly overnight, and becomes a naked beacon in the forest.

Many species from the tropical deciduous forests flower beginning in midwinter (or mid–dry season), each careful not to overlap too broadly with its competitors, thereby being forced to share pollinators, which may be scarce during the dry season. The variation in flowering time is a refreshing manifestation of colors, each species presenting its own dry season tableau without much in the way of competition. Most notable early flower producers are the morning glory trees, *Ipomoea* (Convolvulaceae), which feature showy white blooms in the heart of the dry season, and *amapas*: *Handroanthus chrysanthus* (yellow) and *H. impetiginosus* (rose) (Bignoniaceae), rather large trees compared with other members of the forest, and with a dazzling and dense array of blooms. The yellow-flowered buttercup tree, *Cochlospermum vitifolium* (Bixaceae), is also notable for its brilliant, large yellow blooms that appear when the tree is leafless. The cosmopolitan kapoks, *Ceiba* sp. (Malvaceae), drop their leaves slowly, and flower and fruit gradually, their mango-sized pods bursting open and expelling their fine fibers well into the dry season. Equally prominent but blooming late in the dry season is the small tree *Plumeria rubra* (Apocynaceae), the frangipane, with its brilliant-white terminal flowers. The coral bean tree, *Erythrina flabelliformis* (Fabaceae), sends out large, brilliant-red, spear-like blooms from its naked branches even later, but invariably prior to leafing out.

The window for many flowers is short, as the number of species is great, and all must offer their flowers for pollination to the limited supply of pollinators. After the initial drought of the dry months, some tree or another is usually in flower and taking advantage of the work of pollinators, a situation that somewhat redeems the otherwise unending aesthetic drabness of the tropical deciduous forest during the months of no rain.

Occasionally, rains do occur during the normally dry season, especially late-season hurricanes. The response of trees to these unusual bursts of moisture depends on the species. Some will leaf out; others, more obdurate, will not.

Some trees anticipate the rainy season, leafing out well in advance of the rains, thus gaining a photosynthetic advantage. They accomplish this, however, at the risk of damage posed by an extended dry season. Notable examples of early leafing are *Lysiloma watsonii* (Fabaceae), often called *tepeguaje*, which may be the only green spot in the forest a month or so prior to the advent of rains. Another is *Jatropha cordata* (Euphorbiaceae), which sends out rather large, dark, shiny leaves, usually before other trees stir into action. Its bark exfoliates, and the color and texture of its bark may cause it to be confused with *Bursera* species, especially *B. fagaroides*.

During the dry season, the abundance of cacti in the forest becomes clear. While the cactus population and diversity vary greatly from area to area, cactus numbers stand out when other greens fade and drop out. Especially conspicuous are columnar cacti, which become most diverse in the Balsas Basin. In tropical deciduous forests everywhere in North America, columnar cacti form a significant component of the vegetation, one that may be overlooked when all the trees are leafed out. The most characteristic columnar cactus throughout western Mexico's tropical deciduous forest is *Pachycereus pecten-aboriginum*. It is a prominent component of the forest, found in all regions of the West Coast from Sonora to Chiapas, reaching its greatest height, up to 13 m, in the forests of Guerrero and Oaxaca. Also prominent in restricted habitats is *Pachycereus weberi*, which at a maximum height of 20 m is the largest of all columnar cacti, and several species of *Stenocereus* (*S. fricii, S. martinezii, S. montanus, S. quevedonis*, and, in a restricted area of Oaxaca, the massive *S. chacalapensis*). Prominent in forests of Jalisco through Oaxaca are several species of *Neobuxbaumia*, including abundant *N. mezcalaensis*, a single-stalked giant that demonstrates a distinctive fondness for tropical deciduous forests. *Pilosocereus alensis* and *P. purpusii*, bearded columnar cacti, also frequent the forests, though more sparsely represented than the previous species. In the Balsas depression, several endemic columnar cacti appear, notably the narrowly restricted *Pachycereus tepamo* and the sensational *Pachycereus militaris*, appropriately called Grenadier's Cap in

FIGURE 2.2 Some members of the tropical deciduous forest have spectacular flowering: (A) *Handroanthus impetiginosum* (photo by J. Becerra); (B) *Cochlospermum vitifolium* (photo by A. Lindqvist); (C) *Handroanthus chrysanthus* (photo by A. Molina Hernández, CC BY-NC); (D) *Ceiba aesculifolia* (photo by T. Van Devender).

English. Both are confined to the Tepalcatepec Basin on the east/north side of the Río Balsas, as are *Stenocereus chrysocarpa* and *S. fricii*. On the west side, *Neobuxbaumia multiareolata* and *Stenocereus zopilotensis* appear to be endemic as well. In all, more than 20 species of columnar cacti populate the tropical deciduous forests of Mexico's west coast and often stand out in the dry season as the lone sources of green in a sea of varying shades of brown on hillsides otherwise resembling unending stands of sticks.

But it is the burseras in all their diversity that are the most interesting component of the forests, despite their disappointing blooms. They flower toward the end of the dry season and a variety of species do so simultaneously. In contrast with many flowers of the tropical deciduous forest, their inflorescences are inconspicuous and, unlike many other tropical dry forest stalwarts, are little help to field taxonomists in identifying species. Indeed, unless field botanists are specifically in search of *Bursera* flowers, they may overlook the tiny blooms.

Tropical deciduous forests are targeted with enthusiasm by cattle raisers. During the dry season, the forest can be felled and cleared with relative ease, the deforestation uninterrupted by rains that might cause rapid regrowth. The slash, stumps, and stubble can be burned easily, and the charred land planted with fast-growing forage grasses. Especially notorious is buffelgrass (*Cenchrus ciliare*), an African savanna

FIGURE 2.3 Tropical deciduous forest vegetation in the vicinity of Izúcar de Matamoros dominated by *Bursera* spp. and *Neobuxbaumia mezcalaensis* (photo by L. Venable).

grass that is stimulated to new growth by fire and flourishes with the alternating rain and drought of the seasonally dry and hot climate. And thus, more than 90 percent of tropical deciduous forest vegetation has been cut down, an incalculable loss of biological diversity, watershed protection, climate moderation, and sources of lumber, including immense amounts of firewood. Enormous numbers of burseras have thus been lost since the latter parts of the twentieth century.

Along the Pacific Coast of Mexico and Central America, the coastal plains and flats tend to be vegetated by thornscrub, vegetation composed more of small trees and shrubs than the medium-sized trees of the tropical deciduous forest. There the deeper soils and easier irrigation make the land desirable for crops. And thus, huge tracts of land have been cleared in Sonora, Sinaloa, and parts of Michoacán and transformed into corporate farms. The more hilly and mountainous portions harbor tropical deciduous forest, stimulated by the greater rainfall of mountains and the shade some slopes offer that decreases heat load and evaporation. It is these slopes, often steep, that have been attacked by the ranchers' chainsaws and axes, leading to the overwhelming destruction of burseras' habitat.

CHAPTER 3

Bursera Through Time

The Advantages of Being at the Right Place at the Right Time

Bursera comprises about 114 species, which are notably concentrated in the tropical deciduous forests of the Pacific slopes of Mexico and in lowland canyons south of the Trans-Mexican Volcanic Belt. It is an ancient genus that probably originated in the early Eocene, perhaps more than 50 million years ago (mya) (Becerra et al. 2012). Most species are trees, but some are woody shrubs. Fossil leaves of several species have been discovered: The now extinct *B. serrulata*, an apparent relative of the modern *B. tecomaca*, is present in the early Oligocene (ca. 35-million-year-old) formation in the Florissant Fossil Beds National Monument in Colorado. The fossil *B. inaequilateralis* has been identified from the roughly 50 mya Eocene Green River beds in northwestern Colorado and southwestern Wyoming. These fossil findings attest that in ancient, warmer times the distribution of the genus extended across central North America. The Eocene Era (56 to 35 mya) was a warm period when plants with tropical affinities grew far north of the latitudes that limit most species today. Palms grew in northern Greenland and tropical forests were present in Kentucky and Tennessee (Van Devender 2002). Leaves of two additional fossil *Bursera* species, *B. popensis* and *B. ezequielii*, have tentatively been identified from the Eocene fossil locality in the Carroza Formation in La Popa Basin near Monterrey, Nuevo León, in northeastern Mexico, more than 2,000 km from the Green River fossil beds (Calvillo-Canadell et al. 2013).[1] While the vegetation of the strata in which the leaves are imbedded remains incompletely analyzed, preliminary studies suggest that the climate experienced by *Bursera* at this latitude (26° N, roughly the same latitude as extreme southern Texas) and elevation, 200 m to 600 m, was already

---

1. *Bursera ezequielii* is not to be confused with *Bursera exequielii*, an extant species from La Paz, Baja California. *B. ezequielii* was named after Ezequiel Cerda, who collected the fossil plant material, while *B. exequielii* was named after Exequiel Ezcurra, who wrote the foreword of this book.

demonstrating a drying trend from former tropical conditions and moving toward a seasonally dry climate.

These fossil burseras probably witnessed the transition from the warm Eocene into the cooler, more seasonally variable climate that followed in the Oligocene (35 to 23 mya). The vanishing tropical climate would have sent the humid broadleaf tropical forests, in which some burseras flourish, retreating to lower elevations and southward toward the warmth and greater moisture of the equatorial belt. Meanwhile the former *Bursera* habitat underwent the transition to modern ecosystems such as seasonal forests and grasslands, as the Rocky Mountain vegetation of Florissant now testifies. The vegetation of the Green River fossil region is now a mix of high desert scrub and chaparral.

During the warm and moist Eocene, early *Bursera* species probably inhabited rocky outcrops with quick drainage and thin soils, sites that at times had limited water availability. The genus seems well adapted to climatic conditions that include ample seasonal precipitation and an extended dry season. All species are deciduous, even those whose distribution extends into the tropical perennial forests, and even *B. microphylla*, which survives in plant-hostile deserts and drops its leaves only reluctantly when drought conditions become too drastic. Most burseras survive well in shallow, stony soils. Nonetheless, some species also flourish in more favorable soil and moisture conditions, suggesting that burseras' restriction to habitats of skimpier soil, lesser rainfall, and higher temperatures may be due to their being outcompeted by more aggressive plants in moist tropical forests. They found their favored ecological niche in the long, hot dry seasons and mountainous terrain of Mexico's West. Judging from the proliferation of species there, it appears that they are comfortable indeed in that region.

After the 20 million years or so of a relatively nonseasonal, warm, and wet Eocene, North America underwent an extended drying trend. By the Middle Oligocene and Miocene (30 to 20 mya), the establishment of latitudinal climatic stratification, which persists to the present day, was well on its way: northern and southern latitudes began to experience climates markedly different from those nearer the equator. The most important changes involved the advent of cold or freezing temperatures and long periods of little or no rain. The horse latitudes appeared—the worldwide arid regions at about 30° N and S where deserts abound. This barrier of aridity pinched out tropical species from the south and boreal species from the north. Those emerging dry regimes in Mexico stymied any northward march of burseras and, combined with the threat from cold air masses from the north, limited speciation of burseras there. Horse latitudes are linked closely to sinking air masses originating as moist, ballooning regions of wet, tropical moisture from the equatorial region that descend after depositing their moisture, compressing, heating, and drying the air beneath. This global phenomenon results in a subtropical zone of high pressure and aridity.

Geological events also contributed to the increasing dryness. With the uplifting of the Sierra Madre Occidental and the Trans-Mexican Volcanic Belt, tropical moisture from the Gulf of Mexico and the Pacific Ocean was permanently obstructed from reaching the mid-continent, drying out the Mexican Plateau and the Great Plains to the north. But the rise of mountains in Mexico also helped block the winter cold fronts that descended from the arctic, a development that accompanied the latitudinal climatic stratification following the Eocene. The cold air masses still affect the eastern coast of Mexico far south of the latitude that is frost-free on the west coast. At the same time as the western mountains were constructing barriers against cold air masses, seasonally drier regional climates of the Oligocene annihilated drought-intolerant tropical species. Large leaves became a liability during the months of little or no rain and low humidity, for leaves require water to retain their turgor and lose much water through evapotranspiration. The winners were species that drop their leaves in response to anticipated drought rather than in response to anticipated cold, as is the case with northern temperate deciduous forests. This emerging combination of protection from freezing and more pronounced seasonal droughts provided a stupendous ecological opportunity for those that could sustain the challenge. One of them, *Bursera*, was ready to take over these newly opened habitats.

As the continental crust cooled following the final consumption of the Farallon Plate under the North American Plate, the successor Pacific Plate was traveling northwestward. It glommed on to the western edge of the North American Plate. Its northwestward pull produced Basin and Range extension—crustal stretching—in the American West and northwestern Mexico (Dickenson 2002).[2] The pulling apart of the Earth's crust created widespread faulting as massive blocks broke off the stretching crust. Some of these blocks rose to stupendous heights, while adjacent blocks fell into the void created by the extending crust. Erosion of the newly risen blocks and of the thick blanket of volcanic rock on the Sierra Madre opened a plethora of new lowland canyons, and two conditions necessary for expansion of *Bursera* species emerged: protection from freezing and abundant precipitation during at least some months of the year. These conditions favored the establishment of a new kind of ecosystem: the tropical deciduous forests.[3]

---

2. Some authors believe Basin and Range faulting continues into southern Mexico.

3. Various terms have been used to denote the vegetation of western Mexico. We choose to follow the prominent Mexican ecologist Jerzy Rzedowksi (1978), who coined the terminology *tropical deciduous forest*. This description includes the tropical nature of the forest but also emphasizes the seasonal nature of the forest in that most trees shed their leaves.

Studies on *Bursera*'s diversification indicate that by the Middle Eocene the genus had already given rise to the two subgenera, *Bursera* and *Elaphrium*, and from there the two groups went into rapid radiation, taking advantage of the new dry and seasonal climate to which they were already pre-adapted (Becerra 2005, replicated in De-Nova et al. 2012). At first, they populated the new habitats offered by the multitude of canyons that were formed with the raising and erosion of the Sierra Madre Occidental. The opportunities for diversification only increased as the Trans-Mexican Volcanic Belt started its formation in the central and western side of Mexico. As the uplift proceeded over several million years, extending to the east of Central Mexico, eroded sediments from the rising Sierra Madre Oriental created a vast plain on the Gulf of Mexico coastal region. Although much of this area—primarily in the Mexican states of Tamaulipas and Veracruz—lies within or close to the tropics, it provides no obstacles to the arrival of periodic masses of frigid air plunging south from Arctic regions. These weather systems, called *nortes* by Mexicans, deliver killing frosts deep into the tropics. The rising central plateau (between the Sierra Madre Oriental and Occidental and north of the TMVB) was not protected either: freezing temperatures reach as far south as the Mexico City area. Plants intolerant of hard freezes, however, found refuge in the lowlands of the canyons of the TMVB, well beyond the reach of the arctic air masses from the north. Dozens of new species emerged at that time, claiming new territories for themselves. *Bursera* appears to have been at the right place at the right time when new habitats with climatic and spatial conditions favored the establishment of tropical deciduous vegetation that it is so well adapted to. The new species seem to have shown up as squatters in emerging habitats, staking their rights before other species could put down roots.

The prominence of *Bursera* is particularly striking in the frost-free canyons along the Balsas River depression. Here, the genus often becomes the overwhelmingly dominant woody taxon, surpassing legumes in both diversity and abundance. Their astonishing numbers gave rise to the name *cuajiotales* applied to many of these forests where burseras predominate, derived from the common name *cuajiote* given to a number of different *Bursera* species. *Bursera* is now also prominent on both the Pacific and Atlantic Coasts, where the mountainous terrains provide a critical benevolent protection against cold temperatures. The mountainous terrains have also provided isolated canyons where *Bursera* species may have diverged from one another in a process known as geographic speciation. This probably led to the formation of many narrowly endemic species that are surprisingly abundant in the few places they occur.

CHAPTER 4

Bursera's Anatomical and Physiological Adaptations to the Land

To Exfoliate or Not to Exfoliate, That Is the Question

For everyone curious about this unusual genus, we offer some more general observations: All species of *Bursera* have woody trunks and stems. The plants range in size from shrubs a mere 25 cm high to trees up to 40 m tall. Shrubby species provided with benevolent growing conditions may develop into trees, a variability of form most evident with species from the deserts of Mexico such as *B. arida*, *B. microphylla*, *B. fagaroides*, *B. laxiflora*, and *B. littoralis*. When they are limited to harsh substrates such as cliff faces or south-facing rocky slopes, or are confined to areas with very limited rainfall or strong wind, they may spend their lives as dwarf plants, struggling to survive or even apparently dead. Provide them deep soils and more abundant rainfall, however, and they will grow into proper trees. The only uniformly tall species is *B. simaruba*, and its height does not generally exceed 40 m, even in cultivation. There is only one epiphyte species (more properly hemi-epiphytic), that is, one that grows on other trees, *B. standleyana*, found only in Costa Rica. It establishes itself on a host tree and then sends roots along the trunk and into the ground, as though it were mimicking a strangler fig.

Branching patterns are quite variable in the genus. Many species produce branches close to the ground (0.5 to 3 m), with the main stem quickly losing its identity and sometimes giving the plant a scraggily, gnarled aspect. In mature plants this often results in thick-muscled branches of most agreeable appearance, growing in various directions, many of which invite climbing. In other plants the branching, even though close to the ground, is regularly arranged, giving an aesthetically appealing bonsai appearance.

FIGURE 4.1 Wild branching pattern of a *B. morelensis* tree (photo by J. Becerra).

In some medium-sized species (such as *B. lancifolia*, *B. mirandae*, and *B. multijuga*), branching assumes the graceful, spreading shape of acacias from African savannas, forming fairly flat-topped canopies.

One of the most striking features of this genus is the colorful bark that peels in wispy-thin sheets from the trunks. About half the species, mostly those belonging to the subgenus *Bursera*, share this characteristic; the other half, mostly belonging to the subgenus *Elaphrium*, have gray, nonpeeling bark that ranges from pleasantly smooth to rough (rugose). In Mexico the peeling bark, more accurately referred to as *exfoliating*, combines with the fragrant smell that fruits, leaves, and branches exude when rubbed or crushed. This mixture helps identify a tree as a bursera, even to an inexperienced botanist. But not everywhere. The taxon native to the Galápagos Islands, *graveolens*, which may not belong in *Bursera* (Martínez-Habibe 2012), is commonly called *palo santo*, or holy tree. Its sap also yields fragrant incense. In pre-Hispanic times, Aztecs were familiar with burseras with peeling bark. They labeled such trees *cuajiotes*, a name derived from the word *cuáhuitl*, a combination of *cua* (tree or branch) and *jiote* or *xiotl* (sick skin, or scabies).[1] In some regions, *B. simaruba* is comically—and perhaps aptly—referred to as the *tourist tree*, for the tree's bark is red and peeling, much like the skin of tour-

---

1. Some interpreters have proposed that *cuajiote* means *leprous tree*, but since leprosy was introduced to the Americas by Europeans within the past 500 years, this epithet is probably not accurate.

ists who arrive during winter from the north seeking sunlight and warmth. These conspicuous transplants are a common sight in the burseras' range. We should add that in fall, when leaves have fallen and winds are usually at their lowest point of the year, the tropical deciduous forests often assume a most agreeable silence, with only the sweep of downward gliding leaves as background noise. However, a slight gust can cause the exfoliating sheets of bark to rustle or rattle and startle those nearby. At times, that sound resembles the buzz of a rattlesnake. We testify that the suddenness of the sound breaking the stillness can result in an increased heartbeat in nearby humans.

It is not uncommon for trees found in tropical deciduous forests, including non-burseras, to have peeling bark, and some compilations suggest that anywhere from 9 to 70 percent of the individuals found in tropical deciduous forests exhibit

FIGURE 4.2 A diversity of patterns of *Bursera* trunk exfoliation (photos by J. Becerra and L. Venable).

this feature. If we examine one of these peeling burseras with a magnifying lens, we will find that the outer layer of the periderm (or *phellem*), which is the living layer that produces the cork tissue in stems, is stratified, made up of alternating thin and thick cell tissues that are in constant renewal (Rosell and Olson 2014). The thin cell tissues break easily, tearing in papyrus-like strips or sheets of red, pink, yellow, brown, or green color that are often semitransparent. Beneath the phellem is another layer of green, photosynthetic tissue (or *phelloderm*). Since these plants are leafless for many months of the year, there is a clear advantage in having a trunk or stem that can take over providing photosynthetic products, a function that in other environments would typically be consigned to leaves. Little is known about the photosynthetic contribution of green bursera trunks, but in green-trunked palo verde trees (*Parkinsonia* spp.) of the southwestern U.S. desert (and extending well into South America), trunk photosynthesis can reach 70 percent of annual carbon fixation. The peeling patterns are variable in *Bursera* but are also characteristic of certain species, so that taxonomists can sometimes use the patterns to distinguish species. Given the difficulty of distinguishing among the dozens of species growing together when all are leafless, this can be a taxonomic boon.

On the face of it, peeling bark seems to be a waste of resource, especially since some burseras peel and some don't. Why would a plant willfully surrender something it struggles to create without an obvious benefit? Ecologists hypothesize that exfoliating bark may discourage the establishment of lichens and vines (lianas) that might otherwise intercept light reaching the tree. The ease of removal of the outer layer could also deter the establishment of epiphytic seedlings. Epiphytes grow on the surface of other plants and although they derive their moisture and nutrients from the air, rain, or debris accumulating in their surroundings, they can interfere with photosynthesis of host trees. In addition, the added weight can have a taxing effect, so much so that the additional weight of the epiphytes may break branches or even bring down entire trees during heavy rains or strong winds. The negative effects of lianas have been confirmed for *B. simaruba* in Guanacaste Province, Costa Rica, where the fecundity of female *B. simaruba* appears to be negatively correlated with the degree of coverage by lianas. Experimental reduction of these epiphytes resulted in increased fruit production (Stevens 1983). Thus, lianas seem to be bad news for some plants, and a peeling bark could help reduce them.

The flowers of burseras are tiny and mostly dull in color, yet in some places burseras have spectacular large and beautiful red or orange flowers. Upon close examination, however, it turns out that these flowers actually belong to a mistletoe growing on the bursera branches. Indeed, there is a group of mistletoes in the genus *Psittacanthus* of the Loranthaceae family that specialize in infecting a number of *Bursera* species, with both peeling and nonpeeling bark.[2] *Psittacanthus sonorae* grows on the branches of burseras from the Sonoran Desert region, such as *B. hindsiana, B. fagaroides, B. laxiflora,* and above all, *B. microphylla. Bursera simaruba* is the host of *P. rhynchanthus,* while *P. palmeri* has been observed in central and western Mexico on the crowns of *B. arborea, B. bipinnata, B. cuneata, B. copallifera, B. fagaroides, B. galeottiana, B. grandifolia, B. infernidialis, B. multijuga, B. palmeri, B. sarukhanii, and B. schlechtendalii* (Kuijt 2009; Ortiz-Rodríguez, Guerrero, and Ornelas 2018).

Psittacanthus plants are called "hemiparasites." Hemiparasites are "half parasites," sucking water and nutrients from their host plant but having green leaves and branches that allow them to photosynthesize on their own. Their life cycle starts when a bird poops on a bursera branch—the poop containing sticky seeds of these pesky plants—or after a bird eats the flesh of the fruit and rubs the sticky seeds off its beak. The seed germinates and produces a radicle (embryonic root) whose tip penetrates the bursera bark to find water and nutrients. It is a remarkable organ in the sense that it can discriminate among the host tissues to find a most suitable location to grow inside the host branch. After this intrusive organ gets established, it develops a cushion-like outgrowth called haustorium, a tissue mass by which it attaches to the host. Inside the victim's branches the radicle grows and expands, while on the outside the mistletoe produces branches and leaves. If all goes well, it will produce flowers and fruits and with them feed another hungry bird, often the silky flycatcher (*Phainopepla*), which will transport the seeds and deposit them while defecating on another potential host. With some luck, at least some seeds will survive and grow in a prime location on the host plant, like the crown, where the new mistletoe can get plenty of light and eventually attract pollinators for its flowers and fruit dispersal agents (Ornelas 2019).

In theory, these hemiparasites could use any plant. Yet there is often a striking difference in the abundance of mistletoes on different host species in the wild. Why would some mistletoes prefer to infect burseras when there are other potential hosts? The answer is difficult to ascertain, and it probably involves multiple factors, such as the vulnerability of the host species as well as the advantages that bursera provides to mistletoes above other hosts. We do not know the answer and can only speculate.

To succeed, a mistletoe's invading radicle and haustorium must first resist the chemical toxins of the host. Most plants are full of them, but unlike many other plants, burseras store these toxins in canals that run throughout the outer layers of branches and leaves (as described in chapter 5). Perhaps the radicle of a

---

2. Occasionally, they are found on other plants, but by far, their favorite hosts are burseras.

bursera-specialized mistletoe, in its highly discriminatory wisdom, can navigate inside the bursera branch, evading the canals that contain toxic compounds. Then, as a plus, the mistletoe's striking hummingbird-pollinated flowers do not have to compete for pollinators with the inconspicuous insect-pollinated flowers of burseras, since they flower at different times of the year. Burseras produce flowers when the rainy season is about to start, in May through July, and *Psittacanthus* in September to October (Sandoval Ortega, Martínez, and Arellano-Delgado 2022). But they overlap ripening their fruits, which brings another plus: burseras usually produce masses of fruits that can attract efficient avian fruit dispersers, such as the silky flycatcher (*Phainopepla nitens*) and other flycatchers of the genus *Myiarchus* that can also disperse the mistletoes' fruits. These intelligent birds prefer to visit plants that advertise an abundance of fruits, so mistletoes probably have more success attracting birds to their fruits when surrounded by bursera fruits.

More research is definitively needed to understand the war between mistletoes and burseras. These studies could also answer whether a peeling or a nonpeeling bark serves a host better to fight mistletoes.

In the tropical deciduous forests and deserts of Mexico, epiphytes such as orchids and *Tillandsias* (ball mosses) are also abundant and provide another challenge for which having a peeling bark could be advantageous. Studies from the forests of the state of Morelos have shown that *B. bipinnata*, *B. copallifera*, and *B. glabrifolia* have rugose, nonpeeling bark and tend to host more species and more individuals of *Tillandsia* than *B. fagaroides* trees that have peeling bark (Vergara-Torres et al. 2010). Experimental studies demonstrate that *Tillandsia* seeds adhere more easily to the rugose bark of *B. copallifera* than to the smoother bark of other species of the Morelos forest. Furthermore, when researchers measured the peeling rate of *B. fagaroides*'s bark, they discovered that the degree of exfoliation was highest in the main trunk, lower in the main branches, and still lower in branchlets (López-Villalobos, Flores-Palacios, and Ortiz-Pulido 2008). Interestingly, fewer *Tillandsia* seeds got attached and more seedlings fell with bark peeling from trunks than in main branches and branchlets, supporting the idea that exfoliating bark can reduce epiphytes.

Another plausible explanation for peeling is that it occurs as the bark becomes opaque through development, and shedding it helps the plant maintain the access of light to the photosynthetic phelloderm. An interesting correlation is that all *Bursera* species with peeling bark have photosynthetic trunks, and no *Bursera* without peeling bark have photosynthetic trunks. While the idea of peeling bark to make the trunks photosynthetic sounds plausible, studies that have tested this hypothesis in *Bursera* or other tropical deciduous forest trees with photosynthetic bark have yet to come to our attention. Paloverde trees (*Parkinsonia* sp.) have photosynthetic bark that does not peel, although older trees sometimes develop gray nonphotosynthetic bark on the main trunk, which produces a hoary appearance

FIGURE 4.3 *Bursera microphylla* is the favorite living trellis for the *Psitthacanthus sonorae* mistletoe: (A) infected plant in Bahía de los Ángeles, Baja California, observed in November 2022 (photo by P. Alexander); (B) flowers of *P. sonorae*, observed in Cabo Pulmo, Baja California Sur (photo by P. Hale).

in the tree. Some trees in the genera *Jatropha* (Euphorbiaceae) and *Fouquieria* (Fouquieriaceae) also sport exfoliating bark and greenish trunks. Still, we are left with the undeniable phenomenon found in the burseras: some exfoliate, and some do not.

Succulence

A phenomenon called *succulence* permits plants from many families to store water in structures such as stems, leaves, and roots as a mechanism for coping with drought. Stem succulence is a common feature of tropical dry forest and desert floras. The morphological strategies of water storage can be quite variable among taxa. The celebrated "carrot-like" stem morphology of the *boojum* tree (*Fouquieria columnaris*) of Baja California, for example, is due to its large central trunk pith, which functions as a water storage organ. The Baja California elephant tree, *Pachycormus discolor* (Anacardiaceae), owes its name to *pachy* for "thick" and *kormos* for "stump," referring to the shape of the trunk, which is extensive, swollen, and complete with bark and cork with high water content. Burseras are also stem succulents, one of their notable traits. Members of the genus maintain so much water in the stem and transport tissues that their trunks and branches take on a fat or swollen appearance. The lower the precipitation of the areas where they live, the greater their capacity to store water. So, for example, *B. grandifolia*, which lives in the tropical deciduous forest, has bark that can be twice as thick as that of one of its close relatives, *B. simaruba*, which most often lives in rainforests. The amount of water that a species from the arid desert can store is substantial. *Bursera microphylla* plants from north-central Baja California, for example, store about 1.5 kg of water per cubic meter of trunk. This is less than that stored by many cacti from the same region, which is about 3 to 4 kg of water per cubic meter, but considerably higher than the 0.6 to 0.8 kg of water per cubic meter stored by other nonsucculent shrubs and trees from the same place. Elephant tree does justice to its name, with its heavy-looking, pachyderm-like trunk. Yet much of the weight is water, and when desiccated, the trunks quickly lose that weight. Generally, the water storage capacity of plant stems is closely connected to wood anatomy and the degree to which wood can provide mechanical support: the greater the succulence, the weaker the structure. The higher capacity for water reservoirs seems to require a lighter, low-density wood that can easily break under pressure or even collapse if not well hydrated. Those who have climbed or attempted to climb a bursera tree often discover it to be a foolish pursuit that can end in pain, along with broken limbs in the climber and climbed alike. The meandering arms of such thick-armed and smooth species such as *B. stenophylla* may prove irresistible to the hopeful climber. You have been warned.

While the advantages of storing water in arid environments may seem obvious, the uses for the stored water differ in various plants (Nilsen et al. 1990). Succulence is not merely a reservoir for coping with drought, for *Bursera* species do not use a significant portion of the water stored in their stems to avoid desiccation during the dry season. They have little need for such a resource; they are leafless during that period and leaf evapotranspiration normally associated with photosynthesis is absent. Instead, water stored in the stem appears to serve as a buffering mechanism, available to them just prior to and during the summer rainy season when plants have leaves. This reservoir supplies water during the day to maintain leaf turgor, that is, to prevent leaves from wilting.

FIGURE 4.4 The succulent trunk of *Bursera exequielii* near the coast in Baja California south of La Paz (photo by J. Becerra).

Perhaps even more important, the trees rely on stored water to initiate flower and leaf flushing immediately prior to the onset of the wet season. *Bursera* flowers are small and easy to overlook. Flowering when the canopies of trees in forests they share are crowded with leaves and other trees are laden with blossoms would place them at a disadvantage. Having flowers at a time when competition with leaves is low and insect pollinators are in high need of the sugar and water resources provided by flowers can be a highly adaptive strategy. And since the tropical deciduous forest during the rainy season is a leafy wonderland, flushing new leaves *before* the onset of the rainy season gives a species a temporal advantage in light preemption over other species. In this way, the trees maximize photosynthetic capacity and extend the growing season of the plants (Ávila-Lovera and Ezcurra 2016).

Another unusual characteristic of bursera-rich habitats is their resistance to forest fires. Their tinder-dry appearance late in the dry season belies their high concentration of water, which retards any large-scale fires. This fire resistance has unfortunate consequences for bursera-rich forests. Cattle ranchers wishing to expand grazing potential choose to level entire forests, wait for the downed trees to dry, and then burn the entire mass. The result is a grotesque, blackened wasteland of a formerly productive natural landscape. A few exotic grasses thus replace a diverse and robust forest. Beef for carne asada trumps biological diversity.

Leaves, the Most Variable Trait of Bursera

Bursera provides a remarkable instance of species adaptive evolutionary radiation as the climate of North America has become progressively drier over the past 30 million years. The genus initially was found in newly formed or forming tropical deciduous forests and experienced great speciation success. It subsequently migrated into the deserts that became established a few million years later (Becerra 2005). Throughout this diversification, *Bursera* species developed a series of adaptations to cope with the droughts that moved from occasional episodes to predictable features of the climate. Leaves, trunks, and stems are probably the organs that experienced the major rearrangements to evolve from mesic-adapted toward xeric-adapted morphology and physiology. But as different species colonized or originated in habitats with different geographical and altitudinal dynamics, the precipitation, solar radiance, heat, and natural enemies each species encountered also varied. This no doubt favored the differences in form and function of traits that species now exhibit. Nowhere is this astonishing proliferation of adaptations as evident as in *Bursera* leaves.

To walk in a region of high *Bursera* diversity during the wet season is to be confronted by a fascinating plethora of *Bursera* leaf shapes and arrangement. Remarkable differences appear in leaf size, divisions of the blade, and venation. It is as if these plants are offering a living plant key, a means of distinguishing and remembering each one of them. And indeed, this variation is (we must assume) an unintended gift to botanists: thanks to the leaves, they are readily able to identify different species without flowers, the normal recourse for segregating one species from another. Of course, this gift is fleeting, for every year when the dry season arrives, the lack of rain triggers the shedding of leaves and botanists become stranded woefully in a world of bare trunks and limbs once again, a landscape that may take on the aspect of undifferentiated sticks.

The leaves of flowering plants consist of a petiole (leaf stalk), a lamina (leaf blade), and usually stipules, small leafy appendages located at the base of the petiole. Many burseras are pinnately compound, meaning that the leaf blade is fully subdivided into many leaflets along the midvein in a feather-like arrangement. They are also imparipinnate or odd-pinnate because their leaves, when they are pinnate, have a lone terminal leaflet. The number and shape of leaflets that comprise the leaf are characteristic of each *Bursera* species. Some species are bipinnately compound, meaning the leaf divisions are also divided again (*B. bipinnata*, *B. filicifolia*, and

FIGURE 4.5 A leafless bursera tree in the Zopilote Canyon, Guerrero (photo by B. Vrskovy).

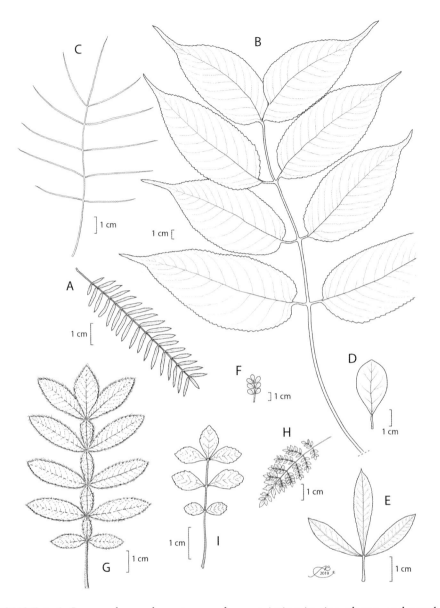

FIGURE 4.6 *Bursera* leaves have tremendous variation in size, shape, and number of leaflets: (A) *B. morelensis*; (B) *B. sarcopoda*; (C) *B. paradoxa*; (D) *B. schlechtendalii*; (E) *B. trimera*; (F) *B. arida*; (G) *B. coyucensis*; (H) *B. bipinnata*; (I) *B. fagaroides* (drawing by A. Barbosa).

B. stenophylla and sometimes *B. graveolens, B. laxiflora, B. littoralis,* and *B. ribana*). A few species are trifoliolate, bearing leaves made up of just three leaflets, as in the case of *B. kerberi, B. trifoliolata,* and *B. trimera.* Several species, such as *B. chemapodicta, B. schlechtendalii,* and *B. simplex,* are unifoliate, meaning that the leaf blade is not divided into leaflets at all.

Leaves are the principal food-producing organs for plants, which accomplish it via photosynthesis. This process incorporates carbon dioxide, water, and light to produce sugars such as glucose and fructose. These can be used for energy to maintain the plant's vigor or can be transformed into the more complex molecules necessary for growth, especially cellulose, the basic structural material in plant cell walls (Givinish 1979). Plants (and leaves) extract water from the ground and carbon dioxide from the air. Photosynthesis is straightforward for plants such as those that live in humid environments, which most of them did 30 million years ago. Plants in arid and semiarid lands, however, face the challenge of carrying on photosynthesis when water, one of the three indispensable ingredients, is in short and often unpredictable supply. To survive in hot and dry climates, *Bursera* has had to come up with a variety of leaf adaptations. For many species, this has meant managing leaf size and modifying leaf traits involved with water and heat control. Under high radiation loads (sunlight), large, undivided leaves rapidly overheat, requiring extensive and water-intensive evaporative cooling. Having small leaves or compound leaves with small leaflets has proved one of the key evolutionary responses of *Bursera* to the transition from their originally wet Eocene-Oligocene environment (40 to 30 mya) to the drylands most of them currently inhabit. And the more open and drier their environment is, the smaller their leaves. For example, *B. arida* and *B. biflora* inhabit the Valley of Tehuacán, where in some places they face a mean annual precipitation of less than 400 mm. These two species have tiny leaf lamina, with an area on average of between 0.5 and 1.5 cm^2, respectively. Other species that inhabit cooler environments at higher altitudes often in cohabitation with oaks and with more than 1,000 mm of mean annual precipitation have large leaves, such as *B. hintonii*, with an average leaf area of 230 cm^2, and *B. simaruba*, which lives in wet tropical forests with precipitation of more than 1,500 mm per year and whose leaf area averages about 185 cm^2. Many *Bursera* species also have very narrow leaflets, as is the case with *B. microphylla*, *B. galleotiana*, and *B. morelensis*. This shape has been associated with greater photosynthetic efficiency in conditions of increased drought, high temperatures, and high irradiance.

By reducing leaf dimensions, *Bursera* has also reduced stomata number. Stomata are tiny pores in the leaf epidermis that open to admit carbon dioxide and emit oxygen (a by-product of photosynthesis). But as the gasses pass through the stomata, water vapor also exits the leaf, in a process called evapotranspiration. That is why plants in general cannot gain carbon dioxide or expel oxygen without simultaneously losing precious water. Thus, balancing food production with water loss is a serious challenge for plants in dry environments. Having fewer stomata or being able to close them means a lower intake of carbon dioxide and a lower rate of photosynthesis. To compensate for this loss, many *Bursera* species have opted for what some other arid plants have done: making the trunk an organ capable of photosynthesis. Trunks of flowering plants evolved originally as organs of structural support and therefore have far fewer or no stomata compared to leaves. Yet trees of many plant families native to dry lands, particularly tropical deciduous forests, have photosynthetic trunks, which are typically more efficient at photosynthesizing with less water loss than leaves.

CHAPTER 5

Bursera Leaves and Their Interactions with Leaf Devourers

Vascular plants (those with specialized tissues for transporting water) appeared on Earth in Silurian times, about 450 mya. They rapidly colonized Earth's terrestrial environment and their leaves and other tissues became a food resource for animals, particularly insects and their relatives. Although leaves are not as nutritious as other plant organs such as fruits, they provide a food source for many organisms, as the abundance of herbivores demonstrates. Historically, insects have been the most significant herbivores of plants, restricting their diets to one or another part of a plant and producing dramatic effects on plant growth and mortality. Vertebrates such as mammalian plant eaters, however, also affect vegetation—the arrangement of plants in the landscape—since most of them depend completely on plants for their sustenance. In many ecosystems, they are the principal plant eaters. Witness how the culinary habits of elephants, giraffes, and wildebeests have shaped African savannas and how bison maintained the Great Plains as grassland.

The leaf provides building materials and is the energy factory of plants, but leaves can be decimated by herbivores with disastrous consequences for plant growth and survival if plant eaters have their way (witness the plundering of landscapes by domestic vertebrates). In response, plants have evolved a series of protective measures against marauding herbivores. Among these is a vast and varied arsenal of chemical substances, from tannins to alkaloids and other products that herbivores find nasty, with names like cyanogenic glucosides, terpenoids, quinones, xantones, acetylenes, amines, and coumarins, to mention a few. There are no plants in the world that do not produce one or another kind of chemical warfare product aimed at deterring or stopping uninvited consumers. One may like to think that compounds such as caffeine, aspirin, and morphine or the chemicals that endow spices with their compelling odors are generous offerings of nature to humans, but all such compounds

TABLE 5.1 Chemical compounds that have been found in some *Bursera* species

SPECIES	CHEMICAL COMPOUNDS
B. aptera	Heptane, 2-Heptanone, 3-Heptanol, Nonane, α-Thujene, α-Pinene, Benzaldehyde, Sabinene, β-Pinene, Myrcene, α-Phelandrene, 3-Carene, β-Phelandrene, Cis-Ocimene, γ-Terpinene, β-Caryophyllene, Germacrene D, Germacrene B, δ-Elemene, γ-Elemene, β-Selenene, α-Eudesmol, Podophyllotoxin.
B. arborea	A-Pinene, Sabinene, α-Copaene, γ-Elemene, β-Caryophyllene, α-Caryophyllene, Germacrene D, β-Selinene, α-Selinene, δ-Cadinene, Germacrene B, Phytol.
B. arida	Heptane, 2-Heptanone, 3-Heptanol, Nonane, α-Thujene, α-Pinene, β-Pinene, Ethyl-hexanoate, Para-Cymene, 2-Heptanol acetate, 1,8 Cineole, Cis-Ocimene, 4-Thujanol, Linalyl acetate, Germacrene D, Germacrene B, γ-Elemene, β-Selenene, Phytol. Ariensin, Naringenin, β-Sitosterol, Betulonic acid, (+)-3-Hydroxymethyl-5-methoxy-6,7-methylenedioxy-1-(3',4'-methylenedioxybenzene)-1,2,3,4-tetrahydronaphthalene-2-carboxylic acid lactone, 2,3-bis-(3,4-Thalene-2-carboxylic acid lactone) 2,3-bis-(3,4-Methylenedioxybenzyl)butane-1,4-diol diacetate (Ionescu 1974).
	Benulin (Ionescu et al. 1977).
B. ariensis	A-Pinene, Sabinene, Isocaryophyllene, α-Caryophyllene, Germacrene D, Germacrene B, Humulene, γ-Elemene, α-Bisabolol, Phytol, Ariensin.
B. aromatica	Nonane, β-Pinene, Limonene, α-Copaene, β-Caryophyllene, α-Cadinene, Vrififlorol, Limonene (Junor et al. 2010).
B. attenuata	A-Thujene, α-Pinene, Sabinene, β-Pinene, Myrcene, β-Caryophyllene, α-Catyophyllene, Germacrene D, Germacrene B, Phytol.
B. bicolor	Heptane, 2-Heptanone, Tricyclene, α-Pinene, Benzaldehyde, Sabinene, β-Pinene, Myrcene, β-Phelandrene, 1,8 Cineole, α-Thujone, Phenylethyl alcohol, Borneol, β-Cedrene, β-Caryophyllene, Germacrene B, Phytol.
B. biflora	2-Heptanol, Tricyclene, α-Pinene, Benzaldehyde, Sabinene, β-Pinene, β-Phelandrene, γ-Terpinene, β-Thujone, Borneol α-Copaene, β-Caryophyllene, cis-β-Farnesene, Germacrene D, Germacrene B, α-Bisabolol, Phytol.

B. bipinnata	Tricyclene, α-Pinene, Benzaldehyde, Sabinene, β-Pinene, β-Phelandrene, Phenylethyl alcohol, Borneol, γ-Terpinene, β-Caryophyllene, Germacrene D, Germacrene B, α-Bisabolol, Phytol.
B. bolivarii	2-Heptanone, 3-Heptanol, Myrcene, Limonene, Cis-Ocimene, 1-Methylhexyl acetate, Trans-Ocimene, Phenyl-ethyl alcohol, β-Caryophyllene, Germacrene D, Germacrene B, α-Eudesmol.
B. bonetti	Tricyclene, α-Pinene, Sabinene, β-Pinene, Myrcene, β-Phelandrene, Cis-Ocimene, Isocaryophyllene, β-Caryophyllene, Germacrene D, Phytol.
B. chemapodicta	Heptane, 2-Heptanone, 3-Heptanol, Nonane, 4-Methyl-2-pentyl acetate, 2-Heptanol, 1-Methylhexyl acetate, β-Caryophyllene, Germacrene D.
B. citronella	Hinokinin, Savinin.
B. confusa	3-Heptanol, α-Pinene, β-Pinene, Ethyl hexanoate, α-Phelandrene, β-Phelandrene, Germacrene D.
B. copallifera	Heptane, 2-Heptanone, Tricyclene, α-Pinene, α-Phelandrene, 1,8 Cineole, α-Thujone, Isocaryophyllene, δ-Elemene, β-Cedrene, β- Caryophyllene, Germacrene D, β-Selinene, Germacrene B, α-Bisabolol, Verticiol, Phytol.
B. coyucensis	A-Thujone, β-α-Thujone, α-Cubebene, δ-Elemene, β-Caryophyllene, Germacrene D, Germacrene B, γ-Elemene, α-Bisabolol, Germacrone, Verticiol, Phytol.
B. crenata	A-Pinene, Sabinene, β-Pinene, Myrcene, β-Phelandrene.
B. cuneata	A-Pinene, Sabinene, β-Pinene, Myrcene, Limonene, β-Cedrene, β-Caryophyllene, Cis-β-Farnesene, Germac-rene D, Germacrene B, Humulene, γ-Elemene, Germacrone, Phytol, Hinokinin, Savinin, Cubebin.
B. discolor	A-Pinene, Sabinene, Limonene, Cis-Ocimene, Trans-Ocimene, γ-Terpinene, δ-Elemene, β-Elemene, β-Cedrene, β-Caryophyllene, Germacrene D, Germacrene B, δ-Cadinene, γ-Elemene, α-Eudesmol.
B. diversifolia	Tricyclene, α-Pinene, Sabinene, Limonene, β-Caryophyllene, Germacrene D, β-Selinene, Germacrene B, α-Bisabolol, Phytol.
B. epinnata	Tricyclene, α-Pinene, β-Pinene, β-Phelandrene, β-Caryophyllene, Germacrene D, Germacrene B, β-Sesquiphelandrene.

(continued)

TABLE 5.1 *(Continued)*

SPECIES	CHEMICAL COMPOUNDS
B. excelsa	Myrcene, α-Phelandrene, β-Phelandrene, β-Caryophyllene, Germacrene D, Germacrene B, Iso-Bursehernin, Guayadequiol, 3,4-Dimethoxy-3',4'-methylenedioxylignano-9,9'.lactone.
B. fagaroides	2-Heptanone, 3-Heptanol, 3-Carene, β-Phelandrene, Isocaryophyllene, α-Cubebene, α-Caryophyllene, Germacrene D, β-Selenene, β-Peltatin A-methyl ether, 5'-Demethoxy-β-peltatin A-methyl ether, (−)-Deoxypodophyllotoxin, (−)-morelensin, 5'-Demethoxy-β-peltatin A-methyl ether, (−)-Yatein, Bursehernin, Acetyl podophyllotoxin, Podophyllotoxin, Deoxypodophyllotoxin, 9'-Acetyl-9-pentadecanoyl-dihydroclusin, 2,3-Demethoxy-secoisolintetralin monoacetate, Dhydroclusin monoacetate, 7',8'-Dehydropodophyllotoxin, 7',8'-Dehydroacetylpodophyllotoxin, 7',8'-Dehydro-trans-p-cumaroyl Podophyllotoxin, Acetylpodophyllo-toxin, 5'-Demethoxy-β-peltatin A Methylether, Acetylpicropodophyllotoxin, Burseranin, Hinokinin.
B. filicifolia	Myrcene, 3-Carene, β-Phelandrene, β-Caryophyllene, Germacrene D, γ-Elemene, α-Bisabolol, Verticiol.
B. fragilis	A-Pinene, Sabinene, β-Pinene, Limonene, β-Caryophyllene.
B. galeottiana	Nonane, Decane, α-Pine, β-Pinene, α-Phelandrene, Meta-Cymene.
B. glabra	Limonene, α-Phelandrene, cis-Ocimene, Cis-Caryophyllene, Trans-Carveol (Cáceres-Ferreira et al. 2019).
B. glabrifolia	2-Heptanone, Tricyclene, α-Pinene, Sabinene, β-Pinene, β-Phelandrene, 1,8 Cineole, β-Cedrene, β-Caryophyllene, Cis-β-Farnecene, Germacrene D, Germacrene B, β-Sesquiphelandrene, γ-Elemene, α-Bisabolol, Phytol.
B. grandifolia	Heptane, α-Copaene, β-Elemene, β-Caryophyllene, α-Caryophyllene, Germacrene D, β-Selinene, α-Selinene, Germacrene B, δ-Cadinene, β-Sesquiphelandrene, Phytol.
B. heteresthes	Isocaryophyllene, δ-Elemene, β-Elemene, β-Cedrene, β-Caryophyllene, α-Caryophyllene, Germacrene D, β-Selinene, Germacrene B, β-Sesquiphelandrene, γ-Elemene, α-Bisabolol, Germacrone, Phytol.
B. hindsiana	Tricyclene, α-Pinene, β-Pinene, Myrcene, β-Phelandrene, β-Caryophyllene, α-Caryophyllene, Germacrene D, Germacrene B, β-Sesquiphelandrene, α-Bisabolol.

B. hintonii	Heptane, α-Pinene, Sabinene, β-Phelandrene, β-Thujone, β-Cedrene, β-Caryophyllene, Germacrene D, Germacrene B, α-Bisabolol, Phytol.
B. hollickii	A-Pinene, β-Pinene, Terpinolene, α-Terpineol, β-Caryophyllene, Humulene (Junor et al. 2008).
B. infernidialis	Heptane, 2-Heptanone, Nonane, β-Pinene, Isocaryophyllene, Germacrene D, Germacrene B.
B. instabilis	A-Pinene, β-Pinene, β-Terpineol, δ-Elemene, β-Caryophyllene, Germacrene D, β-Selinene, α-Selinene, Germacrene B, Phytol.
B. kerberi	2-Heptanone, Tricyclene, α-Pinene, Sabinene, β-Pinene, β-Phelandrene.
B. lancifolia	2-Heptanone, 3-Heptanol, Myrcene, Limonene, Phenylethyl alcohol, β-Caryophyllene, Germacrene B.
B. laxiflora	Tricyclene, α-Pinene, β-Pinene, α-Phelandrene, Limonene, β-Phelandrene, β-Caryophyllene, α-Caryophyllene, Germacrene D, Germacrene B, δ-Cadinene, β-Sesquiphelandrene, Humulene.
B. linanoe	2-Heptanone, Linalyl acetate, Isocaryophyllene, α-Cuebebene, Germacrene D, Germacrene B, β-Caryophyllene, α-Bisabolol.
B. longipes	Heptane, 2-Heptanone, α-Thujene, α-Pinene, β-pinene, Limonene, γ-Terpinene, β-Cedrene, β-Caryophylene, Germacrene D, Germacrene B, β-Selenene, α-Eudesmol, Phytol.
B. microphylla	Tricyclene, α-Pinene, β-Pinene, α-Phelandrene, β-phelandrene, β-caryophylene, α-Humulene, Germacrene D, Verticillene, Phytol, Malabaricatrienone, Malabaricatrienil, Microphyllanin, Ariensin, Burseran, hemiariensin, Picropolygamain, Desmethoxy-yatein, Dihydroclusin 9'-acetate, Podophyllotoxin butanoate. Kaempferol, Catechin, Quercitin, Rutin, Quinic acid, Gallic acid, Ellagic acid, Kaempferol glucoside, Quercitin glucoside, Gallic acid glucoside, Quercitin galloyl glucoside (Vidal-Gutiérrez et al. 2020).
B. mirandae	Heptane, 2-Heptanone, 2-Heptanol, α-Thujone, Linalyl acetate, α-Copaene, β-Caryophyllene, Germacrene D, β-Sesquiphelandrene, α-Bisabolol, Phytol.
B. morelensis	2-Heptanone, 3-Heptanol, α-Pinene, Sabinene, Myrcene, α-phelandrene, Para-Cymene, β-Phelandrene, Iso-caryophyllene, β-Caryophyllene, Germacrene D, Deoxypodophyllotoxin, Morelensin.
B. multijuga	Tryciclene, Sabinene, Myrcene, β-Phelendrene, β-Caryophyllene, Germacrene D, Germacrene B, Phytol.

(continued)

TABLE 5.1 (*Continued*)

SPECIES	CHEMICAL COMPOUNDS
B. odorata	A-Pinene, β-Pinene, Myrcene, Limonene, β-Caryophyllene, α-Caryophyllene, Germacrene D, Germacrene B, γ-Elemene, Phytol.
B. palaciosii	Trans-Ocimene, Isocaryophyllene, β-Caryophyllene, α-Caryophyllene, Germacrene D, β-Selinene, α-Selinene.
B. paradoxa	Trans-Ocimene, Cis-Ocimene, Linalool, β-Caryophyllene, Germacrene D, Phytol.
B. penicillata	A-Pinene, Benzaldehyde, β-Phelandrene, 1-Methylhexyl acetate, β-Elemene, β-Selinene, Germacrene B, Savinin.
B. ribana	Tricyclene, α-Pinene, β-Pinene, Para-Cymene, β-Caryophyllene, α-Caryophyllene, Germacrene D, β-Sesquiphelandrene.
B. roseana	Heptane, Nonane, Sabinene, α-Pinene, β-Phelandrene, β-Terpineol, α-copaene, δ-Elemene, β-Elemene, β-Cedrene, β-Caryophyllene, α-Caryophyllene, Germacrene D, α-Selinene, Germacrene B, β-Selenene, Burseh-ernin, Dextrobursehernin, Morelensin, Deoxypodophyllotoxin, β-Peltatin-A methylether.
B. rzedowskii	Sabinene, β-Pinene, Myrcene, Para-Cymene, Cis-Ocimene, 1-Methylhexyl acetate, Germacrene D.
B. sarcopoda	Heptane, 2-Heptanone, Cis-Ocimene, Trans-Ocimene, β-Cedrene, β-Caryophyllene, Germacrene D, γ-Elemene, Verticiol, Phytol.
B. sarukhanii	Tricyclene, α-Pinene, β-Pinene, α-Phelandrene, Limonene, β-Thujone, β-Caryophyllene, Germacrene D, Germacrene B, Phytol.
B. schlechtendalii	Heptane, 2-Heptanone, 3-Heptanol, Nonane, α-Pinene, Benzaldehyde, Sabinene, β-Pinene, Myrcene, α-Phelandrene, β-Phelandrene, β-Caryophyllene, Germacrene D, Bursehernin.

B. simaruba	A-Pinene, β-Pinene, α-Phelandrene, β-Phelandrene, β-Terpineol, α-Copaene, δ-Elemene, β-Elemene, β-Caryophyllene, α-Caryophyllene, Germacrene D, β-Selinene, α-Selinene, Germacrene B, δ-Cadinene, beta Sesquiphelandrene, Phytol, α-Amyrin, β-Amyrin, Lupeol, Epilupeol, Yatein, β-Peltatin-O-β-D-glucopyranoside, Hinokinin, Bursehernin, 3,4-Dimetoxyphenyl-1-O-β-D-(6-sulpho)-glucopyranoside. Picropolygamain (Peraza-Sánchez and Peña-Rodríguez 1992).
B. submoniliformis	Heptane, α-Pinene, β-Thujone, Isocaryophyllene, δ-Elemene, β-Elemene, β-Caryophyllene, Cis-β-Farnecene, Germacrene D, Germacrene B, β-Sesquiphelandrene, Humulene, α-Bisabolol, Germacrone, Verticiol, Phytol, Savinin.
B. suntui	Heptane, 2-Heptanone, Nonane, Ethyl hexanoate, Cis-Ocimene, β-Caryophyllene, Germacrene D.
B. tecomaca	Cis-Ocimene, Trans-Ocimene, Isocaryophyllene, α-Cubebene, Germacrene D, Germacrene B.
B. trimera	Heptane, 3-Heptanol, Nonane, 2-Heptanol acetate, β-caryophyllene, Germacrene D, α-Eudesmol.
B. vazquezyanesii	A-Pinene, β-Pinene, cis-Pinene, β-Phelandrene, Cis-Ocimene, α-Thujone, Germacrene D, α-Selinene.
B. vejar-vazquezii	2-Heptanone, Sabinene, β-Pinene, α-Thujone, Phenylethyl alcohol, δ-Elemene, β-Caryophyllene, Germacrene D, Germacrene B, β-Sesquiphelandrene, γ-Elemene, α-Bisabolol, Verticiol, Phytol.
B. velutina	Heptane, 2-Heptanone, Nonane, Tricyclene, α-Pinene, Sabinene, α-Phelandrene, Para-Cimene, β-Phelandrene, Cis-Ocimene, Phenylethyl alcohol, Borneol, Carveone, β-Caryophyllene, Germacrene B, β-Sesquiphelandrene, Phytol.
B. xochipalensis	Heptane, 2-Heptanone, α-Pinene, β-Phelandrene, δ-Elemene, β-Caryophyllene, Germacrene D, Germacrene B, α-Bisabolol, Germacrone, Phytol.

Note: All chemical analyses performed by Judith Becerra and collaborators except when cited.

originated in plants many millions of years ago, long before humans were part of the culinary picture (Becerra 1997). The purpose of these defenses, in great part, has been to affect the brain biochemistry, digestion, and overall physiology of insects, to cause them to decrease or cease their feeding on the plants that produce the chemicals. *Bursera* species, like all plants, are participants in this conflict between consumers and victims. *Bursera* produces a variety of defensive compounds often of the terpenoid, phenolic, and hydrocarbon classes (table 5.1). Mixtures of these compounds are called resins and in *Bursera* they are stored in tiny duct-like structures called resin canals. These canals follow the leaf veins that move water and sugar and are also found in the outer layers of trunks and stems. When leaves or other tissues are damaged, canals rupture, releasing their toxin-containing resins. The chemicals they produce affect the nervous system of animals in general, deter insect feeding, inhibit their growth, and poison the offenders. Chemical production of some plants injures nonherbivores, even humans. People in general should not consume poison ivy.

Rubbing or crushing leaves of different *Bursera* species invariably produces a fragrance, each species with its distinct aroma. This is because species differ in the chemical compounds they produce as protection from being eaten by animals or attacked by pathogens. The pungent aroma of crushed *Bursera* leaves is due to the high volatility (ability to evaporate) of monoterpenes and short-chain hydrocarbons, a few of the many chemicals that these plants produce. *Bursera microphylla*, for example, owes its crisp odor to a mixture of mostly α- and β-phelandrene and α- and β-pinene. The pungent smell of *B. schlechtendalii* and *B. chemapodicta* is due largely to a hydrocarbon called heptane (Evans and Becerra 2006). While pleasant to most of us for a few seconds or minutes, inhaling the smell of these leaves for longer periods of time will result in a headache. In contrast, the splendid fragrance of *B. linanoe*, the tree used for perfume and small lacquered boxes, is given by linalyl acetate, which has no recorded ill effects in humans. Most find the aroma intensely pleasurable.

Can these resins prevent herbivores from attacking *Bursera*? The answer invokes a marvel of evolution: In nature, very few insects dare to attack these plants, and the ones that do it have had to modify their digestive and detoxification systems so that they are not poisoned. This is a difficult evolutionary process that often requires gene mutations or some other kind of gene reorganization. One potential reason for each *Bursera* species having its own chemical (and fragrant) signature is to make it more difficult for herbivores to adapt and overcome these defenses. Otherwise, once an herbivore is able to feed and thrive on one plant species, it would be able to attack the foliage of other similarly defended species as well. Thus, it is in the interest of each of these plant species to develop its own peculiar defensive strategies.

While all plants on our planet have developed chemicals that deter most of the great diversity of herbivores, none is equipped to ward off all attacks. Entomologists estimate that between 2 and 8 million species of insects exist on Earth and at least 80 percent of them feed on plants, so it should not be surprising that each plant species has at least one insect species that has been able to adapt its physiology to be immune to the antiherbivore toxins. For example, milkweeds are named for their milky sap that contains an array of chemicals known as cardenolides. These are highly toxic to insects and animals in general because they inhibit cells from maintaining an adequate concentration of calcium and potassium, both of which are indispensable to maintain cell volume. Most herbivores die if they ingest large amounts of these plants compared to their body weight. Yet during their evolution a few species of beetles, true bugs, moths, and butterflies (including the monarchs) gained physiological adaptations that have made them pretty much invulnerable to the milkweeds' cardenolides. This tolerance of a general poison has required extensive physiological modifications that have made them highly specialized, meaning that they cannot eat anything else *but* milkweeds. This sort of evolutionary interaction between two or more species or groups of species affecting each other's evolution is called "coevolution." Monarch butterflies are experiencing a steep decline in numbers as milkweeds are sacrificed when land is cleared for development or agriculture, for the butterflies have no alternate food source. In the same way as milkweeds have coevolved with their herbivores, *Bursera* has coevolved with its own group of herbivores (Becerra 2007).

Bursera's specialized herbivores consist of about 55 species of small jumping beetles in the genus *Blepharida* (Becerra 2004). Their larvae feed on burseras and nothing else, and some of them are so highly specialized that they can feed on no more than a single *Bursera* species. As long as their *Bursera* species is available, they will feed on it, survive, and reproduce, but they are unable to extend their herbivory to other *Bursera* species or any other plant species at all. If they get lucky and find their host plant, however, these small beetles can reproduce in such high numbers that they can easily defoliate a good portion of an individual tree, and if their predation continues year after year, they can kill the tree.

Throughout millions of years, the coevolutionary battle between *Bursera* and *Blepharida* has led to an arms race and a counterattack chase (Becerra 2003a). Researchers using

FIGURE 5.1 Squirt-gun defense of *B. schlechtendalii* (photo by L. Venable).

FIGURE 5.2 A beetle larva of the genus *Blepharida* positions itself along a leaf of *Bursera schlechtendalii* and surgically defuses the squirt-gun defense to avoid the spray of resins (photo by J. Becerra).

FIGURE 5.3 Squirt-gun defense of *B. trimera* (photo by L. Venable).

molecular techniques to estimate the approximate time when each *Bursera* species originated reveal that over time there has been an increase in both the number and the molecular complexity of chemical compounds that these plants produce (Becerra, Noge, and Venable 2009). Species that originated more recently are armed with a more intricate and complex chemical arsenal than species that originated long ago. *Blepharida* beetles have responded to this challenge. After all, life on Earth follows the dictum *adapt or go extinct*. More recently derived species of *Blepharida* have modified their physiology to be able to feed on these more chemically sophisticated plants.

The coevolutionary race has also led some *Bursera* species to add an even more potent line of defense. In these species, resin canals are pressurized. When the canals are severed or punctured by an insect, a high-pressure flow of resins is released, literally a squirt, soaking the attacker. This plant defense represents a daunting challenge for insects: with the new delivery strategy, not only are resins toxic but they also solidify when exposed to air and, depending on the insects' size, can partially bathe or drown the victims. Once the resins harden, they entomb them—not bad for these seemingly powerless, innocent trees.

Squirting noxious chemicals on animal pests is a truly unusual plant adaptation, little known outside *Bursera* and some of its close relatives. And if shooting deadly chemicals at attackers is not extraordinary enough, there is also a counterstrategy that *Blepharida* larvae have developed in turn. One of the authors of this book, Judith, recounts how she discovered it:

Thirty years ago, I was helping lead a field trip for students from the National University of Mexico in the Valley of Tehuacán close to the town of Zapotitlán Salinas, Puebla. On the morning of our third day, I awoke with my ankles and lower legs inflamed with a rash. I had forgotten to dust them with sulfur powder the previous day to deter chig-

FIGURE 5.4 Species of beetles belonging to the genus *Blepharida* that specializes in feeding on *Bursera* plants: (A) *Blepharida sparsae*; (B) *Blepharida schlechtendalii*; (C) *Blepharida flavocostata*; (D) *Blepharida pallida*; (E) *Blepharida multimaculata* (photos by J. Becerra and D. L. Venable).

gers from attacking me while we were hiking up a mountain to conduct a plant census. Unfortunately, this was cow and goat country, and cows and goats bring with them infestations of chiggers. As hiking for me was now painful, the group left me at the base of another mountain where they planned to conduct another field exercise. While waiting in my misery for them to return, I sat on the ground close to a small bonsai-shaped *B. schlechtendalii*, a species abundant in that area. From previous research, I was aware that some of these plants produced copious amounts of resins, and I tested this plant to see if it would squirt when I broke one of its small, unifoliolate leaves.

To my delight, the leaf released a resin squirt that traveled a couple of meters. I repeated the procedure several times more. Sometimes I got a smaller squirt or just a flush of resins that covered most of the leaf.

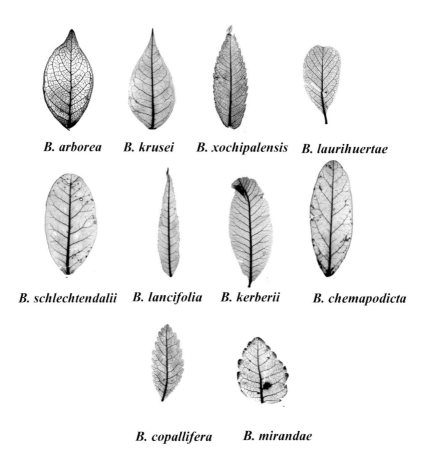

FIGURE 5.5 Different patterns of leaf secondary veins in some *Bursera* species. Of these species, only the ones in the middle (*B. schlechtendalii*, *B. lancifolia*, *B. kerberi*, *B. chemapodicta*) release resins with enough pressure to produce a squirt (adapted from Andrés-Hernández et al. 2012).

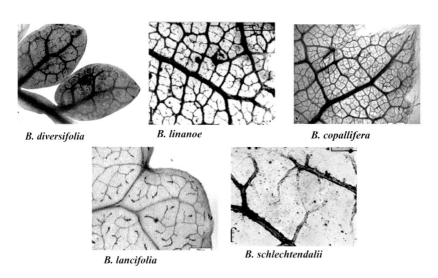

FIGURE 5.6 Patterns of leaf tertiary veins in some burseras. Of these species, only *B. lancifolia* and *B. schlechtendalii* produce a squirt of resins (adapted from Andrés-Hernández et al. 2012).

But then I noticed that some of the leaves on the squirting tree were totally or partially eaten by what were clearly insect jaws. I was naturally surprised that any insect would venture to attack a plant with such a potent defense. The insects responsible for the damage were little yellow larvae that had their backs covered with dollops of poop. By examining these larvae more closely I could see that some of them were laboring at the base of the leaf's midrib, performing what appeared to be a careful and very purposeful operation of puncturing the midrib with their mandibles. And then, after this biting procedure, which sometimes took more than thirty minutes, they turned around to the tip of the leaf and started munching the leaf tissues. At this point the release of resin coming from the wounded tissues was minimal, for the pressure had been released without harm to the insect. The larvae were able to disarm the leaf! And thus, I forgot the burning itch from the chigger bites and cataloged a new observation about the creativity of herbivores in the face of antiherbivore plant evolutionary strategy.

Throughout the years we have had many opportunities to observe this fascinating squirt response in a variety of *Bursera* species as well as the captivating canal-disarming behavior of the *Blepharida* species that feed on them.

It turns out that this leaf defense has also diversified into multiple variants to make herbivore adaptation more difficult (Becerra, Noge, and Venable, 2009). Not only do the chemicals that the plants release differ, but plants have also managed to diversify the anatomy of leaf venation and the location of the canals.

A leaf trait that has perplexed *Bursera*'s anatomists for a century is the great variation in the arrangement of veins. In some species, the primary leaf vein branches into secondary veins that terminate at the leaf margin or tip. In others, the secondaries do not terminate but loop forward to join the next vein. Yet in others the secondaries branch again, and one tertiary vein ends at the margin while another loops forward into the next tertiary (Andrés-Hernández et al. 2012). And in some species veins have grown wider. This degree of variation within a genus is not common in the plant kingdom; that is, most genera tend to have fewer vein variations. In *Bursera*, vein proliferation and elaboration seem to be part of the diversification of herbivore defense strategies. Only a few *Blepharida* species, those with relatively large mandibles, are capable of easily carving wide veins. Also, different venation patterns require that *Blepharida* species disarm canals in different vein locations;

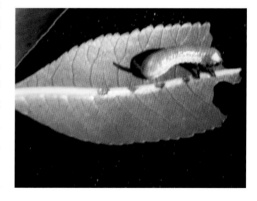

FIGURE 5.7 Another *Blepharida* species (*B. lineata*) is deactivating the resin canals of *B. trimera*, leaving multiple bite wounds on the midrib (photo by J. Becerra).

when there are vein loops, the carving of the vein to relieve pressure might disarm the leaf only partially—the canals within the looping veins can still transport resin to other parts of the leaf margin. We have experimentally transplanted *Blepharida* species that feed on one squirting *Bursera* to another species; although they still attempt to carve the veins, they don't seem to do it properly on the new species and most often end up getting an unexpected flush of resins. When this happens, the larvae quickly withdraw and abandon the leaf. As you can imagine, experimenting with these insects' responses can be grand fun. Science isn't all grunt work.

CHAPTER 6

Bursera Reproductive Traits, or a Genus with Confused Sexuality

Reproductive Systems

The sex life of burseras makes them seem even odder than their appearance. *Bursera* flowers are minute, with a diameter of between 2 and 10 mm and radially symmetric. They are almost always unisexual, meaning they only have male organs (stamens, anthers, and pollen) or female organs (ovary, stigma). *Bursera* species are typically dioecious, which means they produce male-only and female-only plants. So far, so good, but not all species adhere to the typical pattern: a few are polygamo-dioecious, meaning that every now and then some of their populations might have male plants that produce a small quantity of female flowers, or, occasionally, individual plants produce a small proportion of hermaphroditic flowers (with both male and female organs) in addition to their unisexual flowers.

B. fagaroides, which is found from Sonora south into southern Mexico, is probably the champion in having many variations that do not obey the dioecy rule. Across its range there are populations with only male individuals, some with only female individuals, and individuals that carry male flowers plus varying proportions of hermaphroditic flowers. As if this were not complicated enough, some of its populations are made up of exclusively female individuals that probably reproduce by asexual means. We have also observed a few populations with male and female individuals growing along with males that host some hermaphroditic flowers and some with all hermaphroditic individuals.

Among the unruly species are also *B. microphylla* and *B. fagaroides* var. *elongata*, in which some populations are made up of separate female and hermaphrodite-flowered plants (a phenomenon called gynodioecy). *Bursera aromatica*, a species from Jamaica, has both male and hermaphrodite flowers in the same plant (a situation

called andromonoecy). Equally confusing is *B. galeottiana*: in most of its populations, the male plants appear to be inconstant, producing a few hermaphroditic
flowers that mature into fruits (Velázquez-Herrera 2011). *Bursera schlechtendalii*
and *B. morelensis* exhibit the same pattern as *B. galeottiana* but to a lesser extent,
and in only a limited number of populations. *Bursera simaruba* is also polygamo-
dioecious. And then there is the special case of *B. medranoana*, often presumed to
be a hybrid species between *B. schlechtendalii* and *B. morelensis* and for which the
whole species consists of asexual female individuals that produce fruits and seeds
without fertilization (Rzedowski and Ortiz 1988).

While in most vertebrate animals the general directive is for an individual to be
either male or female, dioecy is a rather rare phenomenon in the plant world. Most
flowering plants are cosexual (or hermaphrodites), meaning that both male and female functions are present in the same individual. Only about 6 percent of all angio-
sperm species (flowering plants) are dioecious. But dioecism seems to be an important evolutionary strategy, since, while rare, it has evolved many times. About half
of the 400 or so families of flowering plants have some species that are dioecious.
The most widely accepted hypothesis for the evolution of dioecy is that it functions
to promote outcrossing by nixing the possibility of self-pollination, which can lead
to inbreeding depression. Evolutionary reversions in the opposite direction—from
dioecy to hermaphroditism—seem to be rare in flowering plants, so unusual that
plant reproductive biologists consider dioecy an end point of sexual system evolution. It is understandable, then, that plant scientists consider most interesting the
phenomenon of dioecy breaking down or reverting toward hermaphroditism in
some *Bursera* species. Perhaps the risk of inbreeding is trumped by other variables
that are yet to be discerned.

This breakdown of dioecy has been studied in some detail in *B. microphylla*, high-
lighting how problems in finding mates can lead to some formerly dioecious plants
becoming hermaphrodites. Throughout most of its range in the Sonoran Desert,
this species is dioecious and exhibits an unbiased sex ratio, with male plants and
female plants equally abundant. However, an isolated population in the Waterman
Mountains, Arizona, along the edge of its northeastern distribution, is gynodioecious, consisting mostly of females, some hermaphrodites, and only one male. This
strongly female-biased ratio has resulted in a very limited amount of pollen available
to fertilize the female plants. In contrast, the self-compatible hermaphroditic individuals are not pollen limited.

This suggests that limited pollination may help explain the advantage of these
plants becoming hermaphrodite. However, it is not clear how they have accomplished this change. One explanation could be that the change in reproduction
system is a result of two species hybridizing, since the mixture of genomes from

different species might disrupt the control of producing pure femaleness and male-ness, allowing hermaphrodites to evolve. Alternatively (or in conjunction with hy-bridization), polyploidy, the doubling of chromosome number, could disrupt the sex-determination mechanism, leading to the production of hermaphrodites. We used molecular genomic techniques to test the hypotheses that individuals of the Waterman Mountains are hybrids or polyploids. The results showed no signature of hybridization or polyploidy, so we concluded that these are not the explanations for this reversion from dioecy. The mystery remains unsolved.

Flowers

Bursera flowering begins in early May in anticipation of the summer rains, when the air is hot and dry, and flowering continues until June or, for some species, through July. Individuals of the same species tend to bloom in synchrony, although male individuals often initiate flowering a week to ten days ahead of female flowers, as if anxiously awaiting the first unpollinated female flowers.

The flowers are usually clustered in small inflorescences, but in some species, they can be solitary. Their colors are not particularly striking, ranging from cream to white, a light-green or reddish color, but they do produce nectar and have a sweet smell. These traits are characteristic of insect-pollinated flowers, and while there is no recorded pollination information for many of the *Bursera* species, what is known indicates that bees, both native and honeybees, as well as wasps and flies, are the main visitors of *Bursera* flowers.

Very few *Bursera* researchers have targeted pollination, with good reason. Flow-ers in the genus are normally produced at the beginning of the wet season ahead of leaves, and in *Bursera*, flower traits are not as diagnostic of species as leaves. This produces despair among botanists trained to view flowers as the final arbiter of spe-cies identification. This anomaly—nondescript flowers and diagnostic leaves—and the fact that more than a dozen *Bursera* species may be flowering at the same time in a given location make it difficult to determine which species is which. Tropical deciduous forests are drab and rather unattractive, perhaps even a little boring, in the hot dry period before the onset of the rainy season. Botanical expeditions tend to await the more interesting rainy season to begin field studies, thus often missing the flowering window of *Bursera*.

Despite these botanical roadblocks, some hardy souls have recorded valuable observations for a few species. For example, flowers of *B. copallifera* from a locality in southeast Puebla attract a great variety of insects: at least 66 insect taxa, including bees, wasps, ants, butterflies, flies, moths, and beetles have been recorded visiting

FIGURE 6.1 Collage of *Bursera* flowers (photos by J. Becerra and L. Venable).

the flowers. While the effectiveness of these insects as *B. copallifera* pollinators has not been determined, the most consistent visitors are solitary bees of the genus *Hypanthidium* and honeybees (Rivas-Arancibia et al. 2015). Flowers of *B. morelensis*, a common red-barked cuajiote from Puebla and Oaxaca, are solitary, tiny, and delicate with a light-red color and are very likely pollinated mostly by wasps and bees. Wasps and bees also visit the creamy-green flowers of *B. schlechtendalii* and *B. medranoana*. *Bursera simaruba* is pollinated by *Centris lanipes* bees in the French West Indies and by *Scaptotrigona* and *Melitoma* stingless bees in Yucatán and Central America (Meurgey 2016). *Bursera ovalifolia* as well as *B. simaruba* are also visited by the metallic-green halictid bees of the genus *Neocorynura* in the south of Mexico (Smith-Pardo 2005).

In Costa Rica, *B. simaruba* flowers are also visited by small flies, cerambycid beetles, and other small insects. Small, metallic-green bees are attracted to flowers of cultivated *B. fagaroides* and *B. lancifolia* in Sonora, Mexico. The diminutive size of the flowers would seem to discourage bird or bat pollinators.

Fruits

Bursera fruits are small, nearly round, 0.4 to 1.4 cm long. The botanical term for the type of fruits burseras have is a drupe (the classic example being a cherry or a peach). The drupe of a cherry or peach has a skin (or pericarp) covering a fleshy outer portion of the fruit that we eat (exocarp), which surrounds a hardened inner portion of the fruit, the stone or pit (endocarp), which in turn has an almondlike seed inside.

If you stretch your imagination, a *Bursera* drupe is like a small peach. It too has a pericarp, an exocarp, an endocarp, and a seed. However, unlike the fleshy exocarp of the peach that we eat, the exocarp of *Bursera* is leathery and splits open (dehisces) at maturity to reveal the endocarp, which looks like a seed but is actually hardened fruit tissue (like the peach stone) with its seed inside. For those who know the commercial edible stone fruits better than burseras, the idea of a nonfleshy dehiscent (splitting) stone fruit may seem weird indeed.

FIGURE 6.2 Pollination of *B. simaruba* (photo by B. Peterson).

FIGURE 6.3 *Bursera* fruits are small, often green and reddish (photo by L. Venable).

Thus the black "seed" of *Bursera* is actually a seed surrounded by endocarp. This black pit or stone is totally or partially surrounded by a sometimes white or yellow but usually red pseudoaril. In botanical terms, an aril is a fleshy structure that develops out of a seed stalk and grows around the seed. It is an attractive, often nutritious structure appealing to seed dispersers. While it functions like a fleshy seed coat, it grows out of the seed stalk and covers the real seed coat. It is more readily

FIGURE 6.4 In botanical terms, burseras' fruits are drupes. The leathery exocarp opens at maturity to expose the black pit that encloses the seed. The pit is partially or completely surrounded by a fleshy or papery pseudoaril (photo by L. Venable).

FIGURE 6.5 In some *Bursera* species, the pseudoaril is fleshy and does not cover the stone completely: undehisced fruit (*left*); black stone partially covered by fleshy pseudoaril (*right*) (photo by L. Venable).

distinguished from a fleshy seed coat when it only partially engulfs the seed. To make matters even more complicated, because the black "seed" in *Bursera* is actually a stone, not a seed, botanists do not consider the fleshy outgrowth a true aril, and therefore use the term *pseudoaril*. Nature is intricate and complex, and botanists have risen to the occasion, developing a corresponding vocabulary. This may be annoying to the lay person perhaps, but remember, this intricate complexity and diversity is what makes nature so wonderfully amazing.

After pollination, seeds start developing from ovules in the ovary, which has three chambers (or locules) in species of subgenus *Bursera* and two in species of subgenus *Elaphrium*. In most species where detailed anatomical studies have been performed, only one seed develops per fruit (Becerril 2004; Montano-Arias 2004). The locule carrying the seed expands, while the other locule(s) shrink and remaining ovules are aborted (Ramos-Ordoñez, Márquez-Guzmán, and Arizmendi 2012). However, exceptions occur. In *B. linanoe*, two seeds may initially develop per locule, from which one- or two-seeded fruits develop. *Bursera simaruba* is also known to produce one- and two-seeded fruits (Trainer and Will 1984), and probably other as-yet-unobserved species do too.

Fruits, usually green or yellow, appear by the middle of June and, depending on the species, mature after three months or longer, and they may become red. Maturation involves developing an embryo within the seed, which curiously enough in *Bursera* does not occur until the latest stages of fruit maturation. Some otherwise fully developed fruits never develop an embryo. Thus, they look ripe on the outside but are hollow on the inside. In most species, a good proportion of these "empty" pits remain on plants for as long as "filled" viable pits and often can only be distinguished after careful examination. This is odd, because it is highly

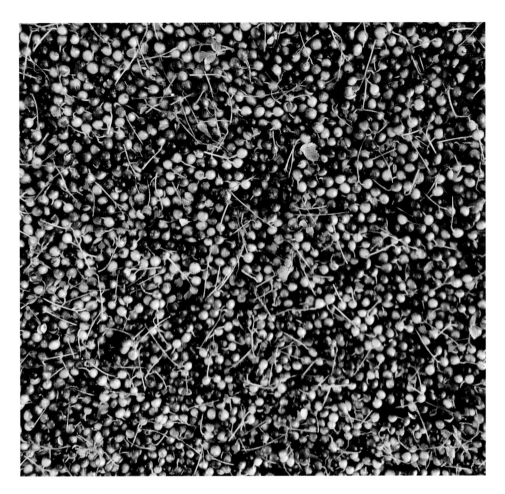

FIGURE 6.6 Fruits of *Bursera glabrifolia* (photo by L. Venable).

unusual—self-defeating—for plants to maintain a fruit without viable seeds. Ordinarily, fruits that are unpollinated have a low number of seeds or are incapable of producing viable progeny due to abnormalities or because of physical damage are aborted early in development. This ensures that precious nutrients are sent to fruits with live embryos rather than being wasted on barren fruits. One possible reason for the maintenance of fruits without embryos is that birds are perhaps more attracted to trees with larger amounts of fruit. Thus, fruits with empty seeds help advertise and disperse fruits bearing viable seeds. Another possible explanation is that dummy fruits can decrease the probability of fruit predation by insects and birds that damage seeds, since these animals injure fruits indiscriminately, that is, whether they have embryos or not (Ramos-Ordoñez 2009).

When *Bursera* fruits ripen, the leathery pericarp valves open and detach, exposing the colorful pseudoaril, which is rich in lipids, sugar, and nutrients. After this grand opening, seed destiny is all up to the birds, for they are the primary agents

FIGURE 6.7 Fruits of *Bursera lina-noe* without the exocarp (photo by D. Cornu).

in seed dispersal in these plants.[1] Rodents and ants may also secondarily disperse (or destroy) their fruits and seeds when they end up on the ground.[2] The presence of the pseudoaril is a strategy that evolved to entice dispersers, and *Bursera* seeds will seldom germinate if this structure is not removed. Seeds transported away from the parent plant are best placed to avoid competition for resources with their mother and siblings as well as to avoid pathogens and predators that specialize in *Bursera* seeds and seedlings.

In Mexico and Central America, the high-lipid-containing *Bursera* fruits are an important dry-season resource for many birds. In *B. morelensis* fruits, for example, 68 percent of the mass is lipid (Ramos-Ordoñez 2009). The caloric content of the pseudoaril is also elevated, higher per weight than comparable fruit resources available to other birds (R. Johnson et al. 1985; Bates 1992). They are a significant food source for resident birds because they are produced when the forests are leafless and insects are scarce. For migrants and wintering birds, *Bursera* fruits are critical

1. In this book, we sometimes use the more familiar word *seed* instead of the more correct word *pit* when it doesn't matter too much for the context. For example, since the units that germinate and disperse are single-seeded pits, pit germination and dispersal are basically the same idea as seed germination and dispersal. There are whole books written on seed dispersal, but we haven't seen any yet on pit dispersal. So sometimes we use *seed dispersal* instead of *pit dispersal*.

2. Interestingly, the fruits of *B. inversa*, a species that looks very similar to *B. simaruba* but we think does not belong to the *Bursera* genus, are consumed and dispersed by spiders and woolly monkeys in the tropics of Colombia (Stevenson, Link, and Ramírez 2005).

because they are abundant when the birds are accumulating fat reserves prior to their northward flights across Mexico and perhaps the Gulf of Mexico. Vireos and tyrannid flycatchers are especially reliant on bursera fruits. In fact, they feed on little else when in bursera country for the winter.

While seed dispersal by means of ingestion by birds or mammals is the dispersal mechanism of excellence for most tree species, particularly in the tropics, different bird species vary in their degree of effectiveness as dispersers, depending on traits such as feeding behavior, gut length, and movement patterns. Birds can be inadequate dispersers for *Bursera* if they chew on seeds and destroy or damage the embryos. Also, retention time in the gut is critical since *Bursera* seeds have a hard coat and require scarification (mechanical or chemical breakdown) to germinate. This is accomplished when the seed is in contact with the acidic gastric juices of the animal digestive tract for a suitable length of time. If seed defecation is not immediate after consumption, it may allow more time to weaken the seed coat and increases the probability that the bird transports and deposits seeds away from the parent plant to a more favorable site for germination and establishment.

Maturation time of fruits among *Bursera* species varies considerably, as do their tendency for having their seeds mature simultaneously or sequentially over a long period of time. An interesting pattern in need of more research is that the species whose fruits mature simultaneously are mostly dispersed by opportunistic birds migrating through during fruiting season. However, at least some of the species of burseras dribble their fruits out a few at a time for months and are associated with overwintering birds, such as vireos that actually set up winter territories around burseras, defend them, and check them regularly throughout the dry season for newly dribbled fruits. For example, in *B. glabrifolia* and *B. hindsiana*, fruits require about 6 months or less to mature, while in *B. bicolor*, *B. biflora*, *B. bipinnata*, *B. grandifolia*, *B. lancifolia*, and *B. submoniliformis*, maturation takes about 7 months. In *B. aptera*, *B. arida*, *B. copallifera*, *B. fagaroides*, *B. microphylla*, *B. morelensis*, *B. schlechtendalii*, and *B. simaruba*, fruits mature between 7 and 11 months after the plants produce them. The asexual *B. medranoana* fruits mature over a period of 12 months after pollination and may overlap with the flowers and fruits produced in the following year (Cortes-Palomec 1998).

The slowly matured fruits of *B. simaruba* are a big food resource on the coasts of Mexico, southern Yucatán, and Central America, and at least 41 species from 10 bird families have been observed eating them (Scott and Martin 1984). Some of them, such as the indigo bunting (*Passerina cyanea*) and the rose-breasted grosbeak (*Pheucticus ludovicianus*), are poor dispersers and are instead seed predators that destroy embryos. But the fruits are also consumed by white-eyed vireos (*Vireo griseus*) that overwinter in Yucatán and do not digest the pits. They feed heavily on the fruits, all the while defending their trees against other birds (Greenberg, Foster, and Márquez-Valdelamar 1995). Likewise, in Santa Rosa National Park in northwestern Costa Rica, *B. simaruba* is consumed by at least 12 bird species, but the most important fruit disperser is the migrant wintering scissor-tailed flycatcher, *Tyrannus forficatus*.

As with *B. simaruba*, in the Río Balsas basin many other *Bursera* species are appealing to a variety of birds that mostly feed on seeds. But they also attract vireos and flycatchers that mainly feed on insects while summering in the United States; when wintering in Mexico, they feed on fruits, predominantly those of *Bursera*. Insects tend to be a rich source of fat and are a good means of satisfying the caloric requirements of birds, a condition shared by *Bursera*'s pseudoarils. These migrants are, again, the ones that often benefit *Bursera* the most in terms of fruit dispersal. For example, *Bursera longipes*, a close relative of *B. simaruba*, is visited by at least 20 species of birds belonging to 9 families during its fruiting season (Almazán-Núñez et al. 2015). However, it is the overwintering tyrannid flycatchers of the genus *Myiarchus* that establish their territories in proximity to these burseras and continuously remove their gradually matured fruits. They consume the pits along with the pseudoaril, routinely defecating the pits later at a distance from the mother plant and in microsites where germination and seedling establishment are high, typically in the shade of other plant species. Thus, they are highly effective dispersers of *B. longipes*. Furthermore, seeds seem to have a higher germination rate after passing through the digestive system of the ash-throated flycatcher, *Myiarchus cinerascens*, and Nutting's flycatcher, *M. nuttingi*, than with other seed-eating birds. The lesser goldfinch, *Spinus psaltria*, and the orange-fronted parakeet, *Eupsittula canicularis*, are very good at detaching pits and pseudoarils, but they discard pits under the mother plant, a location in which recruitment seldom occurs. The orange-fronted parakeet also destroys the plants' seeds when devouring them, thus it does not seem to contribute to the effective dispersal of *B. longipes* seeds.

Overwintering flycatchers are also effective dispersers of *B. aptera*, *B. bicolor*, *B. copallifera*, *B. grandifolia*, *B. lancifolia*, *B. linanoe*, *B. mirandae*, *B. morelensis*, *B. schlechtendalii*, *B. submoniliformis*, and *B. vejar-vazquezii* fruits during the dry season, with the smaller species of flycatchers removing the fruits of species of *Bursera* that produce the smaller fruits and the larger species of birds taking their pick from either larger or medium-seeded *Bursera* species (Rodríguez-Godínez et al. 2022). Resident flycatchers seem to have low impact on *Bursera*'s seed removal because there is an overlap between the dry season and the breeding season of these birds, which occurs from March to May. When that happens, resident flycatchers in tropical forests tend to include a high proportion of protein-rich insects in their diet. Many birds consume *Bursera* seeds in the northwestern Balsas River Basin,

FIGURE 6.8 The ash-throated flycatcher on *Bursera longipes* (photo by P. Pearsal, CC BY-NC).

but the most effective in terms of amounts of fruit taken appear to be members of *Myiarchus*, such as the ash-throated flycatcher (*M. cinerascens*), Nutting's flycatcher (*M. nuttingi*), dusty-capped flycatcher (*M. tuberculifer*), brown-crested flycatcher (*M. tyrannulus*), sulfur-bellied flycatcher (*Myiodynastes luteiventris*), and social flycatcher (*Myiozetetes similis*); and members of *Tyrannus*, including the tropical (*T. melancholicus*), western (*T. verticalis*), Cassin's (*T. vociferans*), and thick-billed kingbirds (*T. crassirostris*). On the Atlantic Coast, seeds of *B. fagaroides* var. *fagaroides* are consumed by overwintering gray vireos (*Vireo griseu*) and gray catbirds (*Dumetella carolinensis*), the last of which seem to serve this plant the best as dispersers, since seeds seem to have a better chance of successful germination after passing through their digestive tracts (Greenberg et al. 1993).

Following this same pattern, fruits of *B. microphylla* in coastal Sonora seem to be effectively dispersed by migrant ash-throated flycatchers and gray vireos (*V. vicinor*), which consume them almost exclusively (Unitt 2000). The elephant tree seeds mature a few at a time over autumn and winter. The vireos set up individually held territories around these trees, defend them, and return to them every year. Fruits

FIGURE 6.9 Gray vireo consuming a pit with pseudoaril of the elephant tree (*B. microphylla*) (photo by P. Deviche).

of *Bursera hindsiana*, on the other hand, while overlapping in distribution with *B. microphylla*, mature synchronously over a few months and do not seem to have specialized fruit consumers. A variety of birds, including Gila woodpeckers (*Melanerpes uropygialis*), cactus wrens (*Campylorhynchus brunneicapillus*), northern mockingbirds (*Mimus polyglottos*), and curve-billed thrashers (*Toxostoma curvirostre*), can potentially function as seed dispersers of *B. hindsiana*, but even Harris's antelope ground squirrels have been observed to feed on them (Bates 1992).

Still, much remains to be learned about variation in morphology and nutrient composition of *Bursera* fruits and how these affect the identity and behavior of their dispersers and seed predators. For example, fruits of some *Bursera* hang from long stems, while in others fruit stems are short, sometimes practically absent. In some species, fruits are solitary while others are grouped in infructescences that contain many fruits. Another interesting factor is the considerable variation among species with respect to the color and the water, sugar, and caloric content of the pseudoaril and how extensively it covers the pit. All the cuajiotes (subgenus *Bursera*) tend to have a pseudoaril completely covering the pit, and the color of the aril tends to be cream or yellow, with some tendencies toward red, like in *B. schlechtendalii* and *B. crenata*. On the other hand, the pseudoaril is more variable in species of subgenus *Elaphrium* (the copales), with the Copallifera group having completely or almost completely covering, usually orange or red, pseudoarils. Most of the remaining copales have the aril covering half or less of the pit. *B. infernidialis* is unusual in having the pseudoaril covering half of one face of the pit but most of the other. And then, the pseudoarils range from dry and papery to thick and fleshy with different water, lipid, and sugar contents (Bates 1992). All these characteristics can hardly escape the eyes of a bird, and one can only wonder about the coevolutionary forces that have shaped the traits in *Bursera* fruits and the behavior of their fruit dispersers.

CHAPTER 7

Bursera and People

For humans, *Bursera* is a friendly and gentle genus, all 100-some species. The same can be said of the family Burseraceae. The greatest damage the plants can inflict per se on humans is to stain the skin and clothing of those who become intimate in excess with the plants and their foliage, fruits, and sap. And, yes, deceivingly weak branches may crack and break under the weight of human climbers, but that is hardly the plants' fault. The trees are mostly leafless for up to half the year, longer in some places, which some view as an aesthetic detriment. Perhaps most negative of all, burseras do not appear to produce anything directly edible.

This lack, if we should call it that, contrasts with the closely related sister family Anacardiaceae, which contains some downright nasty and vicious species. None of us, we hope, would lament the disappearance or even the extinction of poison ivy and poison oak, members of the genus *Toxicodendron*. The poisonwood tree (*Metopium toxiferum*) of southern Florida and the Caribbean is an equally noxious member of the family, less recognizable to unwary vacationing poison-ivy-phobes. Through its ducts seeps the irritant urushiol, which can cause severe dermatitis, bringing misery to the hapless victim. The most popular antidote for the rash, iron-ically, is a potion concocted by steeping the bark of *Bursera simaruba* in water and applying it to the affected area. Poisonwood (unlike poison ivy and poison oak) partially redeems itself by providing splendid lumber but is still dangerous to us—and the woodcutters—due to its abundant resin ducts. Many genera in the Anac-ardieaceae produce urushiol, including several called *hincha-huevos* ("it makes your balls swell"). These include, as we discuss in chapter 10, *Pseudosmondingium multifolium* and *Pseudosmondingium perniciosum*, relatives of poison ivy that are the scourge of the uninitiated in tropical deciduous forests of southern Mexico and are distressingly common in this range.

But along with their harsh cousins, whose resin ducts pump malevolent allergens, the Anacardiaceae include mangoes, cashews, and pistachios, food crops from trees domesticated eons ago and economically important throughout the world. A small percentage of people exhibit allergies to these fruits and nuts (notably cashew juice), but for the most part, the trees that produce them are benign and productive.

So, if they yield no food, of what good are burseras, other than having strange and colorful bark, unusual and intriguing shapes, weird defenses against herbivores, and in at least some of them, agreeable aromas? As we will show, *Bursera*'s practical virtues are many, and they run from sacred and solemn to mundane and commonplace.

Resins

Bursera is best known in Mesoamerica for its ubiquitous use in incense rituals. *Copal* is the common name of some burseras and of their resin after it hardens upon being exposed to air. The word derives from the Náhuatl *copalli*, literally "thanks to this path." Mayas use the term *pom* ("that which is to be burnt") or *copal pom*. In most of North America, copal is mainly derived from *Bursera* resin. Much less frequently and depending on the location, copal can also be made from other plants that have more regional distributions, including several species of pines. Copal derived from burseras, however, hardens and, unlike some pine resins, does not remain sticky and is somewhat water soluble. Thus, it does not cling to skin or clothing and gather dirt and coarse matter like a magnet, a considerable virtue when compared with pine pitch. Yet pines are sometimes more accessible to people who do not inhabit the dry lowlands. In the western Mexican state of Michoacán, one of the states of highest *Bursera* diversity, the Purépecha people of the forested highlands (also known as Tarascans) burn *copal bola* for incense. It is resin extracted from the pines, which are readily available in the territory where they have resided for hundreds of years.

In some parts of southeast Mexico and Central America, copal is gathered from both *Bursera* and the closely related *Protium copal*. *Protium* is a genus in the Burseraceae that shares with *Bursera* major chemical constituents that flow in resin ducts. Neither burseras nor *Protium* grow in the pine-forested highlands of Chiapas and Guatemala where the Highland Maya prospered, so the copal they burned was gathered from the tropical dry and humid deciduous forests of the lower mountain slopes of the Pacific Coast. From there the dried resins were shipped to highland clerics, both Catholic and pagan, and to other consumers. The two regions must have conducted a brisk trade.

In south and central Mexico at present, traditional markets offer sufficient copal to satisfy diverse tastes and budgets (prices vary according to quality and mystique).

FIGURE 7.1 Resin collection from *Bursera bipinnata* in Central Mexico (photo by M. Campos Rivera).

FIGURE 7.2 A Mexican market stand where copal is typically sold along with other medicinal and mystical merchandise (photo by L. Venable).

These varieties are displayed in heaps separated by color and consistency. They include *copal blanco*, *copal lágrima*, *copal oro*, *copal negro*, and *copal de piedra*, with additional varieties appearing in different localities and with different labels. One especially prized variety, sold in the central market of Oaxaca de Juárez, is called *copal cristal* or *copal diamante*. It is so expensive that it is not displayed in open trays, as are other varieties. It is usually kept hidden in secure locations behind the display and only produced upon request.

While copal is usually derived from *Bursera* or a few other plants, popular classification into different types does not appear to adhere to a specific botanical system. Common names reflect more how the product was obtained than the source. *Copal blanco* (white copal), also known sometimes as *copal de santo* or *copal santo* (holy copal), is the preferred product in most areas as it delivers an exquisite fragrance when burned. It is exuded directly from incisions made in the bark of the tree and carefully gathered in containers. In order to prevent contamination with dirt and soil, the chosen receptacle is usually formed from maguey (agave) leaves with "zapatos" shaped from mud and cow dung that functioned as plugs at bases of the maguey leaves. In the twenty-first century, plastic soda bottles are replacing the original receptacles. *Copal lágrima* (tear) is the resin from droplets deposited on the surface of the trunk after environmental or mechanical damage such as incisions made by insects. *Copal oro* (gold), with a subtler aroma, is derived from resin exuded following the complete removal of the bark, while *copal negro* (black) is obtained by beating the bark. The latter is less aromatic and therefore cheaper and so is *copal de piedra* (stone), the resin that is gathered by wasps (Chalcidoidea) and used to cement pebbles and sand grains to form their nests on the underside of rocks. Another incense is *copal tierno* (tender), resin often derived from non-*Bursera* sources, probably pine and other plants, a semicoagulated copal that is sold by the spoonful. It burns and delivers more smoke than aroma but might help repel mosquitoes. Perhaps.

Several species of burseras are known to be sources of incense, but only a few are exploited extensively for commercial copal, specifically, *B. bipinnata*, *B. copallifera*, *B. glabrifolia*, and *B. linanoe*. Which species will be tapped for copal varies with the region and the availability of the species. Other important sources that are less frequently harvested commercially are *B. citronella*, *B. excelsa*, *B. heteresthes*, *B. microphylla*, *B. penicillata*, *B. sarukhanii*, *B. simaruba*, and *B. stenophylla*. Selecting trees for optimum resin yield and ease of harvesting is carried out by the *copaleros*, field harvesters who have become experts in determining whether a particular tree is adequately robust and healthy for extracting the resin. Copaleros usually select mature trees, since young trees do not yield sufficient resin. The copalero selects a tree and slashes a series of cuts or incisions in the bark. The next step is to attach gourds, agave leaves, or plastic soda bottles to the trunk beneath the incision to collect the

FIGURE 7.3 Copals commonly found in Mexican markets: (A) *copal oro*; (B) *copal cristal*; (C) *copal blanco*; (D) *copal lágrima*; (E) *copal negro* (photos by J. Becerra).

resin, much in the way latex is harvested from rubber trees. The resin hardens in the shape of its container and is brought to market without further processing.

For centuries, copal has maintained a conspicuous ceremonial significance throughout Mexico and Central America (Gigliarelli et al. 2015). Much of what we know about its pre-Columbian use comes from Aztec sources. Also known as the Mexica (pronounced as *Mecheeca*), Aztecs rose to power in the mid-fourteenth century, incorporating into their culture much of the beliefs and symbolism of peoples who preceded them in the Mexico City area, often by many centuries.

FIGURE 7.4 Gathering of copal from plants is the occupation of the *copaleros*, who are always male (photo by M. Campos Rivera).

From these predecessors the Aztecs learned the virtues of *Bursera* resin and promoted its mystical significance. When copal is burned over charcoal or embers, it produces a white, intensely fragrant smoke that indigenous peoples of the Mexico City Basin came to associate with Iztacteteo, "White God," a protective entity who aids in the communication between humans and the creators. Millennia before the rise of the Aztecs, the Maya of the lowlands of Yucatán and the Petén and the highlands of Chiapas and Guatemala practiced ritual burning of copal incense. It was recognized as a symbol of the natural forces at work in the universe, as a conduit to open the dialogue with the divine, and as the blood of a plant that feeds the gods (Tripplett 1999). *Popol Vuh*, the Highland Mayan account of their culture and history dating from around the time of the Spanish conquest, contains lengthy references to copal and describes how the sun, moon, and stars arrived on earth, bringing copal with them. These same Maya retain a vigorous role for copal incense in their contemporary rituals that combine pagan and Christian elements.

Bursera copal incense use flourished among the Aztecs, and its importance among their descendants is well documented. The extensive materials recovered from the Templo Mayor in the Aztec capital city of Tenochtitlán (now Mexico City) from the fifteenth and sixteenth centuries contain hundreds of pieces of copal, including many figurines. These were fashioned from an inner core of copal covered with a layer of stucco and formed by a double-sided mold. The figurines were then painted and adorned with paper garments or flags. Copal was also associated with the god Tlaloc ("he who makes things sprout") and the goddess Chalchiuhtlicue ("she of the jade skirt"), both rulers of water and associated with fertility and creation. Archaeologists have unearthed offerings to deities in the shape of small tortillas, tamales, and grains of maize, all composed of copal, leading researchers to believe that smoke from copal was considered to be food for the gods (Lona 2012).

Incense was an integral part of the multiple Aztec festivities. In *Historia general de las cosas de Nueva España*, the sixteenth-century Spanish friar Bernardino de Sahagún (1577), who studied and chronicled indigenous customs and plants, mentions the celebration of Tezcatlipoca, the God of Providence, in which *iztac copalli* (*copal blanco*) as well as *quauhiocopalli* (bark copal) were offered to Huitzilopochtli, deity of war, sun, and the patron of the city of Tenochtitlán. Besides its use in important ceremonies, copal was also burned constantly in the Aztec temples. Sahagún mentions that priests would offer incense nine times each day: four times during the day and five times at night. The four during the day were when the sun first appeared, early morning, noon, and when the sun was setting. The five times at night were from bedtime through shortly before dawn.

The many uses of copal required an abundant supply, which was often obtained from territories conquered by the Mexica. The Tribute Roll, the sixteenth-century central Mexican manuscript that listed the tributes paid by the various tributaries of the Aztec Empire, reports that the

FIGURE 7.5 A priest offers incense at a temple, plate 27 of the codex Fejérváry-Mayer (courtesy of Foundation for the Advancement of Mesoamerican Studies, Inc., http://www.famsi.org/research/loubat/Fejervary/page_27.jpg).

populations of Taxco and Tepecoacuilco (in the state of Guerrero) were each obliged to provide Tenochtitlán with 8,000 lumps of bark copal and 400 baskets of white copal every eighty days.

Copal use not only survived the arrival of the Spaniards but was adopted by them and has long since become a regular component of Catholic liturgical rituals throughout Mexico and Guatemala. An older Guarijío who did field work with one of us (David) in the Sonoran foothills of the Sierra Madre Occidental was officially charged by the local priest with gathering copal for church rituals.

Copal continues to be highly valued by indigenous as well as mestizo people of Middle America for rituals (organized and private), celebrations, and offerings throughout the year, with cleansing, divinatory, and therapeutic functions as well (Purata Velarde 2008). In addition to these spiritual functions, copal is often burned because the aromatic smoke is believed to purify whatever it touches or simply because it makes air and objects smell good. Some ritualistic calendar ceremonies dictate burning copal. One such rite is the annual blessing of the seeds, when supplicants are petitioning for rain, and at ceremonies of thanksgiving for the corn harvest.

In addition to its religious or ritualistic importance, copal has a widespread reputation as a valuable medicine in medico-religious rites. Copal smudging and cleansing are common practices. In smudging ceremonies, the dense smoke is directed over various body parts by fanning, often with large feathers. This practice is notable among the Otomí of the Mexico City area, who also "read" the copal's smoke to

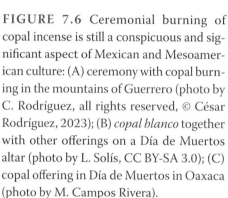

FIGURE 7.6 Ceremonial burning of copal incense is still a conspicuous and significant aspect of Mexican and Mesoamerican culture: (A) ceremony with copal burning in the mountains of Guerrero (photo by C. Rodríguez, all rights reserved, © César Rodríguez, 2023); (B) *copal blanco* together with other offerings on a Día de Muertos altar (photo by L. Solís, CC BY-SA 3.0); (C) copal offering in Día de Muertos in Oaxaca (photo by M. Campos Rivera).

diagnose disease. Reenactment of this ancient tradition has become popular among New Age practitioners as well. Watch your wallet.

Medical applications abound throughout Mexico. The dried resin is crushed, and the powdered residue is steeped into tea taken to help cure bronchitis and other respiratory complaints. Copal ground and dissolved in water is used as an antiseptic and anti-inflammatory poultice and to treat ailments afflicting lungs, stomach, venereal diseases, and even perceived imbalances of the mind. Zapotecs of Oaxaca still employ the use of *copal de memela*, a tortilla-flat copal paste dried and preserved

in banana leaves or corn husks, mixed with water and drunk when fasting. Zapotecs believe it will alleviate the stomach ailment known as "mal del aire." They also
prepare *copal estrella*, a fine *Bursera* resin powder that when ingested for several
days allegedly helps cure "el susto" (sudden fright or hysteria) or continuous "mal
genio" (bad temper). *Bursera graveolens*, also known as *palo santo* throughout Central and South America and the Galápagos Islands, is used to treat acne and as a
mood uplifter. The anti-inflammatory and analgesic qualities of its resin also make
it a popular folk remedy for headaches, including migraines, and for alleviating pain
from tight muscles and sore joints. The resin of *B. bipinnata*, a sacred tree among the
Maya, is used as a gentle cleansing agent to bathe newborns and new mothers after
birth. In the states of Veracruz and Guerrero, copal ashes are applied to snake bites
or scorpion stings (Olavarrieta Marenco 1977). In Sonora, *B. microphylla* is steeped
in alcoholic beverages to make a tincture for gum sores, cold sores, and abscessed
teeth. The dried stems and leaves are used in a tea to relieve painful urination and
as a stimulating expectorant for bronchitis, while the exudate has been used to treat
sexually transmitted diseases.

It seems odd that although copal was, and still is, widely used and highly regarded
as a folk medicine, formal pharmaceutical studies are only beginning to be explored.
The few that exist indicate that *Bursera* resins have natural terpenoid and lignan
compounds that may play a role in their healing properties. Terpenoids can be highly
volatile, and they contribute to the main *Bursera* scents and their antiseptic effects,
while lignans are estrogen-like chemicals, important in the production of diverse
pharmaceuticals. The most notable lignan-type compounds in *Bursera* are podo-
phyllotoxin, deoxypodophyllotoxin, and their derivatives, which are known to deter
the proliferation of laboratory cell lines of human colon adenocarcinoma, glioblas-
toma, breast cancer, melanoma, and other cancers. But they also contain other lignans such as ariensin, yatein, hinoquinin, morelensin, and burseran that have shown
promise to stop cancer cell proliferation (Marcotullio, Curini, and Becerra 2018).

Besides using them as incense and for healing, peoples of tropical North America
have also been incorporating other *Bursera* resin products into their daily lives for
many centuries, well before contact with Europeans. Burseras, like many trees in the
related family Anacardiaceae, are laden with resin ducts, but in *Bursera*, the liquid
is typically nonallergenic. We are unaware of any complaints of dermatitis or other
maladies caused by contact with the plants. On the contrary, many people consider
the liquids that ooze from *Bursera* to be useful or even powerful cures for various
maladies. Their fragrant resins, alone or combined with resins from other plants as
well as other materials, served as varnishes, insecticides, cosmetics, adhesives, and
chewing gum. And they proved most helpful in dental repair and, shall we say, oral
enhancement: the chronicler de Sahagún reported that Aztecs used copal resins

FIGURE 7.7 A pectoral in the shape of a double-headed serpent made of cedro wood (*Cedrela odorata*) and covered with a mosaic of turquoise and red thorny oyster shell. Pine and *Bursera* resins were used as adhesives (copyright The Trustees of the British Museum, CC BY-NC-SA 4.0).

mixed with calcium phosphate to affix precious stones to teeth and to plug tooth cavities. That particular use would serve as a breath freshener as well, at least for a while. The rumored antibiotic properties of some *Bursera* resins may also have been effective in preventing dental deterioration. Mineralized calcium phosphate such as apatite often contains fluorides and combined with *Bursera* resin may also have served as an anticavity agent.

Its value as a high-quality adhesive is manifested in exquisite turquoise mosaics, some of which are now considered the most important objects in the Mesoamerican collections of the British Museum. They are fashioned from small square tiles of turquoise malachite and lignite and shell applied to carved wooden foundations in shapes of masks, a knife, a serpent, and a helmet. Archaeologists suggest that Aztec priests or rulers used them in ceremonies. The artists used *Bursera* resins (probably from *B. bipinnata* or *B. linanoe*) along with pine resin to glue the tiles to the wooden bases.

In northern Sinaloa and southern Sonora, Mayo musicians maintain that the best resin for applying to the bows of their ceremonial violins, which are commercially manufactured, is derived from *B. fragilis*.

While copal is widely available at present, unfortunately it does not seem that the current production system will be sustainable over the long term. For example, many places where burseras grow are heavily stocked with goats and other animals, and few seedlings and saplings escape their grazing and browsing to replace the older trees. In addition, it is unknown how injurious to tree health the practice of making the *V*-shaped incisions in the bark of trunks and branches is. Such incisions probably provide entry points for pests and diseases that may kill mature trees. Furthermore, repeated harvesting without adequate resting periods between extractions may weaken and kill the trees. Most trees are found on communal lands and lack a formal organization to oblige *comuneros* to make sustainable choices. Research into how much resin can be safely extracted and how often is practically nonexistent.

Essential Oil

Bursera delpechiana, commonly known as Indian lavender tree or Indian linaloe, grows in southern India. For more than a century, the tree has been intensively exploited for its essential oils, especially linalyl acetate and linalool, which constitute important ingredients in perfume and pharmaceuticals. As *Bursera* partisans are quick to point out, *delpechiana* is not the tree's legitimate species name, nor is it native to India. Its correct taxonomy is *Bursera linanoe*, a tree native to the lowlands of the western Río Balsas Basin (Noge and Becerra 2010). For centuries before the arrival of the Spaniards, Mexicans valued the tree for its distinctive aromatic resin, which they exploited extensively. *Bursera linanoe* was prized then as it is now, for it is the sole *Bursera* species that produces abundant linalyl acetate, a chemical component of its resin that exudes a peculiarly agreeable aroma. Following the conquest, Spaniards introduced an artisanal industry to extract the oil from plants. Its reputation expanded over the centuries, and in 1912 Scottish entrepreneurs introduced

FIGURE 7.8 A plantation of *Bursera linanoe* at Hyderabad, India (photo by J. M. Garg, CC BY-SA 3.0).

this worthy tree and other closely related species, including *B. glabrifolia*, into India (Burton 1952). They oversaw plantings in the vicinity of Bengaluru (Bangalore) in the state of Karnataka on India's southwest coast, hoping to commercialize the oils. *Bursera linanoe*, which is drought-resistant, prospered in the Indian environment and its cultivation soon spread to Andhra Pradesh on the southeastern coast of India, then on to Thailand and other tropical locations. Agronomists in India discovered that distilling the mature fruits instead of the wood, as had been done in Mexico, yielded oil with a superior aroma and longer persistence than the native Mexican essence. The Indian oil eventually captured the international markets and industrial exploitation in Mexico collapsed. Oil is still extracted from Mexican *B. linanoe* as well as other *Bursera* species, notably *B. graveolens*, but only at an artisanal level. *B. linanoe* (under the name *Bursera delpechiana*) is the only *Bursera* widely cultivated for commercial uses outside its native range.

Bursera Wooden Artifacts

In Sonora and Chihuahua, Mayos, Yaquis, and Guarijíos of the Sierra Madre Occidental carve ceremonial masks and musical instruments from *Bursera* wood, usually *B. laxiflora*. These are still featured in lengthy fiestas throughout the year carried on by peoples rich in traditions and living on the margins of technological society.

But it is central Oaxaca that is famous for carved wooden figurines called *alebrijes*. These are brightly colored, often flamboyant sculptures of phantasmagoric animals, images, or beings, carved primarily from the wood of *B. glabrifolia*, a small tree locally known as *copalillo*. *Copalillo* wood is well suited for sculptures, since it is soft when green, does not split when it dries, contains few knots, sands to a smooth finish, and offers a relatively nonporous surface to which paint adheres but is not absorbed. The sculptures range in size from no more than a few centimeters to nearly two meters in length and proportionally wide and tall.

Crafting *alebrijes* is a relatively recent artistic innovation but has its roots in pre-Hispanic times, with the native Zapotecs' inclination for artistic expression in bright colors and in fantastic and sometimes macabre images. The term

FIGURE 7.9 Guarijío Indian Pascola dance mask made of *Bursera laxiflora* (photo by J. Becerra).

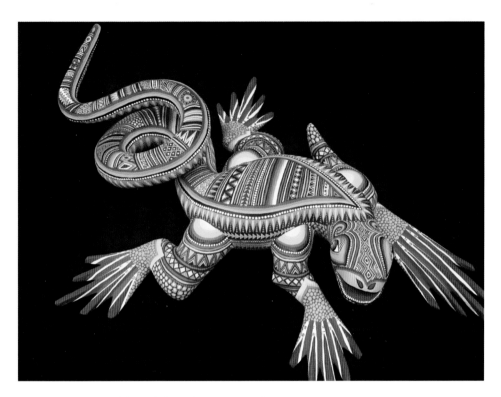

FIGURE 7.10 *Alebrije* (photo by J. Becerra).

alebrije originated in 1936, when it was applied to grotesque figurines fashioned from papier-mâché and painted with intricate patterns and vibrant colors (Bercovitch 2001). These imaginative designs were later adopted and commercialized by Oaxacan wood-carving artists from the Zapotec villages of Arrazola, San Martín Tilcajete, and La Unión Tejalapan in the central valleys of the state of Oaxaca. Wood carvers initially sold a few pieces to craft stores in Oaxaca City to supplement their income, but the sculptures' popularity increased rapidly, and the market expanded. By the 1980s, Oaxacan *alebrijes* had become well established as folk art. Their success has provided employment for scores of villagers who discovered that producing *alebrijes* yielded a better income than farming or tending livestock; this pastime has also allowed them to spend more time carving and painting in a family setting and less time laboring on the countryside or in marketplaces vending their produce and animals.

Alebrije workshops are mostly run by families, some of them extended families, and some of them employing extra workers to keep pace with market demand. What started as a production of small artistic wooden figures has now extended to include designs of larger figures that often require carving thick *copalillo* branches and trunks. In the indigenous town of San Martín Tilcajete, one successful extended

FIGURE 7.11 Making of *alebrijes* in San Martín Tiltajete: (A) their production is often a family affair; (B) men do most of the carving; (C) and (D) women do the painting (photos by L. Venable).

family offers apprenticeships and scholarships to prospective young artists, attracting students worldwide. Men do most of the carving, while women do most of the painting, but the tasks are not exclusively allocated based on gender. Carving is done with hand tools, incorporating machetes, chisels, and knives. Except when a special order is received or commissioned, the woodworkers are usually given artistic license to carve whatever figure they wish. A chunk of wood cut from a tree trunk or branch will "speak" to the artist, inspiring the creation of particular creatures: deer, porcupines, armadillos, iguanas, cats, giraffes, elephants, zebras, deer, dolphins, sharks, rabbits, centipedes, dragons, or any imagined animal form. Animals are carved and painted with exaggerated features that sometimes bear scant resemblance to denizens of the natural world (Hernández-Apolinar, Valverde, and Purata 2006).

Anthropomorphic figures, chimeras, mermaids, devils in naughty pursuits, monsters, and other fantastic motifs, as well as modern artifacts such as helicopters, cars, and planes, are also fair game, and except for mass-produced small objects, no two pieces are alike. Beginning in 2014, with the help of European training, carvers began adding silver and gold leaf and inlay to their designs, with some now evolving into more solemn pieces such as church saints.

Obtaining wood for carving of *alebrijes* has become a major challenge for the carvers, especially to meet the demand for artifacts of large size. Wild *B. glabrifolia* was once one of the most abundant plant species in the area but now the trees have almost completely disappeared from most of the carving communities in the Central Valley of Oaxaca. It is not a fast grower. Consequently, *copalillo* collectors are forced to venture farther and farther into the mountains and canyons that ring the central valleys of Oaxaca to locate wood to supply the carvers. Some carvers have switched to the more plentiful *B. copallifera* and *B. bipinnata*, or to non-*Bursera* woods such as the coral bean tree, *Erythrina coralloides*, and the tropical cedar, *Cedrela odorata*, or the *ahuehuete* (*sabino*), *Taxodium mucronatum*. None of these substitutes, however, are as suitable for producing *alebrijes* as *copalillo*. The community of San Martín Tilcajete has instituted a vigorous program of growing *copalillo* trees from cuttings. But fortune has not been on their side. The plantations feature nearly 1,800 planted trees, but after 7 years agronomists noticed that wood from trees that develop from cuttings has more knots, breaks more easily, and is not as suited for carving as that from trees grown from seeds. Growing of seedlings has also been initiated, yet with very limited success since germination of *copalillo* seeds requires specialized techniques and only a small percentage of seeds germinate. *Comuneros* also acknowledge that the trees either from seed or from cuttings will require a minimum of 20 years to reach a size capable of yielding wood suitable for carving.

A fundamentally different artistic product using *Bursera* wood originates about 250 km to the west. Olinalá is a town of about 9,000 habitants located in the northeastern mountains of the state of Guerrero. Despite its remoteness, it is perhaps the most important center of lacquer handicrafts in Mexico. Olinala's lacquer industry predates the fifteenth-century Aztec conquest of the Tlapanecos and Mixtecos who inhabited this region. The Mexica (Aztec) nobility treasured the brilliantly lacquered and painted gourds, called *jícaras*, for which the town was noted, using them for drinking chocolate, the liquid gold of the Aztec elite (collected as tribute from other conquered peoples). Spaniards who arrived in the region following their conquest of the Aztecs were unimpressed by decorated gourds. They encouraged the artisans instead to produce lacquered boxes, trunks, and chests (*baules*). The wood used to replace the gourds was not abundant near Olinalá. It grew in the distant lowlands and was cut from the tree *Bursera linanoe*. Five hundred years later, lacquered gourds are still being produced, but Olinalá is best known for its exquisite boxes, jewelry cases, and trunks.

Many Mexicans own one or more of these boxes. They are usually small but are readily distinguishable from other handcrafted boxes: when they are opened, the surrounding air becomes charged with the fragrant aroma of linalyl acetate, for which *B. linanoe* is famous. The boxes are lacquered on the outside and brightly adorned with rich patterns and traditional motifs. Generally, decorations have nature themes, ranging from flowers, foliage, and landscapes to rabbits, butterflies, parrots and other birds, deer, and more exotic species. Production of each piece requires a lengthy process. After the wood is brought from the lowlands, it is first cut and sanded to a smooth finish and then a mixture of ground oak ashes, several crushed minerals, and linseed oil is applied with a deer-tail brush. Next, one or several layers of a mixture of minerals that act as glue, natural pigments, and chia oil are applied. Finally, the surface is polished to give it a gloss, lightly carved at various depths to highlight the decoration motives and painted to further enliven the pattern.

FIGURE 7.12 Lacquered *baúl* from Olinalá, Guerrero, Mexico (photo by J. Becerra).

Unfortunately for the crafts market, Olinalá artisans in Guerrero are experiencing the same shortage of raw materials as *alebrije* artists in Oaxaca, since *B. linanoe* is now nearly extinct in some parts of its native range. Small *B. linanoe* plantations have been established but with very limited success. It is clear that protecting those trees that survive and ensuring an adequate supply of wood for artists will require cooperation of artisans, government, scientists, and consumers. Alternatively, perhaps it would be feasible to import the wood from India, where *B. linanoe* is cultivated for its oil. That would be a successful story of repatriation of a Mexican treasure.

The shortage of *B. linanoe* is a serious obstacle to perpetuation of the lacquer craft. Even more ominous, however, is that Olinalá has slowly become surrounded by fields of poppies destined for the heroin trade. As poppy production has expanded, Olinalá has been besieged by *sicarios*, *narcos*, and gang hit men who extort money from shopkeepers. Some craft shops, unable to pay "protection" fees, have closed (Okeowo 2017). The same corrupt forces that have jeopardized the Olinalá crafts have limited our ability to carry out field studies on the *Bursera* species that abound in the region. Since the early twenty-first century, the entire state of Guerrero has become a battleground among organized crime elements, government forces, and traditional folk desperately striving to maintain their way of life.

FIGURE 7.13 Harvesting opium poppies in central Guerrero (photo by C. Rodríguez, all rights reserved, © César Rodríguez, 2023).

Other Uses

Bursera Bark

Some burseras feature bark that produces an aromatic or colorful tea when boiled or steeped in hot water. This is especially true of *B. grandifolia*, the *palo mulato* of the northern tropical deciduous forests. Chips of its bark are widely used to brew into a tea taken for a variety of ailments and used as a coffee substitute. The chips produce a reddish tea (which quickly stains one's urine red) with a slightly astringent taste. Among natives of Sinaloa and Sonora, it is a popular remedy and drink, and many trees exhibit numerous scars where slabs of bark have been excised for brewing into tea. Natives of rural villages often keep a supply of dried bark chips in their homes. Several additional species are believed to have bark with curative properties as well, including *B. fragilis*, *B. laxiflora*, *B. microphylla*, *B. penicillata*, and *B. stenophylla*. All those we have tried produce a tea with a pleasant taste. Whatever curative powers they possess are an additional virtue. The bark can be harvested in moderation without damage to the tree other than the defacing of its bark surface.

Cercas Vivas

A characteristic trait of the landscapes of tropical America is living fences or *cercas vivas*, trees to which several lines of barbed wire are attached to mark the limits of land, deter livestock, and protect private property. Establishment is disarmingly simple: merely sticking thick cuttings into the ground, preferably before the rainy season. These usually develop roots rapidly. As the aspiring trees become established, barbed wire is attached to them and the cutting gradually encompasses the wire with scar tissue. Such fences are extremely cheap to make, and if the posts are correctly selected, they can last for many years, protecting property, animals, and crops while also increasing biodiversity. While a variety of trees can be selected according to the region, throughout Mexico fast-growing bursera species, such as *B. fagaroides*, *B. simaruba*, *B. grandifolia*, *B. bipinnata*, and *B. submoniliformis*, are preferred for fence-post cuttings. The posts often produce flowers and fruits (and copal) faster than seedlings of the same size (an advantage lacking in steel fence posts). Perhaps the most widely used species along coastal states is *B. simaruba*, since a branch can rapidly spring to life, developing roots and branches and, depending on the environmental conditions, doubling or even tripling its thickness within a year. In general, branches of species in subgenus *Bursera* demonstrate a natural inclination to sprout speedily and quickly develop into trees. In other cases, the species are selected not only because they grow fast but also because they can have other uses, such as firewood, copal production, or medicinal applications. *B. graveolens*, highly regarded

FIGURE 7.14 Cerca viva with *B. simaruba* in Panama (photo by J. Slusser, CC BY-SA 3.0).

for its healing properties, is found in southern Mexico only in living fences. Large, ancient living fences of at least fifty-year-old *B. graveolens* grow along old Mexico Route 135 between the towns of Cuicatlán and Teotitlán de Flores Magón in the state of Oaxaca. The original cuttings were probably imported from Central America at a time when people relied more on traditional medicine.

Bursera and the Seris

In areas in Mexico where plant diversity is comparatively low, native peoples have learned to rely heavily on local resources. This is the case of *Bursera* among the Seris, also known as Comcáac, their term for themselves. Seri homelands lie on the central Gulf of California coast of Sonora. Their lands are vegetation-rich Sonoran Desert with annual rainfall of only around 125 mm but often heavy dews. Seri settlements lie immediately adjacent to the waters of the Gulf, which was formerly among the world's richest in marine life. Seris have a long history of persecution by outsiders, notably Spanish military, and later by mestizos encroaching on their lands. Seris appear to have inhabited their territory for more than one millennium, quite probably far longer. Their language is an isolate, meaning it is unrelated to any other known language. They number around 700 and nearly all retain fluency in their aboriginal (Seri) language as well as Spanish, a phenomenon almost unheard of in the Americas. In addition to their exemplary persistence in the face of genocidal aggression from outsiders, Seris possess extraordinary familiarity with intimate details of their lands, which include several islands in the Gulf of California, among them Tiburón Island, the largest in the Gulf. Their familiarity with plants of their homelands and environs is equally remarkable (Felger and Moser 1985).

Among the plants that figure most prominently in their reservoir of important plants are two burseras: *B. microphylla* and *B. hindsiana*. For fabricating items from wood, the most common choice has been that of *B. hindsiana*, also called *torote prieto* in Spanish and *xopínl* (pronounced like *hoping* in English) in the Seri language. It is a small tree with reddish bark, often with gnarled branches, but also frequently with a swollen but straight trunk. Its leaves are far larger than those of *B. microphylla*. Because the wood is rather easily cut and worked into a variety of shapes, it has been frequently used to construct boxes, toys, musical instruments, and fetishes and *santos*, or spiritual objects—in short, anything that needs to be constructed from wood. They carve strips of the wood and fashion them into a culturally distinct headdress to be worn by important Seri *pascolas* (ceremonial dancers.) Seris still fashion their handmade violins from the wood of *B. hindsiana* and use resin from *B. microphylla* for their bows, always melting a blob of the resin on the bottom of the instrument, providing easy access for the violinist. One Seri carved toy boats from the wood and presented one to Yetman as a gift for his son in the early 1970s. The gift came with a name: San Lucas. It was about 40 cm in length. Seri lads would launch such boats at the edge of the sea and propel them along the shore with a long stick they had wedged in the boat's prow. Alas, San Lucas was washed away in a flash flood years later.

Bursera hindsiana is a Sonoran Desert endemic abundant in Baja California but seldom found more than 20 km from the Gulf and less common in Seri lands than *B. microphylla*. Plotting its distribution in mainland Sonora demonstrates that it grows precisely and dramatically within the traditional coastal boundaries of aboriginal Seri territory and does not appear to grow elsewhere. Seris are traditional fishermen and for centuries have been renowned for their expertise in navigating the waters of the Gulf of California. Over the millennia, they have transgressed the Gulf at will, island hopping back and forth between Baja California and Sonora. We suggest the possibility that the Sonoran population of *B. hindsiana* was introduced by Seris importing it from Baja California because of its usefulness.

Bursera microphylla, *torote* in Spanish and *xoop* (similar to *hope* in English) in Seri, has a bewildering array of uses. The Seris still use globs of the resin as glue and formerly maintained a large supply as a caulk to patch holes in boats and pottery or anything else that might need gaps filled. For these uses, they heat a broad knife blade in an open fire and apply a chunk of resin onto the flat surface. The heat softens and melts the resin, making it easily applied to holes, gaps, and fissures. In addition, they use the bark, leaves, fruits, and wood in their pharmacopeia to heal or cure a wide variety of maladies such as sore throats, lung inflammation, and headache, and to heal wounds (Felger and Moser 1985). They treat the sap in some way to make it an effective dye used in basketry. They use chunks of the wood to fashion some artifacts, although the wood is not as desirable as that of *B. hindsiana*. They chew the resin to ward off thirst. They use branches and roots as firewood, for special heating needs, as a brush cover, and they wrap perishables with branches as a preservative. When Yetman's young son was stung by a stingray, two Seri women steeped bark from *xoop* and a creosote branch in very hot water and applied the liquid as a compress to ease the pain. The pain vanished instantly, probably by the hot water denaturing the proteins in the stingray toxin (the child ceased screaming from pain and began giggling in the space of a minute or so). But the wound also healed without a trace, no doubt facilitated by the antiseptic properties of *xoop* and creosote. Indeed, the list of uses of *B. microphylla* and its resin among the Seris is long and complex. The species is deeply entwined in Seri culture.

CHAPTER 8

Where Burseras Grow

Burseras like it hot. They thrive where annual temperature means vary between 20°C and 29°C (68°F and 84.2°F) but do not seem unhappy at a temperature of 45°C (113°F). Unlike plants that require continuous high humidity, they thrive in places with a seasonal pattern of precipitation where rain is abundant during part of the year but absent during several—or most—months and where humidity ranges from extremely low to saturation. But all this is based on the condition that they are protected from hard freezes. Given this life requirement, in North and Central America they have settled on their home in tropical seasonal forests. Some of them, like *B. simaruba* and a few of its very close allies, also seem comfortable in wetter conditions like the ones that pervade in more humid tropical forests. Another substantial number of species seem to have adapted well to drier conditions and are frequent inhabitants of Mexican deserts, with one species—*B. microphylla*—making it into the Sonoran Desert of the United States.

The highest species diversity is found in southern Mexico along the catchment area of the Balsas River (known as the Río Mezcala along a stretch upstream) and its tributaries. With a length of 770 km, the Balsas is one of Mexico's longest rivers. The Balsas Basin is of modest size, roughly 120,000 km². The river flows from east to west in the depression between the Neovolcanic Axis (Trans-Mexican Volcanic Belt) and the Sierra Madre del Sur. The Balsas drainage originates in and flows through the states of Puebla, Morelos, Guerrero, and Mexico and empties into the Pacific Ocean in extreme southeast Michoacán, in what is called El Infiernillo (Little Hell). The climate offers seasonal but often abundant precipitation (between 500 and 1,600 mm depending on the location) and mean annual temperatures of 12.5°C (54.5°F) in the higher mountain region and 31°C (82°F) on the Pacific Coast, which

MAP 8.1 Richness of *Bursera* species across Mexican states (adapted from Rze-dowski, Medina Lemos, and Calderón de Rzedowski 2005).

suffers the highest mean annual temperatures in Mexico. The lower Balsas Basin is the home of at least 58 *Bursera* species.

An intriguing aspect of *Bursera* is that many species have relatively limited dis-tribution range, in terms of both geographic extension and altitude. The majority of species occupy areas of less than 50,000 km^2 (less than the size of West Virginia) and at least two dozen of them exist in just a few localities, totaling no more than 10,000 km^2 (smaller than the size of Puerto Rico). Several have even narrower dis-tribution. Many species also exhibit strict altitudinal limits: while in many places the tropical deciduous forest goes uninterrupted for at least 1,000 vertical m, only a minority of *Bursera* species have an altitudinal range of more than 500 m, and a third of them occupy altitudinal ranges of less than 300 m. The result is a greatly stratified mosaic of species identities across the tropical deciduous forest landscape.

The high *Bursera* species diversity found in the Balsas Basin is related to the high degree of local endemism. Climatic conditions across the Balsas watershed are heterogeneous, mostly due to variation in altitude. Because the western part of the basin is lower than the eastern side, annual mean temperatures are usually higher at the bottom of the western part. Yet environmental conditions in many areas across the whole basin appear similar enough not to impede the growth of almost any *Bursera* species. Despite this, many are restricted to one side or another of the Balsas Basin. Thus, species overlap is not as large as one would expect given the habitat similarities, short distances, and physical connection of these regions. The area of highest diversity on the east side of the Balsas area is in Guerrero between Cuernavaca and Acapulco in the basin of the Río Zopilote, a tributary of the Río Balsas-Mezcala. An area that extends for about 10,000 km^2 is inhabited by at least 36 *Bursera* species: *B. aptera, B. arborea, B. ariensis, B. bicolor, B. bipinnata, B. bolivarii, B. bonetti, B. chemapodicta, B. citronella, B. copallifera, B. diversifolia, B. discolor, B. excelsa, B. fagaroides, B. fragantissima, B. glabrifolia, B. grandifolia, B. heteresthes, B. hintonii, B. krusei, B. lancifolia, B. linanoe, B. longipes, B. mirandae, B. morelensis, B. ovalifolia, B. palmeri, B. roseana, B. rzedowski, B. sarcopoda, B. schlechtendalii, B. submoniliformis, B. suntui, B. tecomaca, B. vejar-vazquezii,* and *B. xochipalensis.*

On the western side of the basin, the area of highest *Bursera* species concentration is the basin of the Río Tepalcatepec in Michoacán, a northwestern tributary of the Balsas with an area of about 10,000 km^2. It is home to at least 32 *Bursera* species: *B. aptera, B. ariensis, B. bicolor, B. bipinnata, B. citronella, B. copallifera, B. coyucensis, B. crenata, B. denticulata, B. diversifolia, B. discolor, B. excelsa, B. fagaroides, B. fragantissima, B. glabrifolia, B. grandifolia, B. heteresthes, B. hintonii, B. infernidialis, B. kerberi, B. krusei, B. lancifolia, B. occulta, B. paradoxa, B. roseana, B. sarukhanii, B. toledoana, B. trifoliolata, B. trimera, B. schlechtendalii, B. velutina,* and *B. xolocotzii.* Despite their geographical proximity, overlap of eastern and western Balsas species is not high, with only about half of the species from the Zopilote basin being found in the Tepalcatepec basin. The explanation for such narrow endemism has so far proved elusive.

Another area of great *Bursera* species diversity is the high basins of the Papaloapan and Tehuantepec Rivers in the state of Oaxaca. The Río Papaloapan originates in the mountains of southern Puebla and empties into the Laguna de Alvarado in the state of Veracruz. Its catchment covers an area of about 47,000 km^2, including the northern part of the state of Oaxaca.

The basin's northern limit is the eastern end of the Trans-Mexican Volcanic Belt, which at this point includes some of the highest mountains in Mexico, including Citlaltépetl, also known as Pico de Orizaba, Mexico's highest peak at 5,636 m. It straddles the state line between Puebla and Veracruz. Parts of the Papaloapan Basin are densely populated and altered by human activities, but pockets of pristine areas with high floristic diversity remain. Freezing temperatures are not unusual on the higher mountains. As slopes descend toward the basin's interior, they are occupied first by cold-adapted grasses, coniferous forests, and oak forests. Then, at an altitude of between 500 and 1,500 m, they are occupied by tropical deciduous forests.

The southwestern part of the Papaloapan Basin forms one of the main tributaries of the Río Papaloapan, the Río Santo Domingo. The Santo Domingo drainage formerly emptied into the Balsas Basin to the west, but recently, geologically speaking (Late Miocene), the river cut its way westward from the lowlands, breached the lofty Sierra Mazateca, and opened up a broad valley, creating a new drainage into the Gulf of Mexico and joining the Río Papaloapan downstream. Thus *Bursera* species living here are a mixture of species that can be found in the east side of the Balsas Basin but also species that are restricted to the Papaloapan basin or may extend a bit farther south into the Río Tehuantepec basin in southern Oaxaca: *B. altijuga, B. aptera, B. ariensis, B. asplenifolia, B. biflora, B. bipinnata, B. bolivarii, B. cinerea, B. copallifera, B. diversifolia, B. discolor, B. excelsa, B. esparzae, B. fagaroides, B. galeottiana, B. glabrifolia, B. heteresthes, B. heliae, B. hintonii, B. isthmica, B. lancifolia, B. laurihuertae, B. linanoe, B. longipes, B. mirandae, B. morelensis, B. schlechtendalii, B. simaruba, B. simplex, B. palmeri, B. pontiveteris, B. submoniliformis,* and *B. zapoteca* (Rzedowski and Medina-Lemos 2021).

The northern portion of the Santo Domingo drainage in the Papaloapan Basin can be very dry, as seen in the semiarid Cuicatlán Valley that receives only about 400 mm during the five months that the rainy season lasts. Yet a good number of *Bursera* species prosper there, and in some places, they are one of the most abundant elements of the xerophylous vegetation. It is possible that burseras appeared there following the breach in the Sierra Mazateca carved by the Río Santo Domingo. This opening allowed masses of humid air to pour through the breach from the moist coastal plain and elevate the humidity west and south of the breach, thus aiding the establishment and perpetuation of burseras in these semiarid valleys of Cuicatlán and Tehuacán. This illustrates how the genus continues to be evolutionarily active, developing adaptations to environments more xeric than tropical deciduous forests.

The ability to survive in arid environments is also exhibited by the *Bursera* species found in the Sonoran Desert. In the middle Miocene, about 15 mya, the peninsula of Baja California was located 300 km to the southeast of where it is today, attached to the coasts of Sonora, Sinaloa, and Nayarit. The entirety of Baja California was part of the North American tectonic plate. From 12 to 15 mya the Pacific Tectonic Plate began its northward march nearly attached to the margin of the North American Plate. The new direction initiated the tearing motion that produced the separation of the Baja peninsula from the mainland and the opening of the Gulf of California. Peninsular burseras would have had to adapt from then on to the dramatic climatic changes—mainly aridification—that the peninsula has endured since then.

The extreme southern tip of the peninsula is still relatively wet, receiving about 850 mm of annual rain, which is sufficient to support a tropical dry forest. Much of the remainder of the peninsula, however, is arid until it terminates at its most northerly limit, the San Jacinto Mountains in Southern California. Geological and climatic changes resulted in separation of *Bursera* into peninsular and mainland populations: some species, such as *B. hindsiana*, *B. laxiflora*, and *B. microphylla*, can now be found on both sides of the Gulf. But others, such as *B. cerasifolia*, *B. epinnata*, *B. filicifolia*, *B. littoralis*, *B. odorata*, and *B. rupicola*, speciated as a result of geographic isolation and now occur only in Baja California.

CHAPTER 9

How to Grow Burseras

Many *Bursera* species are attractive when grown as bonsai and are highly sought after by gardeners and collectors. In regions of warm weather, most *Bursera* species can be grown as potted plants or in the ground as long as they are protected from freezing. Such low temperatures can cause severe harm to mature plants and will most likely kill young individuals, especially seedlings. Allowing the plants to go into dormancy during fall and winter by greatly reducing watering will produce more healthy-looking specimens. Squirting species incorporated as potted plants will produce a very weak squirt or no response at all, thus it is not worthwhile to collect a plant from its natural habitat to reproduce the squirt at home.

Most species from the south of Mexico require protection against excessively high temperatures and intense solar radiation, such as occurs in the hot deserts in the United States. Those conditions are likely to burn or kill these plants. In these regions, plants will respond best in well-drained soils, partial shade, and ample watering during the summer. In more mesic environments, plants should be grown in bright light, to prevent them from taking on a vine-like appearance. They can grow happily in greenhouses but will be easy prey of greenhouse pests such as white flies, aphids, and other homopterans. These sucking insects can readily avoid the plants' defensive resin canals; thus, the application of systemic insecticides may prove necessary to rid the plants of these greenhouse pests.

Bursera plants are easily propagated from seeds as well as through stem cuttings (Bonfil-Sanders, Cajero-Lázaro, and Evans 2008). Some species also produce tubers that can be used to grow new plants. The grower must keep in mind that when flowers of these plants lack adequate cross-pollination, they are likely to produce hollow seeds that lack an embryo and will not germinate. Thus, sometimes a good

FIGURE 9.1 *Bursera microphylla* in a hotel garden in Baja California (photo by J. Becerra).

percentage of seeds, even those collected from field sites, will not be viable. One remedy for this is to collect seeds from different individual plants, always leaving an ample supply of seeds behind for birds. Commercial vendors often pollinate their own stock plants, and the percentage of viable seeds they get is usually higher than in nature. Seeds announce their ripeness when their cover has fallen and the bright-red, orange, or pink pseudoaril is exposed; this is the best time to harvest them. To germinate seeds, it is best to wait for summer (as these seeds respond better to high temperatures and low barometric pressure) (Eslamieh 2013). At that time, remove the pseudoaril and soak the seeds in water or a 5 percent gibberellic acid solution for one to two days before sowing them. Germination occurs most often between one and two weeks. Such events elicit joy in *Bursera* lovers.

FIGURE 9.2 *Bursera bolivarii* growing in a container (photo by J. Becerra).

Stem cuttings and tubers collected in late spring or early summer when plants are still dormant have a higher chance of propagation success. Large branch cuttings of 1 to 1.5 m long are used regularly by Mexican farmers to construct "living fences," using practically any species from their local communities. Commercial *Bursera* propagators use much smaller cuttings, since pieces of as little as 0.5 cm width and

FIGURE 9.3 *Bursera* spp.
growing in a pot (photo by
J. Eslamieh).

15 cm length can develop roots. For best results, the cut should be done from a still-dormant plant that it is about to leaf out, with clean, sharp shears or a fine-toothed saw below a node and the cut covered immediately with rooting hormone. After placement in soil, it is important to shield cuttings from moving for two months. The potting medium should contain at least 50 percent coarse material such as pumice or coarse sand that allows easy drainage, mixed with regular topsoil and slow-release fertilizer.[1]

1. For a more comprehensive overview of *Bursera*'s propagation, see *Cultivation of Bursera* (Eslamieh 2013).

CHAPTER 10

Systematics and Taxonomy

Bursera Belongs to the Burseraceae

The Burseraceae is a family of mostly small to large trees renowned for producing resins of commercial, medicinal, and cultural value throughout human history and for bearing essential oils. Frankincense, myrrh, and copal are some of the best-known Burseraceae products (two of the gifts given by the Magi after the birth of Jesus were Burseraceae). The family consists of about 700 species in 19 genera distributed in the tropics and subtropics around the world in a wide range of mostly tropical or semitropical habitats, including rainforest, tropical deciduous forest, low-elevation oak forest, thornscrub, and desert. The Burseraceae is one of 9 flowering plant families belonging to the order Sapindales that comprise about 5,700 species.

DNA studies have shown that Burseraceae and Anacardiaceae are closest relatives in a group distinguished, among other things, by the presence of resin canals that run throughout their tissues (Wang 2009). For humans, contact with Burseraceae plants almost always results in a fragrant, pleasant experience. But not so with Anacardiaceae, since their canals carry resins that are often foul smelling and provoke potent allergenic reactions in unfortunate victims.

To the nontrained eye, some Anacardiaceae species greatly resemble *Bursera*, but it pays to learn to distinguish them. One of our entomologist friends, looking for insects that commonly attack *Bursera*, once made the mistake of climbing a tree that he thought was a *Bursera* to look for the insects. He was not aware that the tree was an Anacardiaceae species of the genus *Pseudosmodingium* whose common name, *hincha-huevos*, means "it makes your balls swell." He ended up in bed for several days, his body inflamed with large blisters worse than poison ivy that crept over his

FIGURE 10.1 Outcrop with *Pseudosmodingium perniciosum* (Anacardiaceae). This species is found in some of the same habitats as *Bursera*, and because of its exfoliating red bark it is sometimes confused with some burseras, such as *B. grandifolia*, to which it is strikingly similar at first glance (photo by jarturok, CC BY-NC).

body for weeks. The insects know better. The beetles he found in that tree turned out to not be from the bursera-feeding genus, *Blepharida*, but rather from another related genus.

Within the Burseraceae, *Bursera* is part of the tribe Bursereae, along with the genera *Aucomea* and *Commiphora*. Additional DNA studies have also suggested that *Bursera* is most closely related to *Commiphora* (myrrh). But while *Bursera* is confined to the New World, *Commiphora* can be found in India, South America, and especially Africa. The similarities between *Bursera* and *Commiphora* are remarkable and even some botanical experts have been fooled in naming some *Commiphora* as *Bursera* and vice versa, only to have DNA analysis later reveal their mistakes.

One important difference between *Bursera* and *Commiphora* is that *Bursera* species almost always lack spines. Only one described species has branch apices that are thornlike, the Caribbean *B. spinescens*. *Commiphora*, however, has many species with thorns. Perhaps this is not surprising since spines probably come in handy in Africa, where plants have evolved at the mercy of large herbivorous mammals long extinct in the New World. Another trait that distinguishes these two genera is the shape of their seed leaves, called cotyledons. Cotyledons are already present in seeds and form the seedlings' first photosynthetic surfaces after germination. They lie lowest on the stems and can be very different from the plant's subsequent leaves.

FIGURE 10.2 The genus *Commiphora* includes more than 200 species. Many of their features are similar to *Bursera*, especially *Bursera* section *Bursera*: (A) *C. edulis* with fruits; (B) *C. marlothii* with a green fruit; (C) *C. neglecta*; (D) *C. shimperii* with pseudoaril-covered pit and one fruit valve below it (photos by A. M. Viljoen and R. Gill).

The shape and number of cotyledons has been a character that botanists often use to ascertain whether a seedling belongs to one or another group of plants.

Commiphora species have two often broad, heart-shaped or, as botanists call them, unilobate cotyledons (very rarely three), with entire (smooth, untoothed) margins. Seedings of *Bursera* species also have two cotyledons, but instead of having entire margins and depending on the subgroup they belong to, the cotyledons are partitioned into several lobes. Seedlings from the subgenus *Elaphrium* have each

FIGURE 10.3 *Commiphora* species develop two cotyledons that are unilobate and round: (A) *C. mahafaliensis*; (B) *C. africana*; (C) *C. parvilleana*; (D) *C. edulis* (photos by J. Becerra).

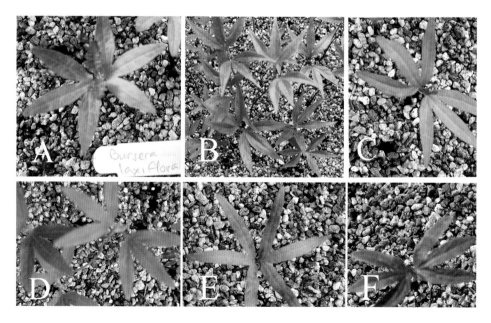

FIGURE 10.4 Species of *Bursera* subgenus *Elaphrium* produce two cotyledons that are divided into three lobes (trilobate): (A) *B. laxiflora*; (B) *B. copallifera*; (C) *B. altijuga*; (D) *B. palmeri*; (E) *B. penicillata*; (F) *B. linanoe* (photos by J. Becerra).

FIGURE 10.5 Species of *Bursera* subgenus *Bursera* have two cotyledon forms: trilobate as in (A) *B. simaruba*; and multilobate as in (B) *B. aptera*; (C) *B. galeottiana*; and (D) *B. microphylla* (photos by L. Venable).

cotyledon divided into three lobes (or trilobate). On the other hand, seedlings of the subgenus *Bursera* have trilobate or multilobate cotyledons. Having trilobate cotyledons is characteristic of *B. simaruba* and its closely related species, also called the Mulato group of the subgenus *Bursera*. The rest of the subgenus has multilobate cotyledons that, as the name implies, are divided into multiple lobes (Andrés-Hernández and Espinoza 2002). This diagnostic trait is not very useful in the field, however, since it comes in handy only in those rare occurrences when you happen to encounter new seedlings.

Across its distribution, *Commiphora* often forms abundant stands of several species, rather like Mexican cuajiotales. Walking along the hills of the Transvaal in northeastern South Africa, one can have the illusion of roaming around in the lowlands of Guerrero or Michoacán—until a kudu or an elephant appears.

Evolutionary Relationships Within the Genus

Bursera is a monophyletic genus that comprises two (also monophyletic) subgenera, *Bursera* (64 spp.) and *Elaphrium* (48 spp.), previously called "section" *Bursera* and section *Bullockia*, respectively. By "monophyletic group" we mean that all the species in a group have a common ancestor and are more related to each other than to any other species. Thus, a monophyletic group consists of an ancestor along with all its (non-extinct) descendants. This concept is important for biologists studying how organisms evolve, how they are classified, and how their traits originated.

Before the advent of molecular studies, the simplest way to tell whether a bursera belonged to one subgenus or the other was its bark characteristics. Exfoliating bark usually meant subgenus *Bursera*, and non-exfoliating bark, subgenus *Elaphrium*. This useful tool fell out of favor when molecular phylogenies confirmed that exfoliating bark did not always correctly discriminate the subgenus. Within the Mexican cuajiotes (subgenus *Bursera*), *B. paradoxa*, *B. silviae*, *B. xolocotzii*, and *B. palaciosii* have gray, smooth, and complete bark. In the Greater Antilles and the Bahamas, *B. aromatica*, *B. brunea*, *B. hollickii*, *B. inaguensis*, *B. spinescens*, and *B. trinitensis* also have nonpeeling bark but belong to subgenus *Bursera*. Likewise, within the copales there are two species (*B. sarcopoda* and *B. mirandae*) with somewhat unusual exfoliating bark (for *Bursera*), but all other traits (and DNA) place them within *Elaphrium*. Setting the bark aside, perhaps the most consistent distinction between the two subgenera, although not that easy to distinguish to the nontrained eye, is the number of locules in the ovary (three in subg. *Bursera* vs. two in *Elaphrium*). Also helpful is the number of valves in the fruit (three in subg. *Bursera* vs. two in *Elaphrium*) and the opening of the fruits along two sutures in the bivalve species, while the fruit of the trivalve ones opens along three sutures. Another distinguishing trait is the presence of well-developed cataphylls (small bract-like leaves that appear before "true leaves" and are short lived) in subgenus *Elaphrium* that are absent or very inconspicuous in subgenus *Bursera*.

Female flowers of species within subgenus *Bursera* generally are 3-merous (merocity refers to the number of sepals in the calyx, the number of petals in the corolla, and the number of stamens in each of the staminal whorls), but occasionally they are 5- or 6-merous, as in some populations of *B. morelensis*. Male flowers in subgenus *Bursera* are most often 5-merous, although in some species they are 3-merous as in *B. trimera* and *B. arida* or 4- or 6-merous as in *B. lancifolia*. Both male and female flowers in subgenus *Elaphrium* are generally 4-merous. Additional distinguishing reproductive characteristics involve the stone (or pit) that holds the seed. It is most often blackish in subgenus *Elaphrium* and often only partially covered by a bright

FIGURE 10.6 A combination of traits that, although not all absolute, can help in the diagnosis of members of the *Elaphrium* subgenus: (A) entire (nonpeeling) bark; (B) presence of cataphylls; (C) bivalvate drupe; (D) 4-merous male and female flowers; (E) pit covered only partially by the pseudoaril (photos by J. Becerra and L. Venable).

red-orange (sometimes white) fleshy pseudoaril. On the other hand, the pit in species of subgenus *Bursera* tends to be pale brown or beige and completely covered by a pale whitish and thin, often papery pseudoaril. Researchers have discovered to their dismay that some individuals have variants to these characteristics that make life difficult for botanists and fellow *Bursera* lovers. But if we put all things together and are fortunate enough to find flowers and fruits in a bursera, we have a high chance of being able to identify what group it belongs to.

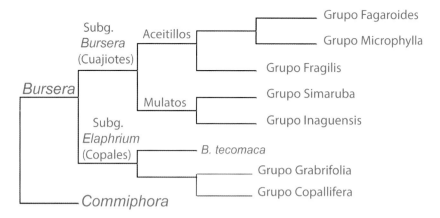

FIGURE 10.7 Evolutionary tree that depicts the classification of the genus *Bursera* into its groups and subgroups (adapted from Becerra 2005 and Becerra et al. 2012).

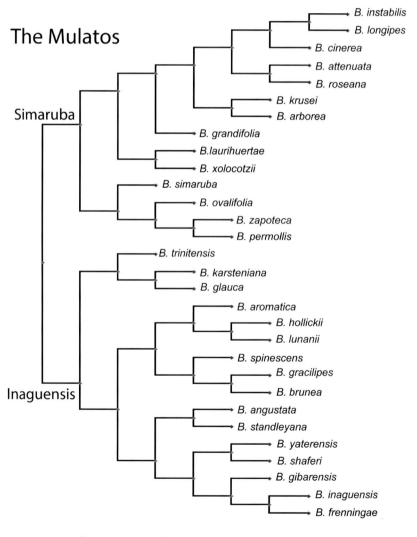

FIGURE 10.8 Evolutionary tree of the species that belong in the Mulatos of subgenus *Bursera* (adapted from Becerra et al. 2012 and Martínez-Habibe 2012).

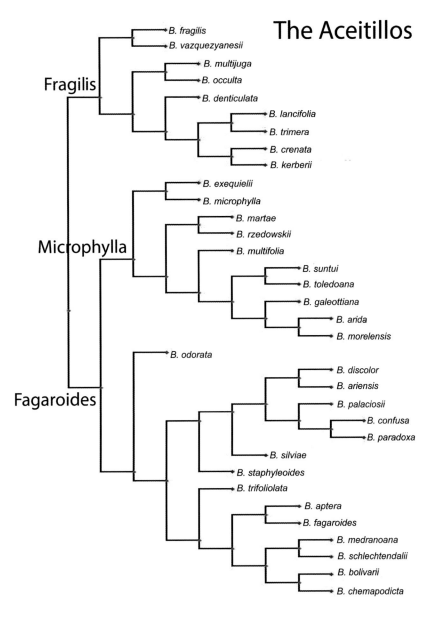

FIGURE 10.9 Evolutionary tree of the species that belong in the Aceitillos of subgenus *Bursera* (molecular evidence provided in Becerra 2005).

Subgenus *Bursera* is further subdivided into the Mulatos, which comprise all the close relatives of *B. simaruba* (the Simaruba group) and those inhabiting the West Indies (the Inaguensis group). These all have trilobate cotyledons and tend to be less aromatic, a condition probably due to the abundance of low-volatility compounds such as triterpenes present in these plants. Continental members have bright-red exfoliating bark, an aspect that not all Caribbean species exhibit. The

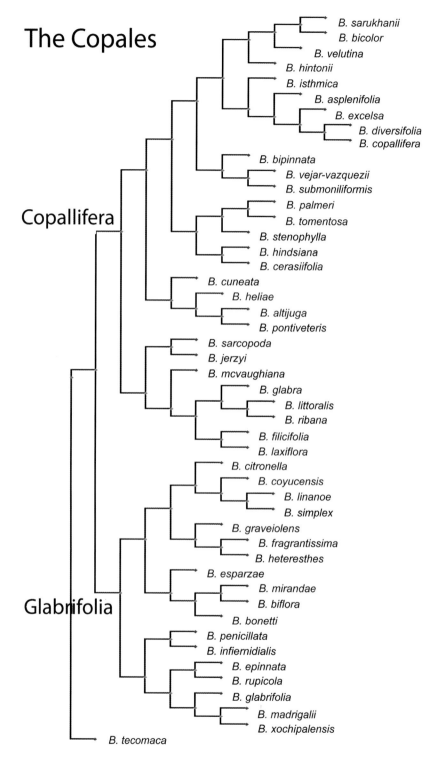

The Copales

Copallifera

Glabrifolia

B. sarukhanii
B. bicolor
B. velutina
B. hintonii
B. isthmica
B. asplenifolia
B. excelsa
B. diversifolia
B. copallifera
B. bipinnata
B. vejar-vazquezii
B. submoniliformis
B. palmeri
B. tomentosa
B. stenophylla
B. hindsiana
B. cerasiifolia
B. cuneata
B. heliae
B. altijuga
B. pontiveteris
B. sarcopoda
B. jerzyi
B. mcvaughiana
B. glabra
B. littoralis
B. ribana
B. filicifolia
B. laxiflora
B. citronella
B. coyucensis
B. linanoe
B. simplex
B. graveiolens
B. fragrantissima
B. heteresthes
B. esparzae
B. mirandae
B. biflora
B. bonetti
B. penicillata
B. infiernidialis
B. epinnata
B. rupicola
B. glabrifolia
B. madrigalii
B. xochipalensis
B. tecomaca

FIGURE 10.10 Evolutionary tree of the species that belong in the copales of the sub-genus *Elaphrium* (molecular evidence provided in Becerra 2005).

remaining species in subgenus *Bursera* form a group with the vernacular name of *aceitillos*, because of the profuse resinous oils they release when a leaf or branch is broken. This abundance of highly volatile essential oils renders them potently fragrant, even pungent to the human nose. Aceitillos all possess multilobate cotyledons. Molecular studies further divide the aceitillos into three groups: the Fragilis, Microphylla, and Fagaroides groups. Species of the Fragilis group most often have toothed (serrated, crenated, etc.) leaves, while the remaining aceitillos have entire margins. Microphylla species tend to have many distinctively small linear leaflets and reddish, exfoliating trunks.

Subgenus *Elaphrium* is currently divided into two main groups, the Glabrifolia and the Copallifera groups, plus one species that diverged before the origin of these two subgroups, *B. tecomaca*. This arrangement is still tentative, for many of the species diverged relatively recently and molecular studies to date have not provided definitive resolution due to fewer genetic differences. The fruit of species of the Glabrifolia group most often have no more than two-thirds of the pit covered by the pseudoaril and have the sepals fused at the base. In turn, species of the Copallifera group have unfused sepals and pits almost completely or completely covered by the pseudoaril.

CHAPTER 11

Bursera

Genus and Species Descriptions

For the plant taxonomist, we present the formal description of the genus:

Bursera Jacq. ex L., 1762.

Small- to medium-sized trees, sometimes shrubs or large trees; rarely epiphytic; rarely subshrubs, dioecious, sometimes polygamo-dioecious, seldom hermaphrodites; with resin canals in vascularized tissues, resin clear or transparent, most often fragrant, containing terpenoid and phenolic compounds, sometimes hydrocarbons, infrequently with aromatic hydrocarbons. Bark red, yellow, or green and papery and exfoliating; or gray; or reddish, smooth, and close. Branchlets (brachioblasts) present. Leaves deciduous, often in rosettes near small branch apices, or alternate on branches, imparipinnate, or sometimes unifoliolate, trifoliolate, rarely bipinnate, rachis frequently winged; cataphylls sometimes present; leaflets entire, crenate, or dentate. Inflorescences axillary or subterminal on branchlets. Flowers almost always unisexual, sometimes bisexual, small, 3-merous to 5-merous, rarely 6-merous, calyx divided almost to base; petals larger than stamens, often white to cream, to yellow, or to green, sometimes reddish; stamens two or more times greater in number than petals, in two usually subequal series, inserted at the base of the disk; male flowers with vestigial pistil; anthers of female flowers generally small and sterile; disk intrastaminal, usually annular; ovary sessile, 3- or 2-carpellate, style usually short, stigma or stigmas divided into 2 or 3 lobes. Fruit a dehiscent 2–3 valve drupe with fleshy to leathery skin, pyrene (stone or pit that contains the seed) cartilaginous to bony, enveloped totally or partially by a red, orange, or yellowish to white or gray arillate structure (pseudoaril). Seed generally one per fruit. Cotyledons 3-lobed or multilobed. n=12. (Rzedowski, Medina Lemos, and Calderón de Rzedowski 2004)

Type: *Bursera gummifera* L. (= *B. simaruba* (L.) Sarg.)

In the following section, we provide brief descriptions of species that we have summarized from various published sources. We have borrowed heavily from some of them, as cited in the species descriptions. Species are endemic to Mexico unless otherwise noted. While we have ascertained specific ethnobotanical information on several species, much of the information in the accounts here is decidedly lacking in detail. It is our hope that researchers will be stimulated to undertake field studies that fill in the frustrating blanks in the human uses of the various species.

Subgenus *Bursera*
Cuajiotes

Trees or shrubs, rarely subshrubs; dioecious or polygamo-dioecious; most often with exfoliating bark, sometimes with entire bark; ovary trilocular; trivalvate fruit; inconspicuous or absent cataphylls. Cotyledons trilobate or multilobate.

Subgenus *Elaphrium*
Copales

Trees or shrubs; dioecious (unless noted); non-exfoliating bark (unless noted); ovary bilocular; bivalvate fruit; well-developed cataphylls. Cotyledons trilobate.

———————

Scientific Name: *Bursera altijuga* Rzedowski, Calderón & Medina (subgenus *Elaphrium*, Copallifera group)

    Common Names: Copal, copalillo

    Shrubs or **trees** less than 8 m tall with gray trunk and non-exfoliating **bark**. **Leaves** 3 to 8 cm long and 1.5 to 4 cm wide, comprising 3 to 11 (most often 5 or 7) leaflets. **Leaflets** ovate or nearly ovate, 0.5 to 2.5 cm long and 0.4 to 1.5 cm wide, edge toothed, softly pubescent. **Flowers** in compact groups to 4 cm long and yellowish-green petals; male and female flowers 4-merous. **Fruits** mostly solitary and glabrous, pit partially covered by an orange pseudoaril, the exposed part black (Rzedowski, Medina Lemos, and Calderón de Rzedowski 2004).

    This species only grows in the limits between the states of Oaxaca and Puebla at altitudes between 1,800 and 2,350 in thornscrub and in oak forests, sometimes cohabiting with *B. biflora*. The latter, however, most often has 1 to 3 leaflets, and its flowers are arranged in open, not compact, inflorescences.

FIGURE 11.1 *Bursera altijuga* Rzedowski, Calderón & Medina, observed in Oaxaca: (A) upper- and underside of leaves; (B) trunk (photos by E. Martínez-Salas, CC BY-NC 4.0).

Scientific Name: *Bursera angustata* Wright ex Griseb (subgenus *Bursera*, Inaguensis group)

Common Names: Almácigo de costa, almácigo de paredón

Trees 4 to 5 m tall, dioecious. **Bark** red, peeling in thin papery sheets. **Leaves** 7 to 14.5 cm long, glabrous, with 7 to 11 lanceolate to elliptic and leathery **leaflets** of 2.6 to 6.3 cm long. Female **flowers** small, in inflorescences 9 to 11 cm long. **Fruits** 7–8 × 5 mm, green, except slightly red at the apex, beige pit covered completely by a bright orange-red, thin pseudoaril.

Bursera angustata is easily recognized by its 7- to 11-foliolate leaves with a petiole 4.5 to 8 cm long and narrow lateral leaflets, lanceolate-elliptic to oblanceolate. Flowering specimens have been collected from March

FIGURE 11.2 *Bursera angustata* Wright ex Griseb, a specimen collected in Cuba (photo by Global Biodiversity Information Facility, CC BY-SA 3.0).

to August and fruiting specimens from October to December (Martínez-Habibe and Daly 2016).

Bursera angustata occurs only in the western provinces of Cuba in low thornscrub associated with serpentine soils (*cuabal*); uneven, bare limestone; and ultramafic slopes. The resin is used topically as antirheumatic.

Scientific Name: *Bursera aptera* Ramírez (subgenus *Bursera*, Fagaroides group)

Common Names: Copalillo, copalaque, coabinillo, cuajiote, cuajiote amarillo, cuajiote verde, cuajiote blanco, cuachital, coxinyotl iztac (Náhuatl)

FIGURE 11.3 *Bursera aptera* Ramírez: (A) trees observed in the state of Puebla; (B) female flower; (C) leaves and fruit (photos by J. Becerra and L. Venable).

Shrubs or **trees** up to 10 m high with green trunks and **bark** that exfoliates in yellow or beige papyrus-like sheets. **Leaves** glabrous, 2.5 to 7.5 cm long, comprising 9 to 17 **leaflets** of 4 to 15 mm long and 2 to 6 mm wide, most often with margins entire, apex mucronate. **Flowers** small, reddish, yellow, or white; solitary, in groups of 2 or 3, or in larger inflorescences; female flowers 3-merous; male flowers 3 or 4-merous. **Fruits** grayish red when mature, solitary or in groups, 6 to 7 mm long and 5 to 6.5 mm wide, terminating in a sharp point, pit completely covered by a yellow or white papery pseudoaril (Rzedowski, Medina Lemos, and Calderón de Rzedowski 2004).

This species can be easily confused with *B. fagaroides*, with which it sometimes occurs, but the rachis of *B. aptera*'s leaves lacks wings, and the plant tends to have slightly smaller leaves, often with more leaflets. *Bursera aptera* has a widespread distribution on the east side of the Balsas depression in Guerrero, Morelos, and in the upper Papaloapan Basin in Puebla and Oaxaca. It inhabits tropical deciduous forest and xerophilous shrub vegetation, often growing in zones of higher aridity than those where *B. fagaroides* is found. Its resin is used as incense and for medicinal purposes (Dávila Aranda and Ramos Rivera 2017).

FIGURE 11.4 *Bursera arborea* (Rose) Riley, individual observed in Nayarit: (A) trunk and bark; (B) leaves (photos by J. Becerra and L. Venable); (C) male inflorescence (photo by E. Huerta-Ocampo).

Scientific Name: *Bursera arborea* (Rose) Riley (subgenus *Bursera*, Simaruba group)

Common Name: Palo mauto

Large **trees** to 30 m tall with **bark** green, becoming reddish and exfoliating in large papery sheets. **Leaves** at first pubescent but essentially glabrous when mature, to 22 cm long and 16 cm wide, comprising 5 to 11 (most often 5 or 7) leaflets. **Leaflets** with entire margins and of acuminate shape to 10 cm long and 4 cm wide. **Flowers** in small inflorescences, stalks about 0.75 mm thick to 8 cm long, white or pink petals. **Fruits** 0.6 to 1.5 cm long, arranged in groups, glabrous at maturity, pit covered with a thin pink aril (Toledo 1982).

This species is a member of a group of closely related and often very similar species called the Simaruba group because it also includes the widely distributed *B. simaruba*. In Mexico, *B. arborea* closely resembles *B. simaruba*, perhaps more than other members of this complex, so that when they cohabit in the same areas it can be a challenge to tell them apart. Matthew Johnson (1992) states that in Sonora, the fruit stalks of *B. arborea* are consistently thinner, and the fruits slightly smaller than those of *B. simaruba*. Also, *B. arborea*'s leaves most often have 7 leaflets, while *B. simaruba*'s leaves tend to consist of 9 to 11 leaflets.

Bursera arborea grows in the Pacific slopes from Sonora to Chiapas at altitudes of less than 1,000 m in tropical deciduous and semideciduous forests.

———————

Scientific Name: *Bursera arida* (Rose) Standl. (subgenus *Bursera*, Microphylla group)

Common Names: Cabrestillo, zapotillo, aceitillo

Small **trees** or **shrubs** with white to reddish-brown exfoliating **bark**. **Leaves** 0.8 to 3 cm long and up to 1 cm wide, with 3 to 11 **leaflets** of 3 to 5 mm long and entire margins. **Flowers** reddish and solitary; male flowers 3 or 4-merous, 2 to 2.5 long; female flowers also 3-merous but smaller (1.5 to 2 mm long). **Fruits** solitary or in pairs over short and pilose peduncles of 1 to 2 mm long, pit completely covered by a pale-yellow pseudoaril (Rzedowski, Medina Lemos, and Calderón de Rzedowski 2004).

This species is remarkable for its tiny leaves, the smallest in the genus. It is found only in the very dry areas inhabited by xerophilous shrub vegetation in southern Puebla and northern Oaxaca at altitudes between 950 and 1,750 m. Plants are common on the dry hills along the roadway between Tehuacán and Zapotitlán, Puebla, alongside other burseras (*B. schlechtendalii*, *B. biflora*, *B. aptera*). Traditionally, the plant latex has been used topically for healing wounds, skin eruptions, white tongue, and skin coloration in the Tehuacán-Cuicatlán valley. Elsewhere it is used as a disinfectant, to cure coughs, and as an antidepressant (Canales et al. 2005; Gorgua Jiménez et al. 2015).

———————

Scientific Name: *Bursera ariensis* McVaugh & Rzed. (subgenus *Bursera*, Fagaroides group)

Common Names: Copal, copal amarillo, copal blanco, copal grande, copalillo, cuajiote, cuajiote blanco, guande, guande blanco, mata perro, papelillo

Trees, sometimes **shrubs**, between 2 and 8 m tall with greenish-gray trunks and **bark** that exfoliates in yellowish or beige papery sheets, sometimes with orange tones. When damaged, plants exude a whitish resin that darkens upon contact with air. **Leaves** hairy, especially when young, 5 to 22 cm long and 2 to 7 cm wide, with

FIGURE 11.5 *Bursera arida* (Rose) Standl.: (A) plant and one of the authors in Puebla; (B) trunk; (C) branch with fruit (photos by J. Becerra and L. Venable); (D) female flower; (E) male flower (photos by E. Huerta-Ocampo).

FIGURE 11.6 *Bursera ariensis* McVaugh & Rzed., a branch with leaves and fruits (photo by L. Venable).

a winged rachis. **Leaflets** 9 to 19, 1 to 1.5 cm long and 0.4 to 1.8 cm wide. **Flowers** sometimes solitary, but most often developing in conglomerates at the end of branches; male flowers 5-merous, reddish-yellow; female flowers 3-merous and usually reddish. **Fruits** 6 to 8 mm long, growing in thick clusters, pit completely covered by a yellow or orange pseudoaril (Rzedowski, Medina Lemos, and Calderón de Rzedowski 2004).

Bursera ariensis grows in the transition zones between tropical deciduous forests and oak forests along Mexico's Pacific slopes from Nayarit to Chiapas. It ranges from 500 up to 2,000 m but is most often found between 1,200 and 1,600 m. Its fresh latex is used as glue; when it hardens, it is used as incense. It is also used to treat colds and to "sacar el frio," an affliction related to inflammation. The large branches are often employed to make living fences.

Scientific Name: *Bursera aromatica* Proctor (subgenus *Bursera*, Inaguensis group)
  Common Name: Siboney
  Andromonoecious **trees** to 12 m tall, with nonpeeling gray **bark** and highly aromatic resin. **Leaves** 19 to 23 cm long, with 3 or 5 leaflets 7 to 10 cm long and 3 to 7 cm wide, largely ovate. **Leaflets** leathery of dull color, with prominent veins in both sides of lamina. **Flowers** grouped in inflorescences of 3 to 11 cm long;

hermaphroditic and male flowers 3-merous, petals greenish. **Fruits** 9 to 11 mm long, 7 mm wide (Martínez-Habibe and Daly 2016).

Endemic to Jamaica, this species is known from the parishes of Hanover, Trelawny, and St. James, on wooded, rocky limestone hills, at an elevation of 440 to 670 m. Flowering specimens have been collected from January to July and fruiting specimens from March to August. It is easy to distinguish from the other two Jamaican endemics: *Bursera lunanii* has simple leaves and *B. hollickii* has shorter leaves (8 to 12 cm long).

FIGURE 11.7 *Bursera aromatica* Proctor, herbarium specimen (photo by Global Biodiversity Information Facility).

Scientific Name: *Bursera asplenifolia* Brandegee (subgenus *Elaphrium*, Copallifera group)

Common Names: Copal, copalillo

Shrubs or **trees** less than 8 m tall with gray trunk and non-exfoliating **bark**. **Leaves** 9.5 to 23 cm long and 2 to 7 cm wide, comprising 13 to 23 leaflets. **Leaflets** 1 to 3.5 cm long and no more than 1.5 cm wide with serrated margins and with

FIGURE 11.8 *Bursera asplenifolia* Brandegee, observed in Malinalco, Mexico: (A) fruits; (B) leaf (photos by I. Avalos, CC BY-SA 4.0).

FIGURE 11.9 *Bursera attenuata* (Rose) Riley, bark and leaves of an individual observed in the vicinity of Tepic, Nayarit (photo by L. Venable).

dense short hairs on the underside, while pubescent in the upper side; primary and secondary veins prominent but almost always without tertiary veins; leaf rachis narrowly winged and with dense short hairs. **Flowers** hairy with greenish-white petals and arranged in inflorescences no more than 7 cm long; both female and male flowers 4-merous. **Fruits** 7 to 8 mm wide, pit almost or completely covered by a yellow-orange pseudoaril (Rzedowski, Medina Lemos, and Calderón de Rzedowski 2004).

This species inhabits tropical deciduous forests and xerophilous shrub vegetation at altitudes of 1,200 to 2,100 m in Oaxaca and Puebla.

Scientific Name: *Bursera attenuata* (Rose) Riley (subgenus *Bursera*, Simaruba group)

Common Names: Papelillo, copal

Trees to 20 m tall, less aromatic than most other *Bursera* species, with green trunks and red, brownish-red, or orange **bark** that exfoliates in thin sheets. **Leaves** large, to 45 cm long, with 5 or 7 leaflets, sometimes 9, perfectly glabrous on both surfaces except for some tufts of hairs in the lower axils of the veins on the under surface. **Leaflets** typically of oval shape, apex ending in a long point. **Flowers** arranged in inflorescences up to 15 cm long, glabrous. **Fruits**, both when immature and ripe, glabrous to 1.2 cm long, pit completely covered by a pale pseudoaril (Rose 1911; Becerra 2003a).

B. attenuata is very closely related to *B. roseana*, perhaps even the same species (Rzedowski, Medina Lemos, and Calderón de Rzedowski 2005; Rosell et al. 2010). It grows in the states of Sinaloa, Durango, Nayarit, and Jalisco.

Scientific Name: *Bursera bicolor* (Willd. ex Schltdl.) Engler (subgenus *Elaphrium*, Copallifera group)

Common Names: Marqueto, tecomaca, tecomate

Trees to 15 m tall (most often 4 m tall) that ramify at short height, with gray, smooth non-exfoliating **bark**. **Leaves** 10 to 30 cm long, comprising 13 to 17 leaflets, the rachis narrowly winged. **Leaflets** linear-lanceolate, sessile, white and hairy on the underside and glabrous and shiny on the upper side, 4 to 10 cm long and 0.3 to

1.5 cm wide. **Flowers** reddish-pink tinged with yellow in petal edges, in inflorescences 7 to 16 cm long, including 8 to 30 flowers. **Fruits** 0.7 to 1.2 cm long, pointed, slightly pubescent, pit almost completely covered by a yellow-white or red pseudo-aril (Toledo 1982).

This species is easy to recognize by its leaves, with a shiny green upper side and a white hairy underside. It inhabits open spaces of the tropical deciduous forest and oak woodland at altitudes between 800 and 1,500 m. It is found from the Balsas Basin to the Isthmus of Tehuantepec in Oaxaca. Its resin is used to prepare a poultice to treat rheumatism.

FIGURE 11.10 *Bursera bicolor* (Willd. ex Schltdl.) Engler, observed in Oaxaca: (A) small tree; (B) leaf upper side and underside; (C) male inflorescence; (D) fruit; (E) pseudoaril covering black pit (photos by J. Becerra and L. Venable).

Scientific Name: *Bursera biflora* (Rose) Standl. (subgenus *Elaphrium*, Glabrifolia group)

Common Names: Copal, copali, mulatillo amarillo

Shrubs or **trees** less than 8 m tall with gray trunk bearing most often non-exfoliating bark. **Leaves** either all unifoliolate and 1 to 3 cm long or trifoliolate and with some leaves with 5 leaflets and up to 7 cm long, pubescent underneath, margin serrated. **Flowers** yellowish green; female flowers arranged in groups of 2 or 3; male flowers arranged in inflorescences of up to 15 flowers. **Fruits** 7 to 9 mm long, pit with one side covered to two-thirds of its length by the orange pseudoaril, the other side with the pseudoaril covering only up to one-third of the length, the exposed part black (Rzedowski, Medina Lemos, and Calderón de Rzedowski 2004).

FIGURE 11.11 *Bursera biflora* (Rose) Standl., observed in Puebla, Mexico: (A) plant with one of the authors; (B) infructescence; (C) unifoliolate leaves; (D) underside of trifoliolate leaf; (E) upper side of trifoliolate leaf; (F) male flower (photos by J. Becerra and L. Venable).

This species inhabits the tropical deciduous forests and xerophilous shrub vegetation of Oaxaca and Puebla.

———————

Scientific Name: *Bursera bipinnata* Engl. (subgenus *Elaphrium*, Copallifera group)

Common Names: Copalillo, copal amargo, copal amargoso, copal chino, copal chino colorado, copal santo, incienso, jaboncillo del país, lantrisco, zocona, copal negro, copal virgen, tetlate, tetlatín, yah yal (Zapotec)

Trees, sometimes **shrubs**, up to 12 m tall, but most often not exceeding 4 m, smooth, clear brown to gray **bark**. **Leaves** most often bipinnate, giving the appearance of some fern leaves; leaf 4 to 12 cm long, 1 to 6.5 cm wide, usually comprising 11 pairs of primary **leaflets** each with 5 to 6 secondary leaflets. **Flowers** white, whitish, yellowish, or greenish with free sepals (not fused), grouped in inflorescences; both male and female flowers 4-merous. **Fruits** glabrous, solitary or in groups, 6 to 9 mm long and 3.5 mm wide, pit almost completely covered by a red pseudoaril, the exposed part black (Rzedowski, Medina Lemos, and Calderón de Rzedowski 2004).

As the multitude of common names suggests, this is a species of wide distribution and many human uses. It ranges from southern Sonora to Honduras and El Salvador. It inhabits tropical deciduous forests, sometimes penetrating into oak woodland forests. Its resin is extensively used as copal in public and private ceremonial activities performed by both mestizo and Indian populations. In some places, it is used as firewood. Its bark and fruits also have medicinal uses.

FIGURE 11.12 *Bursera bipinnata* Engl., observed in Nayarit, Mexico: (A) branch with bipinnate leaves and fruits; (B) male flower (photos by J. Becerra and L. Venable).

Scientific Name: *Bursera bolivarii* Rzedowski (subgenus *Bursera*, Fagaroides group)

Common Names: Aceitillo, cuajiote amarillo

Slender small **trees** to 10 m tall, trunks smooth bluish green; **bark** that exfoliates in large pale-yellow thin strips. **Leaves** up to 12 cm long and 6 cm wide, glabrous, rachis not winged, comprising 3 to 13 bluish green leaflets. **Leaflets** 1 to 5 cm long, mostly obovate (tear-drop shape), margin entire. **Flowers** yellow with a reddish tinge; inflorescences with 1 to 3 flowers. **Fruits** about 1 cm long and 0.6 to 0. 9 cm wide, glabrous, pit completely covered by a thin pale pseudoaril (Toledo 1982).

The uniform, almost teal color and the yellowish exfoliating bark make this a handsome plant. It can be found in the driest precincts at the bottom of the east side of the Balsas Basin in Guerrero and Oaxaca, along with other *Bursera* of restricted distributions such as *B. chemapodicta* and *B. rzedowski*. It is relatively abundant along the slopes of the Río Papagayo, a tributary of the Río Balsas.

FIGURE 11.13 *Bursera bolivarii* Rzedowski: (A) trunk; (B) leaves (photos by J. Becerra and L. Venable); (C) female flower; (D) male flower (photos by E. Huerta-Ocampo).

Scientific Name: *Bursera bonetti* Rzedowski (subgenus *Elaphrium*, Glabrifolia group)

Common Name: Copal

Shrubs or small **trees** to 8 m tall, of gray or reddish-gray smooth, non-exfoliating **bark**. **Leaves** up to 20 cm long and 11 cm wide, with 8 to 19 leaflets, rachis narrowly winged. **Leaflets** glabrous, the margin serrated, 2 to 5 cm long and 0.6 to 1.5 cm wide, apex tapering very gradually to a narrow tip. Lateral leaflets lanceolate sessile, or practically sessile. **Flowers** arranged in very lose inflorescences that can be as large as or larger than the leaves, giving the tree a delicate aspect. **Fruits** 0.6 to 0.8 cm long, glabrous, pit black, its basal half covered by a pale pseudoaril (Rzedowski 1968; Toledo 1982).

This species is restricted to a small area in tropical deciduous forests on the east side of the Balsas Basin at altitudes from 1,100 to 1,450 m.

FIGURE 11.14 *Bursera bonetti* Rzedowski, observed in Guerrero, leaves and bark colonized by lichens (photo by L. Venable).

Scientific Name: *Bursera brunea* (Urb.) Urb. & Ekman (subgenus *Bursera*, Inaguensis group)

Common Name: Gum elemi

Trees to 7 m tall, dioecious, and gray, non-peeling **bark**. **Leaves** typically 8 to 11 cm long and with 5 or 7 leaflets, 2 to 4 cm long. **Leaflets** that resemble paper, with prominent primary and secondary veins. Male inflorescences 10 to 13 cm long with **flowers** 5-merous, sometimes 4-merous (Martínez-Habibe and Daly 2016).

Bursera brunea is known in the Bahamas from Gonaïves Island and one collection from Great Inagua, growing on calcareous soil. It is known to flower in May and June. The plants closely resemble *B. simaruba*, but while *B. simaruba* has exfoliating bark, *B. brunea* does not.

FIGURE 11.15 *Bursera brunea* (Urb.) Urb. & Ekman, herbarium specimen collected in Bahamas (photo by the New York Botanical Garden).

Scientific Name: *Bursera cerasifolia* Brandegee (subgenus *Elaphrium*, Copallifera group)

 Common Names: Torote, copal

 Shrubs or small **trees** to 8 m tall with gray or reddish-gray **bark** that exfoliates in irregular fragments (like scales). **Leaves** unifoliolate, lanceolate, sessile, shining, with margin serrated or with rounded teeth, glabrous or virtually so, 4 to 8 cm long and 1 to 2 cm wide. **Flower** stalks of same length or longer than leaves. **Fruits** 5 to 6 mm long, often solitary, sometimes in groups of 2 or 3, stalks longer than leaf stalks, pit black, one-third to one-half its base covered by an orange pseudoaril (Pérez Navarro 2001).

 Endemic to the Cape region of Baja California Sur, *B. cerasifolia* grows on hillsides and in arroyos.

Scientific Name: *Bursera chemapodicta* Rzed. & Ortiz (subgenus *Bursera*, Fagaroides group)

 Common Name: Cuajiote rojo

 Small **tree** 2.5 to 5 m tall, not always dioecious; **bark** dark red, exfoliating in large papery strips. **Leaves** simple, on stalks to 1.3 cm long, largely ovate with round ending, 3 to 6 cm long and 1.5 to 3.5 cm wide; margin entire, pubescent on the upper

FIGURE 11.16 *Bursera cerasifolia* Brandegee, observed in Baja California Sur: (A) unifoliolate leaves; (B) trunk and bark (photos by J. Becerra and L. Venable).

FIGURE 11.17 *Bursera chemapodicta* Rzed. & Ortiz: (A) details from the bark and a leaf; (B) branch showing leaves and fruits (photos by J. Becerra and L. Venable).

side, velvety on the underside. **Flowers** yellowish with a reddish tinge, pubescent, in small clusters; female flowers 5-merous. **Fruits** 0.5 to 0.7 cm long, glabrous, pit completely covered by the pseudoaril (Rzedowski and Ortiz 1988).

This species is restricted to the bottom of the Zopilote Canyon. Morphologically *B. chemapodicta* is quite similar to *B. schelechtendalli*, except that the former has pubescent flowers and leaves, while the latter is glabrous. Also, *B. chemapodicta*'s resin has a distinctive sweet, pleasant fragrance reminiscent of Lemon Pledge due to its high content of simple hydrocarbons, including nonane and heptane. *Bursera schlechtendalii*'s resin contains hydrocarbons but also large amounts of terpenes such as α-pinene and smells strongly like turpentine (Evans and Becerra 2006).

Scientific Name: *Bursera cinerea* Engl. (subgenus *Bursera*, Simaruba group)

   Common Names: Cuajiote rojo, mulato, palo mulato, camarón, camaroncillo, copalillo

   Trees up to 10 m tall, dioecious, sometimes polygamo-dioecious; trunks green, with **bark** that exfoliates in bright orange-red or brownish-red sheets. **Leaves** bright, mostly glabrous when mature, typically 10 to 45 cm long and 10 to 20 cm wide, with 3 to 5 **leaflets**, apex of leaflets acuminate, terminal leaflet typically obovate (teardrop-shaped). **Flowers** cream to whitish, arranged in inflorescences; male flowers generally 5-merous; female flowers usually 3-merous. Mature **fruits** glabrous,

FIGURE 11.18 *Bursera cinerea* Engl.: (A) individual observed in northern Oaxaca; (B) close-up of its trunk showing the bark; (C) sample of leaves (photos by J. Becerra and L. Venable).

red to brownish, 6 to 10 mm long, the stem holding each fruit no more than 6 mm long, pit completely covered with a red or orange pseudoaril (Rzedowski and Calderón de Rzedowski 1996).

This species inhabits the tropical deciduous forests of Veracruz and Oaxaca. It is common along the roadway between Teotitlán and Huautla in northern Oaxaca. Distinguishing it from *B. simaruba* can be a challenge. *B. cinerea*, however, generally does not inhabit disturbed habitats.

Scientific Name: *Bursera citronella* McVaugh & Rzed. (subgenus *Elaphrium*, Glabrifolia group)

Common Names: Almárciga, lináloe, xochicopal

Trees to 10 m high, highly fragrant; **bark** gray, non-exfoliating. **Leaves** 1 to 5 leaflets, rachis winged. **Leaflets** mostly glabrous, toothed, 2.5 to 4 cm long. **Flow-**

FIGURE 11.19 *Bursera citronella* McVaugh & Rzed., branch with leaves and fruits (photo by D. Espinosa Organista).

ers arranged in a loose inflorescence to 7 cm long. **Fruits** glabrous, 1 to 1.3 cm long, growing in clusters, pit black, its basal half covered by a red pseudoaril (Toledo 1982).

This species is restricted to the western sector of the Sierra Madre del Sur in the states of Colima, Michoacán, and Guerrero, where it grows in tropical subdeciduous forests at altitudes below 1,100 m. The resin is used as incense and is often sold in local markets.

Scientific Name: *Bursera confusa* (Rose) Engl. (subgenus *Bursera*, Fagaroides group)

Common Names: Papelillo

Small **trees**, glabrous, with **bark** gray or green, peeling in sheets ranging in color from yellowish straw to pale reddish. **Leaves** ordinarily with 9 to 19 narrow leaflets. **Leaflets** to 7 cm long, toothed, the teeth usually confined to the middle part of the blade, the long-tapering entire tip often 1 cm long. **Flowers** most often clustered in inflorescences; inflorescences with a very small peduncle, shorter than the stalks of flowers. **Fruits** somewhat wrinkled, in short, compact

FIGURE 11.20 *Bursera confusa* (Rose) Engl., a plant observed in Jalisco (photo by L. Venable).

clusters, pit completely covered by a yellow to orange pseudoaril (McVaugh and Rzedowski 1965).

Bursera confusa is found in Michoacán, Colima, and Jalisco.

Scientific Name: *Bursera copallifera* (Sessé & Moc. ex DC.) Bullock (subgenus *Elaphrium*, Copallifera group)

　Common Name: Copal

　Trees to 5 m tall; trunk often tortuous; **bark** smooth, complete, reddish brown. **Leaves** 9 to 14 cm long, with 19 to 23 leaflets, rachis winged. **Leaflets** rugose, 1 to 2.5 cm long, with toothed margin, dark green on top and light green below, both sides hairy. **Flowers** white, sometimes yellow, sometimes yellow-orange. Inflorescences extensively hairy, to 8 cm long, with many flowers. **Fruits** spherical, to 1 cm long, pit completely or almost completely covered by a pseudoaril (Toledo 1982).

　Bursera copallifera is an abundant component of the tropical deciduous forests in the Balsas Basin and in the canyons along the Río Santiago. It ranges from the states of Nayarit and Zacatecas to Oaxaca.

Scientific Name: *Bursera coyucensis* Bullock (subgenus *Elaphrium*, Glabrifolia group)

　Common Name: Copal de perro

　Small **trees** or **shrubs** to 4 m tall. **Leaves** with 7 to 11 leaflets, with conspicuously long hairs in both sides of the leaf, rachis with extremely wide wing; **leaflets** oval to

FIGURE 11.21 *Bursera copallifera* (Sessé & Moc. ex DC.) Bullock, observed in Guerrero: (A) leaves; (B) flowers; (C) fruits and pit covered by red pseudoaril (photos by J. Becerra and L. Venable).

FIGURE 11.22 *Bursera coyucensis* Bullock, observed in Michoacán: (A) plant with fruits; (B) the leaf rachis is notoriously winged; (C) female flower (photos by J. Becerra and L. Venable).

elliptic, 3 cm long and 1 to 2 cm wide, margin greatly toothed. **Flowers** yellowish red, with long hairs. **Fruits** glabrous, 8 to 9 mm long, grouped in clusters, pit partially covered at the base by a pseudoaril (Toledo 1982).

These plants are found only in tropical deciduous forests between 200 and 650 m elevation on the west side of the Balsas Basin in Guerrero and Michoacán.

Scientific Name: *Bursera crenata* P. G. Wilson (subgenus *Bursera*, Fragilis group)

Common Names: Copal, aceitillo, cuajiote colorado

Trees to 10 m tall, with red exfoliating **bark**. **Leaves** glabrous, unifoliolate, 4 to 7 cm long and 1.5 to 2.2 cm wide, margin conspicuously round-toothed; leaf stalk 0.5 to 0.8 cm long. **Flowers** few; female flowers 3-merous, arranged in short inflorescences. **Fruits** about 0.6 cm long and 0.4 cm wide, in short, compact clusters, pit completely covered by a pale-red pseudoaril (Toledo 1982).

FIGURE 11.23 *Bursera crenata* P. G. Wilson: (A) tree; (B) trunk and bark (photos by
I. Torres García, CC BY-NC 4.0); (C) leaves (photo by B. Vrskovy).

This species grows in tropical deciduous forests in the warmest and driest areas
of the western region of the Balsas Basin in the states of Jalisco, Michoacán, and
Guerrero at altitudes of 250 to 600 m.

Scientific Name: *Bursera cuneata* (Schlecht.) Engl. (subgenus *Elaphrium*, Copallifera group)

   Common Names: Copal, copalillo, cuerecatzundi, cuerica-tzunda, cuiricatzunda
(Purépecha)

FIGURE 11.24 *Bursera cuneata* (Schlecht.) Engl., tree observed in Morelos; (A) leaves; (B) trunk and bark (photos by J. Becerra and L. Venable).

Trees, sometimes **shrubs**, to 10 m tall, of reddish-gray or gray non-exfoliating **bark**, with dense short hairs in all green parts. **Leaves** of 3 to 13 leaflets to 6.5 cm long and 2.3 cm wide, margin roughly toothed, of leathery texture; primary, secondary, and tertiary veins prominent. **Flowers** whitish, in inflorescences to 8 cm long. **Fruits** to 1.2 cm long, glabrous, pit black, almost completely covered by a yellow or orange pseudoaril (Rzedowski and Guevara-Féfer 1992).

This species is distributed from central to southern Mexico in the states of Guanajuato, Hidalgo, Michoacán, Mexico D.F., Morelos, Puebla, and Guerrero; it is often found in oak-tropical deciduous forest transition zones and on basaltic outcrops. It is used in the production of crafts, as firewood, and as incense.

Scientific Name: *Bursera denticulata* McVaugh & Rzedowski (subgenus *Bursera*, Fragilis group)

Common Name: Cuajiote

Trees to 8 m tall, glabrous, of dark brownish-red exfoliating **bark**. **Leaves** with 3 to 5 pairs of leaflets, rachis narrowly winged; lateral **leaflets** 1.5 to 5 cm long and 0.7 to 1.6 cm wide; margin finely toothed. Female **flowers** 3-merous, arranged in small clusters, 1 to 12 flowers. **Fruits** 0.7 to 1 cm long and 0.4 to 0.7 cm wide, arranged in

FIGURE 11.25 *Bursera denticulata* Mc-Vaugh & Rzedowski, a plant in cultivation (photo by B. Vrskovy).

FIGURE 11.26 *Bursera discolor* Rzedowski, observed in Guerrero: (A) trunk and bark; (B) leaf (photos by J. Becerra and L. Venable).

infructescences 1 to 3 cm long, pit completely covered by a pale pseudoaril (Toledo 1982).

This species grows in the southwestern Sierra Madre del Sur and the Balsas Basin in the states of Colima, Guerrero, Jalisco, and Michoacán.

Scientific Name: *Bursera discolor* Rzedowski (subgenus *Bursera*, Fagaroides group)

Common Names: Cuajiote, Cuajiote rojo

Slender **trees** to 10 m tall, with bright and smooth, often bluish-green **bark** that exfoliates in yellow or pale-orange sheets and strips. **Leaves** to 12 cm long and 6.5 cm wide, rachis very narrowly winged, with 3 to 11 leaflets. **Leaflets** olive green on the upper side and teal on the underside, lanceolate and largely glabrous, 1.5 to 3.6 cm long and 0.7 to 1.4 cm wide. **Flowers** purplish red, 5-merous; male flowers occasionally 4- or 6-merous; inflorescences bearing typically 1 to 3 flowers (sometimes more). **Fruits** to 0.8 cm long, in short, small clusters (Toledo 1982).

The distribution of this species includes the Balsas Basin and the canyons and slopes of the Sierra Madre del Sur. It grows in transition areas between tropical deciduous forests and oak forests.

Scientific Name: *Bursera diversifolia* Rose (subgenus *Elaphrium*, Copallifera group)

Common Name: Caraño

Shrubs or small **trees** to 8 m tall. **Bark** gray to reddish gray, non-exfoliating. **Leaves** bipinnate, to 10 cm long and 4 cm wide, rough, wrinkled, glabrous, sometimes pubescent and glossy on top; densely pubescent on the underside. Leaf rachis lightly winged, with 6 to 10 pairs of leaflets, the inferior leaflets most often double pinnate with 3 to 7 leaflets, margins roughly crenate. **Flowers** yellow, of oblong petals, arranged

FIGURE 11.27 *Bursera diversifolia* Rose, observed in Guerrero: (A) trunk and bark; (b) leaf (photos by J. Becerra and L. Venable).

in inflorescences to 3 cm long, with many flowers. **Fruits** to 8 mm long and 6 mm wide, pit almost completely covered by a whitish pseudoaril (Toledo 1982).

This species is found from Guerrero, Mexico, to Guatemala. It is used as incense, and it is probably cultivated in Nicaragua.[1]

Scientific Name: *Bursera epinnata* (Rose) Engl. (subgenus *Elaphrium*, Glabrifolia group)

  Common Names: Copal, torote

  Shrubs or **trees** to 4 m tall with grayish, smooth, non-exfoliating bark. **Leaves** mostly unifoliolate, but also with 3 or 5 leaflets in same branches. **Leaflets** 2 to 4 cm long, densely hairy on both surfaces, margin toothed. **Flowers** arranged in inflorescences of many flowers, petals oblong, spreading at flowering; flower stalks slender, longer than leaf stalks, and often longer than entire leaves. **Fruits** 7 to 10 mm long, solitary or in groups of 2 or 3 (Pérez Navarro 2001).

---

  1. *B. diversifolia* has the characteristics of a hybrid between *B. bipinnata* and *B. copallifera* or between *B. bipinnata* and *B. excelsa*. McVaugh and Rzedowski (1965) consider it so and do not recognize it as a legitimate species. We think there is not sufficient evidence to deny its status as a separate species. Despite its origin, it has long-established reproductive populations sufficient to regard it as a species. Further studies are needed to clarify its taxonomic status.

FIGURE 11.28 *Bursera epinnata* (Rose) Engl., observed in Baja California Sur, Mexico: (A) general aspect of plant; (B) trunk; (C) leaves; (D) fruit and pit covered with pseudoaril (photos by J. Becerra and L. Venable).

Morphologically, *B. epinnata* is very similar to *B. rupicola*, and they inhabit the same region. While the latter is a shrub, *B. epinnata* is more often a tree with a well-defined trunk. Endemic to southern Baja California Sur, *B. epinnata* occurs on hillsides and in arroyos.

FIGURE 11.29 *Bursera esparzae* Rzedowski, Calderón & Medina, observed in Oaxaca: (A) plant; (B) branch with fruits (photos by La Rata Mutante, CC BY-NC 4.0); (C) flowers (photo by C. Domínguez, CC BY-NC).

Scientific Name: *Bursera esparzae* Rzedowski, Calderón & Medina (subgenus *Elaphrium*, Glabrifolia group)

   Common Names: Copal, yàg-yàal (Zapotec)

   Trees or **shrubs**, up to 7 m tall, with gray smooth **bark**; branches dark red, densely hairy when young. **Leaves** 6 to 25 cm long, 3 to 11 cm wide, rachis not winged, regularly with 5 to 11 leaflets. **Leaflets** 1.5 to 8 cm long, densely hairy underneath, with margin prominently toothed. Female and male **flowers** 4-merous, sometimes 5-merous, hairy, deployed in inflorescences up to 7 cm long. **Fruits** hairy, 8 to 10 mm long, pit with one side covered up to two-thirds of its length by the orange pseudoaril, the other side of the pseudoaril covering only up to one-third of the length, the exposed part black (Rzedowski, Medina Lemos, and Calderón de Rzedowski 2004).

This species inhabits both tropical deciduous forests and oak forests. It has been found only in Oaxaca, at altitudes between 1,550 and 1,950 m.

Scientific Name: *Bursera excelsa* (H.B.K.) Engl. (subgenus *Elaphrium*, Copallifera group)

Common Names: Copal, copalillo, tecomajaca, pomó

Trees to 8 m tall of gray trunk, with non-exfoliating **bark**. **Leaves** 11 to 23 cm long and 6 to 10.5 cm wide, rachis winged. **Leaflets** 9 to 15, 2.3 to 5.5 cm long, sparsely hairy on both sides, with margin conspicuously toothed. **Flowers** yellow, densely hairy, arranged in inflorescences 4 to 9 cm long, comprising many flowers. **Fruits** 0.8 cm long, 0.7 to 0.8 cm wide, in short clusters, pit completely covered by a cream-white pseudoaril (Toledo 1982).

This taxon's leaf morphology (size and hairiness) varies significantly across its geographic distribution, which is relatively large for a *Bursera*. It extends from the Pacific lowlands of Sinaloa to Chiapas, Mexico. It is used in traditional medicine

FIGURE 11.30 *Bursera excelsa* (H.B.K.) Engl.: (A) trunk; (B) leaf; (C) branch with flowers and fruits; (D) infructescence (photos by J. Becerra and L. Venable).

to treat tumors and muscle spasms (Acevedo et al. 2015). Several varieties are recognized (McVaugh and Rzedowski 1965). *B. excelsa* var. *excelsa* is found at low altitudes, 1,000 m maximum, and has leaflets that are brown-tomentose beneath. *B. excelsa* var. *favonialis* and *B. excelsa* var. *acutidens* have leaflets that are soft pubescent beneath and tend to inhabit places at higher altitudes, mostly mountainous terrains. *B. acutidens* has only two to three pairs of leaflets.

Scientific Name: *Bursera exequielii* León de la Luz (subgenus *Bursera*, Microphylla group)

Common Name: Torote

Trees up to 4 m tall, dioecious, polygamo-dioecious. **Bark** yellowish-orange, exfoliating in papery strips as stems thicken. **Leaves** with 7 to 11 leaflets, rachis

FIGURE 11.31 *Bursera exequielii* León de la Luz: (A) individual observed near La Paz, Baja California Sur (photo by L. Venable); (B) leaves; (C) details of trunk; (D) male flower (photos by J. León de la Luz, CC BY-NC 4.0).

narrowly winged, 3 to 3.5 cm long. **Leaflets** mostly ovate, 5 to 9 mm long, semi-succulent. **Flowers** in groups of 2 to 5, appearing in the growing season before leaves; male flowers 4-merous, sometimes 5- or 6-merous; female flowers 3-merous, sometimes 4-merous. **Fruits** spherical, pit completely covered by a reddish-yellow pseudoaril (León de la Luz, Medel Narváes, and Domínguez Cadena 2017).

This species is restricted to the tip of El Sargento, Los Cabos, Baja California Sur, where it grows on stabilized dunes close to the beach. *Bursera exequielii* is very closely related to *B. microphylla* and is perhaps a variant of that species. The main difference is that leaves of the latter are mostly linear or lanceolate, while those of *B. exequielii* tend to be rounder.

Scientific Name: *Bursera fagaroides* (H. B. K.) Engl. (subgenus *Bursera*, Fagaroides group)

Common Names: Aceitillo, copal sarzafrás, xixote, cuajiote, cuajiote amarillo, cuajiote blanco, jiote, palo del diablo, papelillo, venadilla, tecomaca, torote, borreguilla

Shrubs or **trees**, to 8 (but ordinarily no more than 4) m tall; highly variable in its morphological and functional traits; dioecious, sometimes hermaphrodites, highly resinous; trunks green with a **bark** that exfoliates in yellowish-gray papery sheets. **Leaves** with no wings on the rachis, with 1 to 5 pairs of **leaflets**, but occasionally unifoliolate or trifoliolate, margin entire or toothed. **Flowers** whitish-green, whitish-yellow, or whitish-pink, some arranged in small inflorescences or solitary; male flowers most often 5-merous (sometimes 3- and 4-merous), female flowers 3-merous. **Fruits** typically 0.5 to 0.8 cm long on short stalks no more than 2 mm long and terminating in a sharp point; after the pit matures, it is covered by a yellow or red pseudoaril (Rzedowski, Medina Lemos, and Calderón de Rzedowski 2004).

Bursera fagaroides is a complex of taxa in need of revision. Rogers McVaugh and Jerzy Rzedowski (1965) distinguished three subspecific entities: var. *fagaroides*, var. *purpusii*, and var. *elongata*. *Bursera fagaroides* var. *elongata* has 3 to 6 pairs of leaflets of lanceolate shape. *Bursera fagaroides* var. *fagaroides* does not have oblong to elliptic

FIGURE 11.32 *Bursera fagaroides* (H. B. K.) Engl. var. *elongata*, from Sonora (photo by J. Becerra).

FIGURE 11.33 *Bursera fagaroides* (H.B.K.) Engl. observed in Morelos: (A) small trees; (B) leaves; (C) trunk; (D) male flower; (E) female flower (photos by J. Becerra and L. Venable); (F) *B. fagaroides* as bonsai (photo by S. Ross).

leaflets with dentate margin. *Bursera fagaroides* var. *purpusii* also has oblong to elliptic leaflets with margin mostly entire. However, field observations suggested later that the second proposed subspecies often cannot be distinguished from the third, and molecular analysis showed that the third is probably an independent species (Becerra and Venable 1999; Becerra 2003b). *Bursera fagaroides* is often difficult to distinguish from *B. aptera*.

Bursera fagaroides var. *fagaroides* is a wide-ranging species, as the long collection of common names suggests. It grows mostly in xerophilous shrub and tropical deciduous forests in the Mexican high plateau, in Aguascalientes, Coahuila, Guanajuato, Queretaro, San Luis Potosí, and Zacatecas, but it also inhabits sections of the Balsas Basin from Michoacán to Jalisco. Populations of *B. fagaroides* var. *purpusii* are most frequently found on the west side of the Balsas Basin at altitudes between 400 and 600 m. *Bursera fagaroides* var. *elongata* grows from the Pacific slopes of Sonora to Nayarit, perhaps to Oaxaca. These plants are often used as firewood and as living fences. Medicinal properties are attributed to them, with the gum used for treating scorpion and insect stings. In some places, they are considered toxic, and extracts are used to kill ants. The bark is also employed in tanning. *Bursera fagaroides* is the bursera sold most often in nurseries outside Mexico and it is the one grown most frequently as bonsai.

Scientific Name: *Bursera filicifolia* Brandegee (subgenus *Elaphrium*, Copallifera group)

   Common Names: Torote, copalquín

Trees to 10 m tall. **Bark** of mature trunks and larger branches are light gray while small branches are yellowish gray. **Leaves** to 10 cm long, bipinnate, bright green, densely hairy beneath, rachis narrowly winged. **Leaflets** 5 to 13 in mature leaves, 0.3 to 2 cm long, 1.5 to 12 mm wide, margin slightly toothed, the apex of the terminal leaflet round. Female inflorescences 5 to 7 cm long, with up to 3 **flowers**. **Fruits** to 1 cm long, reddish at maturity, pit covered up to two-thirds of its length by a red or orange pseudoaril, the exposed part black or dark brown (Pérez Navarro 2001).

FIGURE 11.34 *Bursera filicifolia* Brandegee, observed in Baja California Sur (photo by J. Becerra and L. Venable).

Another *Bursera* endemic to southern Baja California.

Scientific Name: *Bursera fragilis* S. Watson (subgenus *Bursera*, Fragilis group)

Common Name: Torote amarillo, papelillo, torote copal, incienso, torote jolopete, to'oro chutamo (Mayo)

Shrubs or small **trees** to 8 m tall with green smooth trunks; **bark** most often pale gray or straw colored, sometimes very dark green, exfoliating in papery strips. **Leaves** with 3 to 9 leaflets, glabrous. **Leaflets** lanceolate to elliptic, 3 to 7 cm long and 0.7 to 2 cm wide, margins finely and regularly toothed. **Flowers** up to 1 cm long with yellowish-white petals, solitary or in inflorescences 6 cm long. **Fruits** 0.6 to 1.0 cm long, pit covered with a thin, papery orange pseudoaril (M. Johnson 1992).

This species inhabits hills, slopes, and canyons in thornscrub, tropical dry forest, and the lower edges of oak woodlands of eastern Sonora, southwest Chihuahua, Durango, and Sinaloa. It is sometimes confused with *B. lancifolia*, a close relative that is very similar but grows in southern Mexico from Guerrero and Queretaro to Oaxaca. *Bursera fragilis*, however, has pale-green-colored bark, larger white flowers (about

FIGURE 11.35 *Bursera fragilis* S. Watson, plant observed in Sonora: (A) trunk; (B) inflorescence (photos by L. Venable); (C) leaves (photo by A. Búrquez).

1 cm), and larger inflorescences (about 6 cm long), while *B. lancifolia* has bright-red, sometimes orange exfoliating bark, smaller cream flowers (to 6 mm long), and inflorescences 2 to 4 cm long. Also, molecular studies suggest that *B. fragilis* and *B. lancifolia* have different species as closest relatives and hence are not likely to be conspecific. But further research is needed to establish the limits of *B. fragilis*'s southern geographic range. According to Howard Scott Gentry (1942), *B. fragilis*'s gum is used as a poultice for backaches, bruises, and bone breaks. It is also used as incense in Mayo and Guarijío ceremonies.

Scientific Name: *Bursera fragrantissima* Bullock (subgenus *Elaphrium*, Glabrifolia group)

    Common Name: Copal

    Trees to 6 m tall, with non-exfoliating gray **bark**, highly fragrant (hence the species name). **Leaves** to 12 cm long, typically trifoliate, occasionally with 5 leaflets, leaf stalk of 7 to 12 cm long. **Leaflets** generally of rhomboid shape with acuminate apex, glabrous except on veins and rachis, and with margin noticeably toothed. **Flowers** white, in inflorescences about 20 cm long. **Fruits** 1.2 cm long and 0.6 cm wide, pit black, its basal half covered by a red pseudoaril (Toledo 1982).

FIGURE 11.36 *Bursera fragrantissima* Bullock, collected in Mexico (photo by the New York Botanical Garden, CC BY 4.0).

    This species grows in Guerrero and Michoacán in relatively humid habitats mostly at altitudes between 1,000 and 1,400 m, sometimes in oak forests.

Scientific Name: *Bursera frenningae* Correll (subgenus *Bursera*, Inaguensis group)

    Common Name: Frenning's gum elemi

    Shrubs or **trees** to 13 m tall, dioecious. **Bark** reddish or reddish brown, often shed in papery sheets. **Leaves** 8 to 10 cm long, typically with 3 to 5 sessile or practically sessile **leaflets**, 5.6 to 6.3 cm long, broadly oblong-elliptic to elliptic-oblanceolate, apex mucronate. Male **flowers** 5-merous, yellowish green, arranged in inflorescences 5 to 8 cm long; female flowers 3-merous. **Fruits** 7 to 8 mm long, 5 to 7 mm wide (Martínez-Habibe and Daly 2016).

    Bursera frenningae is distributed in the Bahamas and the Caicos Islands on hard-packed sand near the seashore, in open coppices, and in coastal rocky thickets. It flowers from June to October and fruits throughout the year, especially June to

FIGURE 11.37 *Bursera frenningae* Correll: (A) trunk and bark; (B) leaf; (C) leaves and fruits (photos by E. Freid).

November. It is difficult to distinguish from *B. inaguensis* at first sight since the leaves are strikingly similar, but *B. frenningae* can be identified by its tree habit and its red and peeling bark, while *B. inaguensis* is a shrub with gray nonpeeling bark, and slender longer inflorescences about 9 cm long.

Scientific Name: *Bursera galeottiana* Engl. (subgenus *Bursera*, Microphylla group)

Common Names: Cuajiote colorado, copal, cuajiote rojo, breo, copal mulato, xiote colorado, xixote, xixote colorado

Trees or **shrubs** 2 to 8 m tall, with deep-red trunk and **bark** that exfoliates in small sheets of the same color, young branches slightly hairy, dioecious, sometimes polygamo-dioecious. **Leaves** 4 to 7 cm long and 1 to 4 cm wide, with pubescent stalks up to 7 mm long; leaf blade divided into 5 to 29 linear **leaflets** up to 20 mm long and 1 mm wide. **Flowers** yellow, solitary or in pairs, often in groups at the branch tips with pubescent peduncles no more than 0.5 cm long; male flowers typically 5-merous; female flowers 3-merous. **Fruits** 6 to 8 mm long, pit completely covered by a yellow pseudoaril when young that changes to orange at maturity (Rzedowski, Medina Lemos, and Calderón de Rzedowski 2004).

FIGURE 11.38 *Bursera galeottiana* Engl.: (A) individual observed in the state of Oaxaca; (B) close-up of the bark; (C) branch with fruits; (D) male flowers (photos by J. Becerra and L. Venable).

This species is found only in two disjunct areas, one in Querétaro and Guanajuato and the other in Puebla and Oaxaca. It inhabits tropical deciduous forests where they grade into oak forests and xerophilous shrub. It is used as an analgesic, a healing herb, and to treat abscesses.

Scientific Name: *Bursera gibarensis* M. C. Martínez, Daly & J. Pérez (subgenus *Bursera*, Inaguensis group)

Common Name: Copal

FIGURE 11.39 *Bursera gibarensis* M. C. Martínez, Daly & J. Pérez: (A) plant observed in Cabo Lucrecia, Banes, Cuba; (B) branch with leaves (photos by J. L. Gómez-Hechavarria).

Subshrubs to 30 cm tall, densely branching. **Leaves** 2.1 to 3.2 cm long, most often with 3 leaflets, sometimes 5; petiole and rachis sparsely pubescent; all **leaflets** sessile, resembling paper, 11 to 20 mm long and 2.3 to 4.5 mm wide, narrowly elliptic, with midvein highly prominent and the rest of venation not readily visible, apex mucronate. Male **flowers** 5-merous, arranged in inflorescences to 1.4 cm long. **Fruits** 6 to 7 mm long and about 4 mm wide (Martínez-Habibe and Daly 2016).

Bursera gibarensis is endemic to xerophytic coastal scrub that grows in the cavities in karst (dogtooth limestone) substrates in Hoguin Province, Cuba. The species is known to flower and fruit in August.

Scientific Name: *Bursera glabra* (Jacq.) Triana & Planch. (subgenus *Elaphrium*, Copallifera group)

Common Names: Aliia, bálsamo de incienso, bálsamo real

Shrubs or small **trees** to 6 m tall with reddish-brown **bark**, smooth and not peeling. **Leaves** in clusters at the end of short branches, 2.5 to 5.5 cm long, with 3 to 11 leaflets, rachis slightly winged. **Leaflets** densely pubescent on both sides when young, but mostly glabrous when mature, 1.5 to 2.5 cm long, toothed in the last

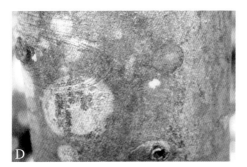

FIGURE 11.40 *Bursera glabra* (Jacq.) Triana & Planch., observed in Guanacaste, Costa Rica: (A) branch with leaves; (B) underside of a leaf; (C) branch with fruits and leaves; (D) trunk (photos by D. H. Janzen, CC BY-NC-SA 3.0).

two-thirds of the leaflet. Male **flowers** 4-merous, rarely 5-merous. Infructescences short, with 1 to 4 **fruits**; pseudoaril orange red, covering three-fourths of the black pit (Castro Laportte 2013).

Bursera glabra is native to Costa Rica, Colombia, and Venezuela.

Scientific Name: *Bursera glabrifolia* (H.B.K.) Engl. (subgenus *Elaphrium*, Glabrifolia group)

   Common Names: Copalillo, copal blanco, copal hembra, zomplante

   Trees to 12 m tall, of reddish-gray non-exfoliating **bark** in trunk and reddish bark in small branches. **Leaves** to 12.5 cm long and 6 cm wide, rachis narrowly winged, 0.4 to 2 mm on each side, with 5 to 11 leaflets. **Leaflets** bright on the upper side, 0.8 to 3 cm long and 0.5 to 2 cm wide, margin crenated, with prominent veins on the underside. **Flowers** arranged in inflorescences, petals yellow and hairy; female and male flowers 4-merous. **Fruits** 9 to 13 mm long, spherical or subspherical, arranged in small groups, sometimes solitary, pit covered up to two-thirds of its length by a yellow or orange-red fleshy pseudoaril, the exposed part black (Rzedowski, Medina Lemos, and Calderón de Rzedowski 2004).

This species inhabits the tropical deciduous forest and areas of transition to woodland forest vegetation in the states of Mexico, Oaxaca, Puebla, Michoacán, Morelos, and Guerrero at altitudes of 1,400 to 2,200 m. In Oaxaca it is used to treat fever, inflammation, and body weakness (Acevedo et al. 2015). It provides the wood of choice for carving *alebrijes* in the Central Valleys of Oaxaca and is excessively harvested there.

Scientific Name: *Bursera glauca* Griseb. (subgenus *Bursera*, Inaguensis group)

   Common Names: Ayúa prieta, ayúa prieta sin espinas, ayuda prieta, ayuda sin espinas, azucarero, copal

FIGURE 11.41 *Bursera glabrifolia* (H.B.K.) Engl., observed in Oaxaca: (A) leaf and fruits; (B) pit covered with pseudoaril (photos by J. Becerra and L. Venable); (C) female flower; (D) male flower (photos by E. Huerta-Ocampo).

FIGURE 11.42 *Bursera glauca* Griseb., a branch showing leaves (photo by J. L. Gómez, C C BY-NC).

FIGURE 11.43 *Bursera gracilipes* (photo by B. Vrskovy).

Shrubs or **trees** to 6 m tall with peeling **bark**, branches slender and reddish. **Leaves** 3 to 6 cm long, with 1 to 5 leaflets (rarely 7), glaucous, leaf petiole 3 to 4 mm long. **Leaflets** sessile, 3.8 to 4.2 cm long, narrowly oblong-elliptic to oblong. Male **flowers** 5-merous, petals lanceolate, in inflorescences short, to 2.6 cm long with peduncles 4 to 11 mm long, few-flowered. **Fruit** 6 to 7 mm long (Martínez-Habibe and Daly 2016).

Bursera glauca is endemic to serpentine soils (soils of extremely high content of minerals such as magnesium and heavy metals) in Cuba (Camaguey, Holguin, Guantanamo, and Santiago de Cuba provinces), the Dominican Republic (Independencia), and Haiti (Artibonite and Nord-Ouest).

Scientific Name: *Bursera gracilipes* Urb. & Ekman (subgenus *Bursera*, Inaguensis group)

Common Name: Copal

Shrubs or small **trees** to 6 m tall. **Leaves** 2 to 3 cm long, with 3 to 5 leaflets. **Leaflets** 17 to 22 mm long and 6 to 9 mm wide, oblong-elliptic, membranaceous, glossy green with mucronate apex. Male **flowers** 4-merous, arranged in inflorescences to 2.8 cm long, producing +/− 10 flowers; female flowers 3-merous, arranged in inflorescences to 1.8 cm long, 1- to 3-flowered. **Fruits** 1 to 1.2 cm long, 0.7 cm wide, ovoid or ellipsoid, green but turning reddish at maturity, fruiting pedicel 0.8 to 1 cm (Martínez-Habibe and Daly 2016).

Known only from Pedernales and Barahona in the Dominican Republic, in dry forest on calcareous soil. Known to flower from June to September and to produce fruits in September.

———————

Scientific Name: *Bursera grandifolia* (Schltdl.) Engl. (subgenus *Bursera*)

Common Names: Mulato, jiote blanco, chicopun, chutama, guande blanco, palo mulato (Spanish); napitaro (Guarijío); to'oro mulato (Mayo); iweri (Tarahumara)

Large **trees** to 20 m tall, with dark-green trunks and bright orange-red **bark** that exfoliates in large brownish-red strips or sheets. **Leaves** large (as is reflected in the species name), 14 to 37 cm long and 10 to 26 cm wide, comprising 3 to 7 pairs of leaflets. **Leaflets** 4 to 15 cm long and 2 to 4 cm wide, acuminate (narrow pointed tip) and edges entire, veins prominent, the blades soft and velvety, bright green above, gray on the underside. **Flowers** densely grouped in fuzzy inflorescences, with white petals tinged with pink; male flowers 5-merous; female flowers 3-merous. **Fruits** 6 to 12 mm long and 5 to 8 mm wide, pubescent, fruit stalks shorter than the fruits, pit completely covered by a thin whitish-pink pseudoaril (Toledo 1982).

FIGURE 11.44 *Bursera grandifolia* (Schltdl.) Engl., observed in Sinaloa, Mexico: (A) trunk (photo by LauraReginaAC, CC BY-NC); (B) leaves (photo by jarturoq, CC BY-NC); (C) fruits (photo by E. Guevara, CC BY-NC-SA).

A species of wide geographic distribution, *B. grandifolia* grows in northwest Mexico in Sonora and southwest Chihuahua and ranges south to Costa Rica. The trees are conspicuous in tropical seasonal forests and especially abundant in the tropical deciduous forests in the state of Guerrero. These plants are sometimes used for living fences and firewood. The bark and leaves are commonly brewed into a refreshing tea, also used as a tonic to restore vigor and to alleviate fever (Camou-Guerrero 2008).

Scientific Name: *Bursera graveolens* (Kunth) Triana & Planch. (subgenus *Elaphrium*, Glabrifolia group)

   Common Names: Aceitillo, azafrán, gomilla, palo de brujo, palo santo, sasafrás, nabanché, mizquixochicopalli

   Trees, sometimes **shrubs**, to 15 m tall, highly fragrant, with gray **bark**. **Leaves** pinnate, sometimes bipinnate, to 30 cm long and 18 cm wide, with 7 to 11 leaflets. **Leaflets** 3 to 9 cm long and 1 to 4 cm wide, the apex largely acuminate, margin roughly toothed, of membranaceous texture. **Flowers** yellowish, white, or green, arranged in inflorescences that typically are as large as the leaves. **Fruits** glabrous, reddish at maturity, 0.6 to 1.0 cm long, pit black, about two-thirds covered by an orange-red pseudoaril (Rzedowski, Medina Lemos, and Calderón de Rzedowski 2004).

FIGURE 11.45 *Bursera graveolens* (Kunth) Triana & Planch., from Galápagos Islands: (A) tree with whitish trunk covered with lichens; (B) leaves (photos by J. Becerra and L. Venable).

FIGURE 11.46 *Bursera graveolens* (Kunth) Triana & Planch., observed in Oaxaca, Mexico: (A) smooth and nonpeeling trunk; (B) leaves; (C) seedling with trilobate cotyledons (photos by J. Becerra and L. Venable).

This is often considered a wide-ranging species, growing from southeast Mexico to Colombia, Venezuela, Peru, and Ecuador (including the Galápagos Islands). However, it very probably includes two or more species that look alike but may not even be congeners. Using a DNA phylogenetic analyses, José De-Nova et al. (2012) found that *B. graveolens* from a population from Teotitlán del Camino, Oaxaca, Mexico, was very closely related to *B. heteresthes*. Also, in her revision of *Bursera* of Venezuela, Mercedes Castro Laportte (2013) reports that in that country, *B. graveolens* has trilobate cotyledons. However, María Cristina Martínez-Habibe (2012), also using molecular phylogenetics, found that the species inhabiting the Galápagos Islands is more closely related to *Commiphora* than to *Bursera*. It would be interesting to observe the cotyledons of *B. graveolens* from the Galápagos Islands, as cotyledons of *Commiphora* are typically heart-shaped rather than trilobate as in typical copales like the *B. graveolens* observed in Venezuela. In Mexico, *B. graveolens* is sometimes cultivated and often found in living fences. All over its geographic range, the species is highly appreciated for

FIGURE 11.47 *Bursera heliae* Rzedowski & Calderón, observed in Oaxaca, Mexico (photo by L. Venable).

FIGURE 11.48 *Bursera heteresthes* Bullock, from Guerrero (photo by L. Venable).

its medicinal properties. The bark is used in an alcohol infusion to alleviate inflammation, rheumatism, and skin tumors. As a tea, it is used for digestive and respiratory problems (Nakanishi et al. 2005).

***

Scientific Name: *Bursera heliae* Rzedowski & Calderón (subgenus *Elaphrium*, Copallifera group)

Common Names: Copal blanco, copal colorado, copal tecomaca, tecomaca, cecomacal, yàg-yàal (Zapotec)

Trees, sometimes **shrubs**, to 8 m tall, with non-exfoliating gray **bark**. **Leaves** of rough, wrinkled texture, up to 7 cm long and 5.5 cm wide, with 3 to 5 (infrequently 7) leaflets. **Leaflets** with dense short hairs and toothed margin, 0.8 to 4.5 cm long and 0.7 to 3.5 cm wide; the terminal leaflet usually larger than the lateral ones. **Flowers** 4-merous, arranged in inflorescences up to 6 cm long, densely haired, with white to yellowish petals. Mature **fruits** red, spherical, up to 0.8 cm wide, glabrous, pit covered up to five-sixths of its length by an orange-yellow pseudoaril, the exposed part black (Rzedowski and Calderón de Rzedowski 2002).

This species is restricted to the Río Tehuantepec Basin in Oaxaca. It has been extensively used as incense.

***

Scientific Name: *Bursera heteresthes* Bullock (subgenus *Elaphrium*, Glabrifolia group)

Common Names: Copal, copalillo

Shrubs or **trees** to 10 m tall, with gray, non-exfoliating, and smooth **bark** with many lenticels. **Leaves** trifoliolate, occasionally with 5 leaflets and rachis widely winged. **Leaflets** with bright-green upper side, toothed margin, sometimes with dense short hairs, 5 to 14 (but most often 8 to 10) cm long and 3 to 10 (but most often 5 to 8) cm wide. **Flowers** whitish, grouped in lax inflorescences. **Fruits** 0.6 to 1 cm long, glabrous, reddish, pit covered partially by a pseudoaril that turns red at maturity (Frias Castro 2008; Rzedowski and Calderón de Rzedowski 2009).

This is a species of wide distribution, from southern Jalisco to Guatemala. It grows from sea level to altitudes of 1,600 m and inhabits tropical deciduous forests, oak forests, and more humid forests as well. Across its range there is high individual variation of leaflet shape. It is often used in living fences.

Scientific Name: *Bursera hindsiana* (Bentham) Engler (subgenus *Elaphrium*, Copallifera group)

    Common Names: Red elephant tree, copal, torote prieto, xopínl (Comcáac)

    Shrubs or small **trees** to 5 m tall with non-exfoliating grayish-red **bark**. **Leaves** most often of 1 leaflet, sometimes of 3 to 5 leaflets often not completely separated,

FIGURE 11.49 *Bursera hindsiana* (Bentham) Engler, observed in Sonora, Mexico: (A) branch with leaves and fruit; (B) trunk and bark; (C) pits with pseudoaril; (D) seedling with trilobate cotyledons (photos by J. Becerra and L. Venable).

to 5.5 cm long, with winged rachis. **Leaflets** ovate or obovate, 0.8 to 3.5 cm long and 0.6 to 2.5 cm wide, soft, hairy, the margins irregularly toothed. **Flowers** white, in few-flowered clusters or solitary. **Fruits** red and green, pit black, about two-thirds covered by an orange pseudoaril (M. Johnson 1992).

This species is common in portions of the arid northwest of Mexico, growing in desert scrub in central coastal Sonora and in much of the lowlands of Baja California. *Bursera hindsiana* is extensively used by the Comcáac (Seri Indians) as wood for producing artifacts and as medicine.

————————

Scientific Name: *Bursera hintonii* Bullock (subgenus *Elaphrium*, Copallifera group)

   Common Names: Copal, copal manso

   Trees, occasionally **shrubs**, up to 14 m tall, with gray trunk and non-exfoliating **bark**, dioecious, sometimes polygamo-dioecious. **Leaves** large, 20 to 35 cm long and

12 to 20 cm wide, densely haired on both their upper side and underside, rachis prominently winged, wings toothed. **Leaflets** most often 11 to 17, occasionally 21; lateral leaflets up to 16 cm long and 7 cm wide with the terminal leaflet a bit larger than the lateral ones, with their margin serrated. Young leaves whitish, mature ones green, becoming reddish as they get old. **Flowers** green and hairy, arranged in inflorescences up to 20 cm long. **Fruits** about 1.3 cm long and 0.8 cm wide, pit covered completely or almost completely by a yellow pseudoaril, the exposed part black (Rzedowski, Medina Lemos, and Calderón de Rzedowski 2004).

FIGURE 11.50 *Bursera hintonii* Bullock, observed in Guerrero (photo by L. Venable).

This species inhabits the transition areas between tropical deciduous and oak forests at altitudes above 1,300 m in the states of Mexico, Michoacán, Guerrero, and Oaxaca. It is used as incense, in living fences, and in traditional medicine. Fruits are used by children as slingshot projectiles.

————————

Scientific Name: *Bursera hollickii* (Britt.) Fawc. & Rendle (subgenus *Bursera*, Inaguensis group)

   Common Names: Hollick's birch, red birch, gray bark birch

   Trees up to 30 m tall with reddish-gray, nonpeeling bark. **Leaves** 8 to 12 cm long, producing 3 to 7 leaflets 3.5 to 6.4 cm long, ovate, leaflet apex short-acuminate.

FIGURE 11.51 *Bursera hollickii* (Britt.) Fawc. & Rendle: (A) observed in Jamaica (photo by D. L. Whyte); (B) leaves.

Leaflets leathery, dull green, midvein conspicuous, secondary veins inconspicuous. Infructescences 4 to 7 cm long. **Fruits** 8 to 10 mm long, green, obovoid, pit beige, covered by a red-orange pseudoaril (Martínez-Habibe and Daly 2016).

Bursera hollickii grows only in Jamaica, where it is one of the most striking trees of the tropical dry forest. It can be found in the parishes of Clarendon, St. Andrew, and St. Catherine, in dry thickets of limestone woodland, at 300 m. This species resembles *B. simaruba* because of the size and number of leaflets, but in *B. hollickii* the bark is not peeling, and its leaflets are leathery. It is larger than the other three native *Bursera* species, *B. lunanii*, *B. aromatica*, and *B. simaruba*. Only a few populations remain, and it is considered critically endangered.

Scientific Name: *Bursera inaguensis* Britt. (subgenus *Bursera*, Inaguensis group)

Common Names: Torchwood copal, fragrant bursera, almaciguillo

Shrubs or small **trees**, up to 4 m tall with **bark** grayish, smooth. **Leaves** glabrous, 8 to 10 cm long, with 3 to 7 leaflets, light green on both sides, not strongly veined, upper side faintly shining, petiole slender, 2 to 5 cm long. Lateral **leaflets** sessile or the stalks no more than 0.5 mm long, oblong to oblanceolate, leathery, and faintly glossy, apex mucronate. Male **flowers** 5-merous, 3 mm long, petals whitish and lanceolate, arranged in inflorescences 5 to 6 cm long. **Fruits** 6 to 7 mm long, female infructescences 9 to 10.5 cm long, pit beige (Martínez-Habibe and Daly 2016).

FIGURE 11.52 *Bursera inaguensis* Britt., observed in Bahamas: (A) trees have a gray and nonpeeling bark; (B) branch with inflorescences and leaves; (C) close-up of male flowers (photos by B. Stock).

FIGURE 11.53 *Bursera infernidialis* Guevara & Rzedowski, observed in Michoacán: (A) bark; (B) leaf (photos by J. Becerra and L. Venable).

Bursera inaguensis occurs in the Bahamas (Great Inagua Island) and central Cuba in evergreen forest formations and on rocky scrublands. Flowering specimens have been collected from June to August and fruiting specimens from August to September.

Scientific Name: *Bursera infernidialis* Guevara & Rzedowski (subgenus *Elaphrium*, Glabrifolia group)

Common Name: Copal

Trees 3 to 6 m tall, of reddish-gray non-exfoliating **bark**. **Leaves** 3 to 8 cm long, typically trifoliolate, exceptionally with 4 or 5 leaflets. **Leaflets** 1.8 to 4.5 cm long and 0.7 to 1.5 cm wide, toothed margin, pubescent when young, mostly glabrous at maturity. **Flowers** yellowish cream, in inflorescences 3 to 3.5 cm long, of 3 to 10 flowers. **Fruits** 0.7 to 0.9 cm long, glabrous, in infructescences with 1 to 3 fruits, pit black, partially covered by a bright-red pseudoaril (Toledo 1982).

This species is restricted to an area encompassed by western Jalisco, central Michoacán, and southwestern Guerrero, where it inhabits tropical deciduous forest. It is a common tree in the surroundings of Zicuirán, Michoacán.

Scientific Name: *Bursera instabilis* McVaugh & Rzedowski (subgenus *Bursera*, Simaruba group)

Common Names: Papelillo, palo mulato

Trees to 8 m tall; **bark** that exfoliates in large reddish-brown thin sheets, leaving the trunk with a grayish-green surface, with abundant lenticels (pores). **Leaves** highly variable in shape and size, with 1 to 5 leaflets on the same plant. **Leaflets** ovate, sometimes asymmetric, margin entire, apex slightly acuminate, glabrous on the upper side, somewhat hairy on the underside; unifoliolate leaves 4 to 8 cm long and 2.5 to 4 cm wide; leaflets of pinnate leaves a bit smaller. **Fruits** 0.6 to 0.8 cm long, pit completely covered by a pale, sometimes red pseudoaril (Toledo 1982).

Bursera instabilis grows along the Pacific Coast from Nayarit to the Isthmus of Tehuantepec in Oaxaca.

FIGURE 11.54 *Bursera instabilis* McVaugh & Rzedowski: (A) leaves (photo by L. Venable); (B) trunk, bark, and leaves, observed in Jalisco (photo by A. Frias, CC BY-NC 4.0).

FIGURE 11.55 *Bursera inversa* Daly: (A) individual plant; (B) leaves; (C) bark; (D) female flowers; (E) infructescence; (F) cotyledons (adapted from Castro Laportte 2013, CC BY-NC 4.0).

Scientific Name: *Bursera inversa* Daly (not a *Bursera*)

    Common Name: Resbalamono

    This species is native to South America. While it is currently classified as *Bursera* (Daly 1993), molecular phylogenetic studies suggest that it is closer to *Commiphora* than to *Bursera* (Martínez-Habibe 2012). *B. inversa*'s cotyledons have unlobed entire margins like those of *Commiphora*, while in all other *Burseras* whose cotyledons have been studied, they are multilobate or trilobate. This further suggests that *B. inversa* does not belong within the genus *Bursera*. Also, it appears to have 15 staminodes on the female flowers, not seen in any burseras.

FIGURE 11.56 *Bursera isthmica* Rzedowski & Calderón, a plant observed in Oaxaca: (A) small trees; (B) leaf; (C) underside of leaf; (D) fruit (photos by filimonios, CC BY-NC).

Scientific Name: *Bursera isthmica* Rzedowski & Calderón (subgenus *Elaphrium*, Copallifera group)

Common Names: Copal, coyul

Trees, sometimes **shrubs**, up to 8 m tall; **bark** gray and non-exfoliating. **Leaves** up to 23 cm long and 10 cm wide, rachis prominently winged, with 5 to 15 leaflets. **Leaflets** 1.5 to 7 cm long and 1 to 3.5 cm wide, lightly pubescent on the upper side, while densely pubescent on the underside, of leathery texture, edge coarsely toothed (some of the teeth bigger than the others). **Flowers** 4-merous, arranged in inflorescences, with white petals; female inflorescences up to 6 cm long; male inflorescences up to 15 cm long. Mature **fruits** spherical, 0.6 to 0.7 cm wide, glabrous, pit covered

FIGURE 11.57 *Bursera itzae* Lundell, a specimen collected in Guatemala (photo by United States National Herbarium, CC BY-NC 3.0).

up to two-thirds of its length by an orange-yellow pseudoaril, the exposed part black (Rzedowski and Calderón de Rzedowski 2002).

This species is restricted to tropical deciduous forests below 200 m elevation in the Isthmus of Tehuantepec in Oaxaca.

Scientific Name: *Bursera itzae* Lundell (subgenus *Bursera*, Simaruba group)

Common Names: Copal; palo mulato

This Central American species is very probably a synonym of *B. simaruba* (Rossell et al. 2010).

Scientific Name: *Bursera jerzyi* Medina (subgenus *Elaphrium*, Copallifera group)

Common Name: Copal

Trees up to 14 m tall, with gray trunk and non-exfoliating **bark** with abundant lenticels. **Leaves** not fragrant when crumpled up, in groups at the end of branches 26 to 55 cm long and 15 to 28 cm wide, generally with 7 leaflets, sometimes with 9. **Leaflets** elliptic, slightly pubescent, with short hairs, the edge with round teeth, of membranaceous texture. **Fruits** in groups, spherical and glabrous when mature, of 1.3 to 1.5 cm long and 0.8 to 1.2 cm wide, pit completely covered by a pseudoaril, pale yellow or white when immature (Medina-Lemos 2013).

This species is endemic to the coast of Oaxaca. It inhabits tropical deciduous forests from sea level to 75 m of altitude. It is similar to *B. sarcopoda*, but the latter has red, exfoliating bark. It is considered a critically endangered species and threatened by commercial tourism development in its habitat.

Scientific Name: *Bursera karsteniana* Engl. (subgenus *Bursera*, Inaguensis group)

Common Names: Palu di sia kòrá, pal'i siya cora, palu di sia dushi, mara blanca, isicagua blanca, isicana, West Indian birch tree

Trees to 10 m tall, dioecious; exfoliating brownish-red **bark**. **Leaves** in groups often at the end of branches, with 1 to 5 leaflets, with stalks red at the base. **Leaflets** 3.5 to 7 cm long and 2.5 to 5 cm wide, glabrous when mature, most frequently ovate, entire margin, almost sessile. Male and female **flowers** 3- or 4-merous, arranged in short inflorescences, with few flowers. **Fruits** 5 to 9 mm long and 4 to 7 mm wide,

FIGURE 11.58 *Bursera jerzyi* Medina: (A) tree; (B) branch; (C) leaf (photos by C. Domínguez-Rodriguez, CC BY 4.0); (D) trunk; (E) fruits (adapted from Medina-Lemos 2013).

FIGURE 11.59 *Bursera karsteniana* Engl.: (A) tree observed in Curaçao; (B) leaves; (C) male flowers; (D) fruits (photos by G. van Buurt and C. de Haseth, CC BY-NC 3.0).

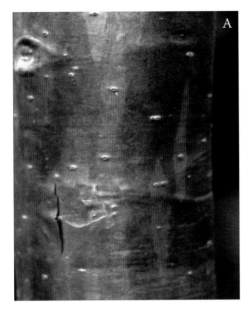

FIGURE 11.60 *Bursera kerberi* Engl.: (A) trunk and bark of an individual observed in Nayarit; (B) leaves (photos by J. Becerra and L. Venable).

reddish when mature, pit completely covered by a red pseudoaril (Castro Laportte 2013).

This species can be found in Trinidad and Tobago, Curaçao, the Dominican Republic, and along the coasts of Colombia and Venezuela. It inhabits xerophilous scrub from 0 to 350 m of altitude. It flowers between February and March and in September. It produces fruits all year long. Its wood is extremely popular for all manner of use, including living fence posts.

Scientific Name: *Bursera kerberi* Engl. (subgenus *Bursera*, Fragilis group)

    Common Name: Tecomaca

    Trees to 10 m tall, of green, sometimes bright-red exfoliating **bark**. **Leaves** always trifoliolate, glabrous. **Leaflets** 5 to 8 cm long and 2 to 4 cm wide, lanceolate, apex ending in a tail, margin sharply serrated. Male **flowers** 5-merous, occasionally 4-merous; female flowers 3-merous; flowers arranged in few-flowered inflorescences. **Fruits** about 0.7 cm long and 0.4 cm wide, pit completely covered by a pale pseudoaril (Toledo 1982).

    This species has a wide geographic distribution, from Nayarit to Guerrero and the state of Mexico.

Scientific Name: *Bursera krusei* Rzedowski (subgenus *Bursera*, Simaruba group)

    Common Name: Palo de león

    Trees to 8 m tall, not very fragrant; **bark** yellowish, exfoliating in large sheets. **Leaves** typically trifoliolate, occasionally with 1 or 2 leaflets. **Leaflets** velvety, lan-

FIGURE 11.61 *Bursera krusei* Rzedowski: (A) trunk; (B) leaves (photos by J. C. Calvillo García).

ceolate to ovate, 7 to 20 cm long and 4 to 8.5 cm wide, ending in a long tip, margin entire. **Flowers** cream white with pink lines on petals; male flowers 5-merous; female flowers 3- or 5-merous; flowers arranged in inflorescences with many flowers, velvety. **Fruits** 0.5 to 0.6 cm when dry, longer when fresh, velvety, grouped in small clusters, pit completely covered by a yellow pseudoaril (Toledo 1982).

These trees grow on the coast of Guerrero and on the Isthmus of Tehuantepec in Oaxaca in tropical deciduous forests.

Scientific Name: *Bursera lancifolia* (Schltdl.) Engl. (subgenus *Bursera*, Fragilis group)

Common Names: Cuajiote, cuajiote chino, chaca

Trees to 15 m tall, glabrous; **bark** deep red, copper, or orange. **Leaves** with 3 to 9 (most often 5 to 7) leaflets, exuding a strong turpentine odor when crushed and abundant resin. **Leaflets** lanceolate, 4 to 9.5 cm long and 0.8 to 2.5 cm wide, margin finely serrated, upper surface glossy, central vein prominent. **Flowers** cream, to 6 mm long; female flowers 3-merous, sometimes 5-merous; male flowers 5-merous, sometimes 4-merous. Inflorescences of 2 to 18 flowers, 2 to 4 cm long. **Fruits** reddish, obliquely oblong, 0.8 to 1.2 cm long, ending in a conspicuous point, peduncle bent upward, arranged in infructescences 1 to 5 cm long, pit completely covered by a yellow pseudoaril (Toledo 1982).

Abundant in tropical deciduous forests at altitudes of 600 to 950 m on the east side of the Balsas Basin south and east to the coasts of Guerrero and Oaxaca. Small disjunct populations are found in Morelos and Querétaro (Rzedowski and Guevara-Féfer 1992). The wood was formerly employed in making matches. The resin is sometimes still used as glue, and as emetic and purgative.

Scientific Name: *Bursera laurihuertae* Rzed. & Calderón (subgenus *Bursera*, Simaruba group)

Common Names: Mulato, jit kiek

Tree to 15 m tall (although most often no more than 8) of wide crown and red, sometimes yellowish **bark** that exfoliates in large and thin strips; white resin. **Leaves**

FIGURE 11.62 *Bursera lancifolia* (Schltdl.) Engl.: (A) tree observed in Guerrero; (B) trunk and branches (photos by J. Becerra and L. Venable); (C) leaves (photo by J. Jacobo, CC BY-NC); (D) branch with leaves and fruits (photo by R. Cano).

ordinarily all simple (unifoliolate) to 9 cm long and 4.5 cm wide, occasionally with 3 to 5 **leaflets**, narrow to widely ovate, margin entire, apex often with a shallow depression. Female **flowers** 4-merous in inflorescences to 4 cm long, often including one single yellow flower; male flowers 5-merous, in inflorescences to 6 cm long. **Fruits** to 1.1 cm long and 0.6 cm wide, obliquely ovoid, pit completely covered by a pale-pink pseudoaril (Rzedowski and Calderón de Rzedowski 2000b).

FIGURE 11.63 *Bursera laurihuertae* Rzed. & Calderón: (A) leaves (photo by M. Pérez, CC BY-NC); (B) branches; (C) trunk (photos by B. Vrskovy).

This species grows in Oaxaca, and it is particularly abundant in the Isthmus of Tehuantepec. It is very similar to *B. schlechtendalii*, but *B. laurihuertae* often has trifoliolate leaves and its flowers are grouped in inflorescences, not solitary as in *B. schlechtendalii*. It is employed in traditional medicinal uses, and it is also used to construct living fences.

Scientific Name: *Bursera laxiflora* S. Watson (subgenus *Elaphrium*, Copallifera group)

Common Names: Torote prieto, to'oro chicuri (Mayo, Yaqui), xoop caacöj (Comcáac)

Shrubs or small **trees** to 10 m tall with **bark** dark purple-brown. **Leaves** once-pinnate or bipinnate, 2.5 to 12 cm long, glabrous, the rachis slightly winged. Primary **leaflets** 1 to 15, secondary leaflets (when present) 3 to 7, margin unevenly toothed. **Flowers** white to pale yellow, solitary or grouped in few-flowered inflorescences. **Fruits** 6 to 8 mm long, glabrous, pit black, partially covered by an orange or yellow pseudoaril (M. Johnson 1992).

This species inhabits northwestern Mexico, flourishing in desert scrub, thornscrub, and tropical deciduous forest from north-central Sonora and southwest Chihuahua to Sinaloa and in south-central Baja California at altitudes up to 1,065 m. Its bark is darkish purple, often lending a purplish tint to hillsides in thornscrub, where it is frequently a dominant plant.

The gum is used medicinally for treating toothaches (Gentry 1942). It is also used by the Comcáac (Seri) to make a tea for colds, sore throat, and coughs and for treating scorpion stings and black widow spider bites (Felger and Moser 1985). It is the preferred wood among the Mayo (Yoreme) of Sonora for producing ceremonial masks and other artifacts.

FIGURE 11.64 *Bursera laxiflora* S. Watson, observed in Sonora: (A) general aspect of a plant; (B) inflorescence; (C) branch with leaves and dried inflorescences (photos by J. Becerra and L. Venable).

Scientific Name: *Bursera linanoe* (La Llave) Rzedowski, Calderón & Medina (subgenus *Elaphrium*, Glabrifolia group)

Common Names: Copalillo, linanoé, linaloé, ulinoé, xochicopal tehomahaca, copalihyacmemeyalquahuitl (Nahua)

Trees up 10 m tall with reddish-gray trunk; dioecious, sometimes polygamodioecious; resin producing a pleasant, sweet odor. **Leaves** 6 to 15 cm long, 3 to 10 cm wide, rachis winged, 2 to 2.5 mm on each side, entire, with 3 to 11 leaflets. **Leaflets** of membranaceous texture, 1.2 to 4 cm long and 0.8 to 2 cm wide. **Flowers** arranged in inflorescences; petals white. **Fruits** red, 9 to 11 mm long, slightly compressed on both sides, arranged in groups of up to 8 or solitary, pit often wider than long, covered up to two-thirds of its length by an orange pseudoaril, the exposed part black (Rzedowski, Medina Lemos, and Calderón de Rzedowski 2004).

This species inhabits the tropical deciduous forest and xerophilous shrub vegetation of Oaxaca, Puebla, Morelos, and Guerrero at altitudes of 650 to 1,500 m. *Bursera linanoe* is easy to confuse with *B. glabrifolia*, except that the latter inhabits forests at altitudes of 1,400 to 2,200 m and its fragrance is markedly different. *B. linanoe* was one of the most important medicinal plants of the Nahua pharmacopeia (De Vos 2017). The royal physician Francisco Hernández de Toledo (1615), sent by the Spanish Crown to record Mexican materia medica in the 1570s, describes *tecomahaca* as "endowed with same properties as and used in place of myrrh. Soothes pain caused by flatulence and cold, benefits uterus, strengthens stomach and relieves ulcers. Calms nervousness, toothaches, tones the brain and weakened nerves," while the Spanish physician and botanist Nicolás Monardes (1565) in his *Historia medicinal* adds that "plasters reduce swellings, any cold illness, orifice seepage, tooth ache."

The resin of *B. linanoe* is still extensively used as incense, for medicinal purposes and to extract oil for fragrance. The wood is used to make a wide range of boxes. It is grown commercially in India (Becerra and Noge 2010).

FIGURE 11.65 *Bursera linanoe* (La Llave) Rzedowski, Calderón & Medina, observed in Oaxaca (photo by L. Venable).

Scientific Name: *Bursera littoralis* León de la Luz & Pérez Navarro (subgenus *Elaphrium*, Copallifera group)

Common Names: Elephant tree, torote

Shrubs to 1.5 m tall of gray trunks with non-exfoliating **bark**. **Leaves** with 7 to 11 leaflets, sometimes bipinnate, rachis lightly winged. **Leaves** 2.5 to 5 cm long and 1.2 to 1.5 cm wide of membranaceous texture, a bit pubescent. **Leaflets** bright upper side with reddish veins, margin with rounded teeth. **Flowers** yellowish white, in short inflorescences. **Fruits** solitary, 6 to 9 mm long, pit with two-thirds of its length covered by an orange or red pseudoaril, the exposed part black (León de la Luz and Pérez-Navarro 2010).

FIGURE 11.66 *Bursera littoralis* León de la Luz & Pérez Navarro: (A) plant observed in Baja California (photo by G.M.E., CC BY-NC 3.0); (B) trunk of an individual grown in a greenhouse; (C) leaves (photos by J. Becerra).

FIGURE 11.67 *Bursera longipes* (Rose) Standley: (A) tree observed in Guerrero, Mexico; (B) leaves with trunk background (photos by J. Becerra and L. Venable).

FIGURE 11.68 *Bursera lunanii* (Spreng.) C.D. Adams & Dandy ex Proctor (photo by C. Martínez-Habibe).

This species is found only along the coast of the southern tip of Baja California Sur. It differs from *B. filicifolia*, in that *B. littoralis* grows in a compact habit along the coast, where it is constantly buffeted by strong winds that inhibit upright growth. In greenhouse conditions, it grows tall as *B. filicifolia*. Thus, it may be an ecotype of *B. filicifolia*.

Scientific Name: *Bursera longipes* (Rose) Standley (subgenus *Bursera*, Simaruba group)

Common Name: Cuajiote rojo

Trees to 13 m in height of reddish, exfoliating **bark**. **Leaves** 10 to 29 cm long and 9 to 16 cm wide, with 7 to 13 leaflets, glabrous; **leaflets** 2.5 to 12.5 cm long and 1.2 to 3.4 cm wide, edge entire, apex acuminate. Male **flowers** 4- and 5-merous; female flowers 3- or 5-merous, cream colored, grouped in inflorescences to 25 cm long. **Fruits** 1 to 1.5 cm long and 0.7 to 1 cm wide, glabrous, pit completely covered by a cream, yellow, or orange pseudoaril (Toledo 1982).

This species is distributed in the eastern side of the Balsas Basin in the states of Guerrero, Michoacán, Oaxaca, and Puebla.

Scientific Name: *Bursera lunanii* (Spreng.) C.D. Adams & Dandy ex Proctor (subgenus *Bursera*, Inaguensis group)

Common Names: Bastard birch-gum, black birch

Trees 3 to 15 m tall with branches nearest to trunk upcurving and spreading. **Bark** grayish to dark brown, rough, sometimes shed in plates (not papery sheets). **Leaves** simple, 6 to 8 cm long, petiole 4 to 5 cm long, lamina elliptic to obovate, somewhat leathery, glossy, green. Male **flowers** 4-

to 5-merous, creamy white, in inflorescences with few flowers, 4.5 to 7 cm long. **Fruits** 8 to 9 mm long and 6 mm wide, in infructescences 3 to 6 cm long, pit beige (Martínez-Habibe and Daly 2016).

Bursera lunanii is a Jamaican endemic found in the parishes of Clarendon, Kingston, St. Ann, St. Andrew, St. Catherine, St. Elizabeth, and St. Thomas, Jamaica, in dry woodlands and low thornscrub. It is easy to distinguish from its Jamaican congeners by its simple, oblong-elliptic leaves and nonpeeling bark.

Scientific Name: *Bursera macvaughiana* Cuevas & Rzedowski (subgenus *Elaphrium*, Copallifera group)

   Common Names: Copal

   Trees to 10 m tall, of gray trunks with non-exfoliating **bark**. **Leaves** to 25 cm long and 8 cm wide with 5 to 15 leaflets, rachis narrowly winged, wings no more than 2 mm wide on each side, a bit pubescent on the upper side, densely hairy on the underside. **Leaflets** up to 5.5 cm long and 2 cm wide, edge irregularly toothed.

FIGURE 11.69 *Bursera macvaughiana* Cuevas & Rzedowski, observed in Colima (photo by P. Gonzalez Zamora, CC BY-SA 4.0).

Flowers tiny, yellow green, in many-flowered inflorescences to 20 cm long. **Fruits** reddish green, no more than 9 mm long, glabrous, pit with one-half to two-thirds of its length covered by an orange pseudoaril, the exposed part black (Cuevas and Rzedowski 1999).

   This species inhabits tropical deciduous forest at altitudes between 1,100 and 1,800 m. It is restricted to a small mountainous area between Jalisco and Colima.

Scientific Name: *Bursera madrigalii* Rzed. & Calderón (subgenus *Elaphrium*, Glabrifolia group)

   Common Name: Copal

   Trees to 9 m tall with gray **bark**. **Leaves** 12 to 30 cm long, 8 to 13 cm wide, leaf rachis conspicuously winged, comprising 5 to 15 leaflets. **Leaflets** 4 to 11 cm long and 1 to 4 cm wide, with prominent veins on the underside and edges

FIGURE 11.70 *Bursera madrigalii* Rzed. & Calderón, specimen collected in Michoacán (photo by the New York Botanical Garden, CC BY 4.0).

with rounded teeth. **Flowers** of cream-color petals, arranged in inflorescences up to 20 cm long. **Fruits** 7 to 17 mm, arranged in large infructecenses to 30 cm long, pit covered at least half length by an orange pseudoaril, the exposed part of the pit black (Rzedowski and Calderón de Rzedowski 2002).

This species is found only in the vicinity of Morelia, Michoacán, where it inhabits the transition between tropical dry forest and woodland forest at 1,550 to 2,040 m altitude.

Scientific Name: *Bursera martae* J. Jiménez Ram. & Cruz-Durán (subgenus *Bursera*, Microphylla group)

Common Name: Copal macho

Shrubs up to 4 m tall; **bark** reddish gray, with fissures but only lightly exfoliating. **Leaves** unifoliolate, glabrous, 4.1 to 6.4 cm long and 2 to 2.8 cm wide, with prominent veins, edged with small round teeth. **Flowers** solitary, groups of 2 or 3, with white petals; male flowers 5-merous; female flowers 3-merous. **Fruits** solitary or in pairs, subspherical, 5 to 7 mm long, pit completely covered by a pale-green pseudoaril (Jiménez Ramírez and Cruz Durán 2001).

This species has so far been found only in the vicinity of Tecomazúchil, Guerrero, in the Balsas Basin at altitudes between 1,390 and 1,470 m.

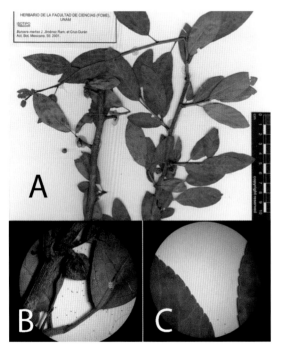

FIGURE 11.71 *Bursera martae* J. Jiménez Ram. & Cruz-Durán, collected in Guerrero: (A) herbarium specimen of branches with leaves and fruits (photo by Instituto de Biología México); (B) close-up of a fruit; (C) close-up of leaves showing the round-toothed margin (photos from Jiménez Ram and Cruz-Durán 2001).

Scientific Name: *Bursera medranoana* Rzedowski & Ortíz (subgenus *Bursera*, Fagaroides group)

Common Names: Cuajiote, cuajiote rojo

Trees up to 5 m tall, with deep-red trunk and **bark** that exfoliates in sheets of the same color. **Leaves** typically with 5 to 11 leaflets, occasionally unifoliolate or tri-foliolate; **leaflets** up to 3 cm long, the terminal usually larger than the lateral ones. **Flowers** solitary or in groups of 2, with greenish-white or yellow petals, 3-merous; male flowers absent; all individuals produce only female flowers. **Fruits** 6 to 7 mm long, pit completely covered by an orange-red pseudoaril at maturity (Rzedowski and Ortiz 1988).

This species grows only in tropical deciduous forest on the steep cliffs of Tolantongo Canyon in the Mezquital Valley in the state of Hidalgo along with several congeneric plants, including *B. morelensis*.

FIGURE 11.72 *Bursera medranoana* Rzedowski & Ortíz: (A) tree observed in La Barranca de Tolantongo, Hidalgo; (B) deep-red bark, peeling in large papery sheets of the same color; (C) leaves (photos by J. Becerra and L. Venable); (D) female flower with nonfunctional stamens (photo by E. Huerta-Ocampo).

Scientific Name: *Bursera microphylla* A. Gray (subgenus *Bursera*, Microphylla group)

   Common Names: Elephant tree, torote, torote colorado, copal, xoop (Comcáac)

   Shrubs or small **trees** to 8 m tall; most often dioecious, sometimes gynodioecious, unfrequently hermaphrodite; **bark** of main trunk whitish yellow, exfoliating in thin sheets; branches cherry red; trunk and lower branches often thickened out of proportion to the height of the plant. **Leaves** 3 to 8 cm long with 7 to 35 small, linear leaflets. **Leaflets** 6 to 12 mm long and 1 to 2.5 mm wide, glabrous. **Flowers** yellowish white or greenish, single or in few-flowered clusters. **Fruits** brownish red, pit completely covered by a yellow-orange pseudoaril (M. Johnson 1992).

   Bursera microphylla is the most arid-adapted bursera growing in the Sonoran Desert, from southern Arizona and California to Sonora, and in Baja California. In the tropical dry forest of southern Baja California, on the slopes of the Sierra de la Laguna and thereabouts it reaches its largest size as a dominant tree. Elsewhere it is rare to locally common in washes, on gravelly plains, and on rocky limestone or igneous slopes. In Sonora, the Comcáac (Seri) have used this plant extensively for fuel, medicine, dyeing cloth and other artifacts, and as glue.

Scientific Name: *Bursera mirandae* C. A. Toledo (subgenus *Elaphrium*, Glabrifolia group)

   Common Names: Copal, copal santo

   Trees up to 8 m tall, sometimes **shrubs**; trunk generally reddish gray with **bark** that exfoliates in unusual thick sheets or sometimes with gray, non-exfoliating bark. **Leaves** 5 to 11 cm long and 2.5 to 4 cm wide, leaf rachis not winged or inconspicuously winged. **Leaflets** 7 to 17, 0.6 to 2.1 cm long, irregularly toothed. **Flowers** arranged in inflorescences up to 20 cm long, petals white or greenish. **Fruits** red when mature, 7 to 8 mm long, subspherical, not compressed, pit covered up to two-thirds of its length by an orange or red pseudoaril, the exposed part black (Rzedowski, Medina Lemos, and Calderón de Rzedowski 2004).

   This species is found in the states of Oaxaca, Puebla, and Guerrero at altitudes of 1,450 to 1,650 m. Its wood is used as fuel and its resin as incense.

Scientific Name: *Bursera morelensis* Ramírez (subgenus *Bursera*, Microphylla group)

   Common Names: Copalillo, cuajiote rojo, cuajiote, palo colorado, palo mulato, xixote

   Trees up to 13 m tall with red **bark** that exfoliates in thin sheets. Leaves glabrous, 5 to 11 cm long and 1.5 to 4.5 cm wide. **Leaflets** 15 to 51, 0.7 to 2.2 cm long and 1.4 to 2.5 mm wide. **Flowers** yellow, pink, greenish, or white; male flowers

FIGURE 11.73 *Bursera microphylla* A. Gray: (A) plant observed in La Paz, Baja California; (B) branch with leaves and fruits; (C) female flowers; (D) male flowers; (E) hermaphrodite flower from a population in Arizona; (F) cotyledons (photos by J. Becerra and L. Venable).

FIGURE 11.74 *Bursera mirandae* C. A. Toledo, observed in Oaxaca, Mexico: (A) fruit; (B) leaves; (C) branch with leaves and inflorescences; (D) exfoliating bark (photos by J. Becerra and L. Venable).

arranged in small inflorescences up to 5 cm long, generally 5-merous, sometimes 3-merous; female flowers solitary, infrequently in pairs or in short inflorescences, typically 3-merous, less often 4- or 5-merous. **Fruits** 0.5 to 1 cm long, asymmetrically valvate, pit completely covered by a pale-yellow pseudoaril (Rzedowski and Guevara-Féfer 1992).

Bursera morelensis is an abundant member of tropical deciduous forests in the states of Guerrero, Morelos, Puebla, Oaxaca, San Luis Potosí, Guanajuato, Querétaro, and Hidalgo. It is believed to have medicinal properties and its wood has been used to make matches and as firewood.

Scientific Name: *Bursera multifolia* (Rose) Engl. (subgenus *Bursera*, Microphylla group)

   Common Names: Copalillo, cuajiote rojo, papelillo

   Shrubs or small **trees** of dark-red trunks with **bark** that exfoliates in grayish sheets, all glabrous except for very young branches, which are lightly pubescent; dioecious, sometimes polygamo-dioecious. **Leaves** with 15 to 19 leaflets. **Leaflets**

FIGURE 11.75 *Bursera morelensis* Ramírez, observed in Hidalgo: (A) the red bark exfoliates in thin sheets; (B) close-up of the tree; (C) *Blepharida verdeae* larva consuming a leaf (photos by J. Becerra and L. Venable); (D) female inflorescence with young fruit; (E) male inflorescence (photos by E. Huerta-Ocampo).

FIGURE 11.76 *Bursera multifolia* (Rose) Engl.: (A) plant in cultivation collected in Zacatecas; (B) branch with leaves (photos by J. Eslamieh).

FIGURE 11.77 *Bursera multijuga* Engl., observed in Jalisco: (A) typical leaf; (B) two trees in a living fence with a field of blue agave in the background (photos by J. Becerra and L. Venable).

linear-oblong, 1 to 1.3 cm long and 2 to 3 mm broad. **Flowers** yellowish; male flowers 3-merous, occasionally 4-merous. Fruits solitary, on short, bent stalks (Rose 1906; Toledo 1984).

These plants are known only from the surroundings of San Juan Capistrano, Zacatecas.

Scientific Name: *Bursera multijuga* Engl. (subgenus *Bursera*, Fragilis group)

    Common Name: Palo colorado

    Trees up to 12 m tall with red **bark** that exfoliates in thin sheets, the most interior sheets of reddish-yellow color. **Bark** with many small orange pores (lenticels). Plants with abundant resin but weakly fragrant. **Leaves** glabrous, with 17 to 23 leaflets. **Leaflets** 3 to 4.5 cm long and 0.5 to 0.7 cm wide, with a serrated edge. Leaf upper side bright green, underside a bit hairy. Male **flowers** arranged in inflorescences up to 5 cm long, generally 5-merous, sometimes 3-merous; female flowers solitary, infrequently in pairs or in short inflorescences, typically 3-merous, less often 4- or 5-merous; flower petals yellow, greenish, or white. **Fruits** 0.5 to 1 cm long, pit completely covered by a pale, grayish-yellow pseudoaril when mature (McVaugh and Rzedowski 1965).

    Bursera multijuga is found in the states of Aguascalientes, Colima, Jalisco, Nayarit, Michoacán, Sinaloa, and Zacatecas.

Scientific Name: *Bursera occulta* McV. & Rzed. (subgenus *Bursera*, Fragilis group)

    Common Names: Papelillo

    Trees to 10 m tall, glabrous, with exfoliating yellow **bark**. **Leaves** with 7 or 11 leaflets. **Leaflets** 2.5 to 4.5 cm long and 0.8 to 2 cm wide, oval-lanceolate, leaf tip noticeably acuminate, margin conspicuously serrated. Inflorescences 3 to 5 cm long. **Fruits** 0.5 to 0.7 cm long, pit completely covered by a pale pseudoaril (McVaugh and Rzedowski 1965).

This species is found only in a small area west of the Sierra Madre del Sur in the states of Michoacán and Jalisco.

Scientific Name: *Bursera odorata* Brandegee (subgenus *Bursera*, Fagaroides group)

Common Names: Torote, torote blanco

Shrubs or **trees** to 4 m tall of pale orange-reddish **bark** that exfoliates in thin sheets. **Leaves** 3 to 6 cm long with

FIGURE 11.78 *Bursera occulta* McV. & Rzed., herbarium specimen collected in Michoacán (photo by the New York Botanical Garden, CC BY 4.0).

FIGURE 11.79 *Bursera odorata* Brandegee, observed in Baja California Sur: (A) general appearance of plants; (B) fruits, one showing pseudoaril (photos by J. Becerra and D. L. Venable).

3 to 9 leaflets. **Leaflets** elliptic to ovate, 5 to 10 mm wide and 1 to 1.2 cm long, glabrous, often with reddish veins. **Flowers** of short peduncles, solitary in small inflorescences. **Fruits** 6 to 10 mm long, in small clusters, glabrous, pit completely covered by a whitish-yellow to orange pseudoaril (Pérez Navarro 2001).

These plants are endemic to Baja California Sur. The identity of the species is currently in flux and some authors believe it could be the same as *B. fagaroides* var. *elongata* (Rzedowski, Medina Lemos, and Calderón de Rzedowski 2005).

Scientific Name: *Bursera ovalifolia* (Schltdl.) Engl. (subgenus *Bursera*, Simaruba group)

Common Names: Mulato, mulato colorado, mulato verde, palo jiote, palo mulato

Trees, sometimes **shrubs**, up to 25 m tall, less aromatic than most other *Bursera* species; with green trunks and red, brownish-red, or orange **bark** that exfoliates in thin sheets. **Leaves** glabrous or almost glabrous when mature, with 3 or 5 (sometimes 7) leaflets. **Leaflets** typically of oval shape, 1.5 to 15 cm long and 1.5 to 7 cm wide, abruptly ending in a long point. **Flowers** arranged in inflorescences up to 20 cm long, with petals white to cream colored; male flowers typically 5-merous; female flowers 3-merous. **Fruits** glabrous, 0.6 to 0.9 cm long, pit completely covered by a pale pseudoaril (Rzedowski, Medina Lemos, and Calderón de Rzedowski 2007).

FIGURE 11.80 *Bursera ovalifolia* (Schltdl.) Engl., observed in Oaxaca (photo by J. C. Bautista Martínez).

This species inhabits tropical deciduous and semideciduous forests from sea level to 1,850 m from Jalisco, Michoacán, Oaxaca, and Chiapas, Mexico, to Costa Rica. *Bursera ovalifolia* leaf sizes and shapes are varied. It is similar in its morphology to *B. attenuata* and to the Costa Rican *B. standleyana*.

Scientific Name: *Bursera palaciosii* Rzed. & Calderón (subgenus *Bursera*, Fagaroides group)

Common Names: Papelillo, cuajiote

Shrubs or small **trees** 2 to 6 m tall, with non-exfoliating, sometimes weakly exfoliating rough, gray-white **bark** and with whitish, mildly irritant resin. **Leaves** with 1 to 7 leaflets (most often trifoliolate), 4 to 9 cm long and 3 to 6 cm wide. **Leaflets** 1 to 5 cm long, of variable shape from ovate to lanceolate. Edge of the leaflet entire or unevenly serrate. **Flowers** solitary or in groups at the end of small branches with white to pinkish or greenish petals; female flowers 3-merous; male ones 5-merous. **Fruits** 4 to 5 mm wide, pit 3.5 to 4 mm wide, completely covered by a whitish pseudoaril (Rzedowski and Calderón de Rzedowski 2000a).

Bursera palaciosii resembles *B. staphyleoides*, a species that grows in Michoacán. *B. palaciosii*, however, has solitary fruits. It is found in tropical deciduous forest in

FIGURE 11.81 *Bursera palaciosii* Rzed. & Calderón, observed on the coast of Jalisco: (A) lanceolate serrate leaflets; (B) trunk and bark (photos by J. Becerra and L. Venable).

southwestern Jalisco in the Universidad Nacional Autónoma de México's Estación de Biología Chamela and in environs from 100 to 500 m elevation.

Scientific Name: *Bursera palmeri* S. Watson (subgenus *Elaphrium*, Copallifera group)

    Common Name: Copalillo

    Trees, sometimes **shrubs**, to 8 m tall, with gray or reddish-gray non-exfoliating **bark**; all tender and young parts very hairy. **Leaves** comprising 3 to 9 leaflets, with rachis manifestly winged; wings sometimes toothed. **Leaflets** ovate to lanceolate, 2.5 to 6 cm long and 0.7 to 3 cm wide; tip of leaf shortly acuminate, margin roughly toothed, with prominent veins on the underside, tomentose in both sides. **Flowers** whitish, densely congregated in hairy inflorescences up to 8 cm long. **Fruits** red when mature, 1 to 1.4 cm long, with a pointy end, on stalks 1 to 3 cm long, pit partially covered by a red, yellow, or orange pseudoaril when mature (Rzedowski and Guevara-Féfer 1992).

FIGURE 11.82 *Bursera palmeri* S. Watson, leaves and fruits observed in Jalisco (photo by L. Venable).

    This is one of the few *Bursera* that grow in the southern portion of Mexico's central High Plateau. It is found in the states of Aguascalientes, Durango, Guanajuato, Jalisco, Michoacán, Querétaro, and Zacatecas in tropical deciduous forests transitioning to oak forest, grassland, and secondary vegetation at altitudes of 1,600 to 2,200 m. *Bursera palmeri* used to be abundant, but its numbers have now been greatly diminished. Its resin is used as incense, and its wood is sought for the manufacture of wooden spoons and other crafts. The principal threat to its survival, however, is its popularity as firewood (Rzedowski and Guevara-Féfer 1992).

Scientific Name: *Bursera paradoxa* Guevara & Rzedowski (subgenus *Bursera*, Fagaroides group)

    Common Names: Copal, Cabello de angel, Pinillo

    Small **trees** 3 to 6 m tall, with pale-gray, non-exfoliating smooth **bark**. **Leaves** up to 11.5 cm long and 9 to 10 cm wide, comprising 13 to 19 leaflets. **Leaflets** linear, 5 to 6 cm long and less than 1 mm wide, glabrous. **Flowers** reddish, arranged in inflorescences of 1 to 8 flowers; male flowers 5-merous; female flowers 3-merous. **Fruits** grayish at maturity, 5 to 8 mm long, pit completely covered by a pale pseudoaril (Guevara-Féfer and Rzedowski 1980).

FIGURE 11.83 *Bursera paradoxa* Guevara & Rzedowski, observed in Michoacán: (A) tree; (B) branch with leaves; (C) trunk with gray non-exfoliating bark; (D) seedling showing its multilobate cotyledons at the base and leaves above (photos by G. I. Casas, CC BY-NC-SA 3.0).

Bursera paradoxa's leaves with linear leaflets are highly unusual for this genus, making it very easy to distinguish it from other *Burseras*. It is also unusual in that its bark is non-exfoliating despite its classification in the normally exfoliating subgenus *Bursera*. Of limited range, it is confined to the lowest part of the Balsas Basin in central Michoacán and northwestern Guerrero.

Scientific Name: *Bursera penicillata* (DC.) Engl. (subgenus *Elaphrium*, Glabrifolia group)

Common Names: Torote copal, torote prieto, torote incienso, árbol de chicle, mostoche, to'oro chutama (Mayo)

Upright **trees** to 12 m tall; **bark** gray or reddish gray, smooth to slightly scaly and non-exfoliating. **Leaves** 12 to 38 cm long, rachis winged. **Leaflets** 3 to 15, 2.5 to 12 cm long and 1 to 4 cm wide, the blades finely pubescent on both surfaces, the margins strongly toothed. **Flowers** white, arranged in inflorescences up to 14 cm long. **Fruits** 1 to 1.3 cm long, 0.8 to 1.1 cm wide, pit black, partially covered by a red, orange, or pale pseudoaril (Rzedowski and Guevara-Féfer 1992).

This species prospers in tropical deciduous forests and appears sporadically in thornscrub and transitional oak woodlands from southeastern Sonora and southwest Chihuahua to Michoacán. According to Gentry (1942), the leaves are used to treat the common cold and the gums for toothaches. It is also used as incense and in living fences. *B. penicillata* exudes a powerful and agreeable aroma detectable before the tree is spotted.

FIGURE 11.84 *Bursera penicillata* (DC.) Engl., observed in Nayarit, Mexico (photo by L. Venable).

Scientific Name: *Bursera pereirae* Daly

Common Name: Falsa-amburana

This species inhabits the scrubby upland vegetation called *cerrado* in Brazil. Recent molecular phylogenetics suggest that *B. pereirae* does not belong within the genus *Bursera* (Martínez-Habibe 2012).

FIGURE 11.85 *Bursera pereirae* Daly: (A) tree during the dry season; (B) male inflorescence; (C) close-up of leaves and fruits; (D) trunk and bark (photos by Árvores do Bioma Cerrado).

Scientific Name: *Bursera permollis* Standl. & Steyerm. (subgenus *Bursera*, Simaruba group)

    Common Name: Jiñocuabo

    Trees to 18 m tall; **bark** smooth, of reddish-brown color and peeling in large sheets or small scales. **Leaves** to 22 cm long and 19.5 cm wide, rachis not winged. **Leaflets** 1 or 3, occasionally 5, ovate, apex abruptly and shortly acuminate and

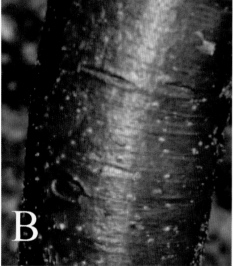

FIGURE 11.86 *Bursera permollis* Standl. & Steyerm., observed in Costa Rica: (A) leaves; (B) trunk and bark (photos by D. H. Janzen, CC BY-NC-SA 3.0).

margin entire. **Flowers** pale yellow, in inflorescences to 7 cm long. **Fruits** elliptic or ovoid, 7 to 9 mm long, reddish when mature, sparsely pubescent, in infructescences to 6.5 cm long (Porter and Pool 2001).

This species grows in Chiapas, Guatemala, Honduras, and El Salvador, at altitudes most often between 650 and 1,400 m, where it can be locally abundant. It resembles *B. grandifolia* and *B. zapoteca* from Mexico.

Scientific Name: *Bursera pontiveteris* Rzedowski, Calderón & Medina (subgenus *Elaphrium*, Copallifera group)

Common Names: Copal, copalillo

Shrubs or **trees** up to 7 m tall, with gray **bark**, dioecious or polygamo-dioecious. **Leaves** to 20 cm long and 13 cm wide, rachis not winged, petioles up to 8 cm long, trifoliolate or with 5 leaflets. **Leaflets** 2 to 8 cm long, the terminal longer than the laterals; stalk that supports the leaflet 1 to 4 mm long; edge of leaflets deeply toothed. **Flowers** white, grouped in inflorescences. **Fruits** solitary or in groups, 7 to 9 mm long, pit black, covered partially by an orange pseudoaril (Rzedowski, Medina Lemos, and Calderón de Rzedowski 2004).

This species inhabits tropical dry forest vegetation in Oaxaca and Puebla.

Scientific Name: *Bursera ribana* Rzed. & Calderón (subgenus *Elaphrium*, Copallifera group)

Common Names: Copal, copalillo

Shrubs or small **trees** 2 to 6 m tall with gray **bark**; twigs dark red. **Leaves** imparipinnate (in a few branches bipinnate), less than 11 cm long and 8 cm wide, rachis widely winged. **Leaflets** dark green and a bit bright on their upper side, most often 2.5 to 6.5 cm long, with margins deeply serrated with 2 to 5 teeth on each side. **Flowers** white, grouped in inflorescences at the end of small branches along with leaves. **Fruits** 5 to 6 mm wide, pit covered at the bottom two-thirds by an orange pseudoaril (Rzedowski and Calderón de Rzedowski 2000a).

FIGURE 11.87 *Bursera pontiveteris* Rzedowski, Calderón & Medina, observed in Oaxaca: (A) leaves; (B) trunk (photos by J. Becerra and L. Venable).

FIGURE 11.88 *Bursera ribana* Rzed. & Calderón, observed in Jalisco: (A) leaves; (B) trunk and bark (photos by J. Becerra and L. Venable).

Bursera ribana has a restricted distribution along the coasts of Jalisco and Michoacán at altitudes of 5 to 450 m, in tropical deciduous and semideciduous forests. It resembles *B. laxiflora*, but the latter is not found in the southwest of Mexico.

Scientific Name: *Bursera roseana* Rzed., Calderón & Medina (subgenus *Bursera*, Simaruba group)

Common Names: Copal, papelillo, cebolleta

Trees to 20 m tall (although most often less than 12) with green trunks and red, brownish-red, or orange **bark** that exfoliates in thin sheets. **Leaves**' underside

FIGURE 11.89 *Bursera roseana* Rzed., Calderón & Medina., observed in the state of Mexico: (A) trunk and leaves; (B) female flower; (C) male inflorescence (photos by L. Venable and E. Huerta-Ocampo).

typically hairy at least when young, up to 45 cm long and 22 cm wide, with 3 to 7 (sometimes 9) leaflets; mature **leaflets** bright and glabrous on the upper side, typically of oval shape, 4.5 to 15 cm long and 2 to 6 cm wide, abruptly ending in a long point. **Flowers** arranged in inflorescences up to 13 cm long; petals white or greenish; male flowers typically 5-merous, sometimes 4-merous; female flowers 3- or 4-merous. **Fruits** glabrous, 0.9 to 1.2 cm long, pit completely covered by a pale pseudoaril (Rzedowski, Medina Lemos, and Calderón de Rzedowski 2007).

This species inhabits tropical deciduous and semideciduous forests at altitudes typically between 1,200 and 1,900 m, often found growing in pine and oak forests as well. It has been found in the states of Mexico, Nayarit, Zacatecas, Aguascalientes, Jalisco, Colima, Michoacán, and Guerrero.

***

Scientific Name: *Bursera rupicola* León de la Luz (subgenus *Elaphrium*, Glabrifolia group)

Common Names: Torote, elephant tree, copalillo

Shrubs to 3 m tall, with gray trunks and non-exfoliating **bark**. **Leaves** with only 1 leaflet, rarely with 3, up 5 cm long and 3.5 cm wide, with toothed margin, bright green on the upper side, petioles red, densely pubescent. **Flowers** yellowish white, hairy, in groups of 2 or 3; male flowers 5-merous; female flowers 4-merous. **Fruits** solitary or in groups of 3 or 4, 0.9 to 1.2 cm wide, pit covered two-thirds of its length by a scarlet-red pseudoaril, the exposed part black (Pérez Navarro 2001).

FIGURE 11.90 *Bursera rupicola* León de la Luz: (A) individual observed in Baja California Sur; (B) branch with leaves and flowers; (C) branch with fruits (photos by J. León de la Luz, CC BY-SA 4.0).

This species has a distribution restricted to the vicinity of Los Cabos in Baja California Sur, Mexico, where it grows in a tropical dry forest that develops along small canyons, hanging from granitic walls.

Scientific Name: *Bursera rzedowskii* Toledo (subgenus *Bursera*, Microphylla group)

Common Names: Cuajiote rojo, aceitillo

Trees or **shrubs** to 7 m tall with abundant resin and reddish exfoliating **bark**. **Leaves** simple (unifoliolate), narrowly elliptic or ovate, glabrous, 2.3 to 7.5 cm long and 1.3 to 2.5 cm wide, margin entire. **Fruits** solitary, glabrous, 0.5 to 0.8 cm long and 0.4 to 0.6 cm wide (when dry), fruit stalk 0.1 to 0.6 cm long, pit completely covered by a pale-yellow pseudoaril (Toledo 1982).

Bursera rzedowskii is a narrow endemic that grows in tropical deciduous forests in a few localities in the lowlands along the Río Mezcala in the Balsas Basin, in Guerrero.

FIGURE 11.91 *Bursera rzedowskii* Toledo: (A) trunk, bark, and leaf; (B) male flower (photos by L. Venable and E. Huerta-Ocampo).

FIGURE 11.92 *Bursera sarcopoda* P. G. Wilson: (A) leaves are conspicuously serrated (photo by J. Becerra); (B) trunk; (C) fruits (adapted from Medina-Lemos 2013).

Scientific Name: *Bursera sarcopoda* P. G. Wilson (subgenus *Elaphrium*, Copallifera group)

    Common Name: Copal

    Trees or **shrubs** to 8 m tall, with reddish-brown trunk and unusually thickly exfoliating **bark**. **Leaves** large, to 60 cm long, with 5 to 11 leaflets. **Leaflets** 5 to 16 cm long and 5 to 11 cm wide, edge conspicuously serrated, densely pubescent on both sides. **Flowers** reddish, grouped in inflorescences that can be up to 60 cm long. **Fruits** in groups, conspicuously longer than wide, up to 1.1 cm long and 0.7 mm wide, glabrous when mature, pit covered no more than one-half of its length by a yellow pseudoaril (Toledo 1982).

    This species occupies the most humid areas of the dry deciduous forests and the driest areas of the subdeciduous forests from Jalisco to Guerrero at a wide altitudinal range (from sea level to 1,800 m).

Scientific Name: *Bursera sarukhanii* Guevara & Rzedowski (subgenus *Elaphrium*, Copallifera group)

    Common Name: Copal

Trees to 6 m tall with conspicuously bright lead-colored, non-exfoliating **bark**. **Leaves** 15 to 28 cm long and 9 to 17.5 cm wide, with 9 to 13 leaflets, rachis winged. **Leaflets** exceptionally hairy, lanceolate, margin noticeably toothed. **Flowers** purplish red, in inflorescences with many flowers, densely haired, 2.5 to 9 cm long. **Fruits** largely glabrous, 0.8 to 1.0 cm long and 0.5 to 0.6 cm wide, ending in an obvious point, in infructescences 5 to 11 cm long, with 3 to 10 fruits, pit black, two-thirds covered by an orange-red pseudoaril (Guevara-Féfer and Rzedowski 1980).

This species is restricted to an area encompassed by western Jalisco, central Michoacán, and southwestern Guerrero, where it inhabits tropical deciduous forest. It is abundant in the vicinity of Zicuirán, Michoacán.

Scientific Name: *Bursera schlechtendalii* Engl. (subgenus *Bursera*, Fagaroides group)

Common Names: Aceitillo, copal, copal negro, mulato rojo

Squat **shrubs**, but sometimes **trees** 1 to 10 m tall; dioecious, sometimes hermaphrodite; glabrous; very resinous, exuding a strong turpentine smell; dull-red **bark** that exfoliates in large narrow, thin sheets. **Leaves** simple (unifoliolate), leaf blade most often less than 6 cm long and 2.5 cm wide. **Flowers** usually solitary, sometimes in small groups, with yellow or reddish petals; female flowers 3-merous, infrequently 5-merous; male flowers 3-merous, sometimes 5-merous. **Fruits** green, sometimes becoming reddish at maturity, 4 to 8 mm long, pit completely covered by a yellow or red pseudoaril (Toledo 1982).

This is a wide-ranging species growing from Zacatecas, Coahuila, and Tamaulipas to Yucatán and Guatemala in tropical deciduous forests and xerophilous shrub vegetation. It varies consider-

FIGURE 11.93 *Bursera sarukhanii* Guevara & Rzedowski, observed in Michoacán: (A) leaves and flowers; (B) leaves and fruits; (C) seedling with cotyledons (photos by V. W. Steinmann).

FIGURE 11.94 *Bursera schlechtendalii* Engl.: (A) plant from Puebla; (B) trunk with bark peeling off in large papery sheets; (C) leaves are simple, and their underside is glabrous (photos by J. Becerra); (D) female flower; (E) male flower (photos by E. Huerta-Ocampo); (F) fruits (photo by L. Venable).

ably from region to region both in terms of plant size and leaf size and shape. In some areas, such as the arid lands of the Valley of Tehuacán, it grows abundantly, often assuming an attractive bonsai shape, with leaves 1 to 3 cm long. In habitats with greater rainfall, it tends to lose its compact shape, and leaves are most often of oval shape to 6 cm long. It is used to treat the flu (Acevedo et al. 2015).

B. schlechtendalii is the most convenient bursera on which to demonstrate the squirt response to insect herbivory (see figures I.3 and 5.1).

———

Scientific Name: *Bursera shaferi* Urb. (subgenus *Bursera*, Inaguensis group)

    Common Name: Almácigo

    Trees to 6 m tall, dioecious, with red **bark** peeling in thin papery sheets; branches dark brown. **Leaves** 7 to 9 cm long and 2 to 3 cm wide, most often simple, occasionally with 2 to 3 leaflets to 9 cm long and 3 cm wide. **Leaflets** narrowly lanceolate, tip acuminate, base rounded, leathery, glossy, dark green. Infructescences short, to 2.2 cm long. **Fruits** 6.5 to 7 mm long, 5 mm wide, obovoid, green except slightly red at the tip, in short infructescences to 2.2 cm long, pit beige, completely covered by a thin, bright orange-red pseudoaril (Martínez-Habibe and Daly 2016).

Bursera shaferi is a Cuban endemic that grows on limestone hills (*mogotes*) in scrubland and semideciduous forests.

Scientific Name: *Bursera silviae* Rzed. & Calderón (subgenus *Bursera*, Fagaroides group)

Common Names: Mulato, mulato verde

Shrub or **tree** up to 7 m tall. **Bark** green, showing little or no exfoliation; young branches white or pale yellow; resin whitish or yellowish. **Leaves** with 1 to 7 leaflets of membranaceous texture; leaf blade 3 to 7 cm long; lateral leaflets 1 to 3 cm long, the terminal leaflet bigger. **Leaflets** ovate, elliptic or oblong, margin entire to

FIGURE 11.95 *Bursera shaferi* Urb. (photo by B. Vrskovy).

FIGURE 11.96 *Bursera silviae* Rzed. & Calderón, observed in Oaxaca: (A) trunk and bark; (B) branch with leaves and fruits (photos by C. Domínguez-Rodríguez, CC BY-NC 4.0).

crenate or serrate; terminal leaflet rhomboid. **Flowers** solitary or in groups of 2 to 4 with purplish-red petals; male flowers 3- or 4-merous; female flowers 3-merous. **Fruits** up to 5 mm long, solitary or in groups, pit completely covered by a yellow pseudoaril (Rzedowski and Calderón de Rzedowski 2008).

　　Bursera silviae is endemic to the coast of Oaxaca. It is closely related to *B. fagaroides*, but while the latter has an obviously exfoliating bark, *B. silviae* does not.

Scientific Name: *Bursera simaruba* (L.) Sarg. (subgenus *Bursera*, Simaruba group)

　　Common Names: Copalillo, palo mulato, papelillo, palo retino, chaca, jiote, jiote colorado, quiote, mulato, palo colorado, chocogüite, chohuite, tzaca, suchicopal, cohuite; chachah, hukúp (Maya); chacaj, lon-sha-la-ec (Chontal); tusun, ta'sun (Totonaca); yala-guito (Zapoteca); gumbo-limbo, West Indian birch, almácigo, almácigo colorado, azucarero

FIGURE 11.97 *Bursera simaruba* (L.) Sarg.: (A) trunk and peeling bark; (B) leaves; (c) fruits; (D) male flowers; (E) cotyledons (photos by A. Hernández, J. Cubilla, K. Irf, and D. L. Nickrent).

Trees up to 35 m tall (but most often are between 5 and 20 m), with a diameter at chest height of 40 cm to 1 m; dioecious, sometimes polygamo-dioecius; less aromatic than most other *Bursera* species; trunks green and with a **bark** that exfoliates in narrow, bright orange-red shreds. **Leaves** bright, mostly glabrous when mature; **leaflets** with acuminate tips, 3 to 13, commonly 4 to 9 cm long and 1.8 to 3.5 cm wide, the terminal leaflet typically oval shape. **Flowers** with pink, pale yellow-green, or white petals, arranged in inflorescences; female flowers 3-merous; male flowers 4- or 5-merous. Mature **fruits** glabrous, red to brownish, of 1 to 1.5 cm long, ending in a point, the stem holding each fruit no more than 15 mm long, pit completely covered with a red pseudoaril (Toledo 1982).

This cosmopolitan species has the largest geographic extension of the *Burseras*. In the Gulf of Mexico lowlands, it ranges from the coasts of Florida, the Antilles, Tamaulipas, and Veracruz to the Yucatán Peninsula and from Sonora to Chiapas on the Pacific Coast. It continues to Central America, Colombia, Venezuela, Guyana, and northern Brazil. It grows in tropical or subtropical humid forests of 0 to 1,200 m of altitude, higher in cultivation. It is the species most often used for living fences due to its rapid growth. Its wood is not highly valued, for although it is soft and easy to work with, it tends to tarnish—turning black—and if it is not dried immediately, it rots quickly. Despite its drawbacks, the wood is sometimes used as veneer and to manufacture tool handles, boxes, matches, and toothpicks. In the past, its resin was used as glue, varnish, and to seal and protect wood. Parts of the tree are also the source of a variety of purported medicinal properties, and the fruits are used as food for chickens and hogs.

Scientific Name: *Bursera simplex* Rzed. & Calderón (subgenus *Elaphrium*, Glabrifolia group)

Common Names: Copal, copallillo

Shrubs or **trees** less than 10 m tall with gray trunk and non-exfoliating **bark**. **Leaves** most often unifoliolate, 2 to 5 cm long and no more than 2.2 cm wide, clustered at the end of branches; mostly glabrous. **Flowers** of cream-colored petals about 5 mm long; the male ones arranged in inflorescences with 1 to 7 flowers; female

FIGURE 11.98 *Bursera simplex* Rzed. & Calderón, observed in Oaxaca (photo by L. Venable).

flowers most often solitary, sometimes in groups of 3. **Fruits** 10 to 13 mm long, one side of pit covered up to two-thirds of its length by a deep-red pseudoaril, the other side covered only up to one-third of the length, the exposed part pale, not black (Rzedowski, Medina Lemos, and Calderón de Rzedowski 2004).

This species is endemic to the Tehuantepec River Basin in Oaxaca.

Scientific Name: *Bursera spinescens* Urb. & Ekman (subgenus *Bursera*, Inaguensis group)

Common Name: Copal

Shrubs 1.5 to 2 m tall, highly branched. **Bark** grayish, non-exfoliating; branches pale brown, with thorny short shoots. **Leaves** simple, thick and leathery, almost succulent, glossy green, petiole no more than 1 mm long; lamina 5 to 10 mm long and 3.5 to 5 mm wide, oblong-elliptic, tip and base rounded. Male **flowers** 3-merous, creamy white, fleshy, arranged in very short inflorescences, 1- to 5-flowered. **Fruits** 5 to 6 mm long, 4 mm wide, green with reddish-purple tip or sometimes completely red, in infructescences to 1 cm long, pit beige (Martínez-Habibe and Daly 2016).

FIGURE 11.99 *Bursera spinescens* Urb. & Ekman, the only currently described *Bursera* to have thorns (photo by B. Vrskovy).

Bursera spinescens occurs in low thorn-scrub over dogtooth limestone, restricted to the southernmost region of Hispaniola, in the contiguous provinces of Jimaní (Haiti) and Barahona and Pedernales (Dominican Republic). This is the only species in the genus known to have thorns.

Scientific Name: *Bursera standleyana* L.O. Williams & Cuatrec. (subgenus *Bursera*, Simaruba group)

Common Name: Indio desnudo

Trees/lianas, most often 7 to 10 m tall, sometimes reaching 22 m above the ground; stems conspicuously smooth, reddish with papery **bark**. **Leaves** glabrous with 1, 3, or 5 leaflets, rarely 7. Leaf petioles short, reddish brown. **Leaflets** obovate, rhomboid, sometimes wider than longer, margin entire, caudate or cuspitate at the tip. Inflorescences whitish. **Fruits** globose 6 to 9 mm long, reddish at maturity, glabrous, pit completely covered by a white pseudoaril (Daly 1993).

This species is endemic to the Pacific slopes of Costa Rica. It flowers from February to April. It is the only *Bursera* species to grow as an epiphytic vine.

Scientific Name: *Bursera staphyleoides* McV. & Rzed. (subgenus *Bursera*, Fagaroides group)

Common Name: Cuajiote rojo

Trees 3 to 5 m tall; trunk smooth, green, with bark exfoliating in thin papery strips. **Leaves** unifoliolate or trifoliolate, finely toothed, glabrous, 3 to 6.5 cm long, ovate to elliptic ovate, tip gradually tapering to a sharp point. Infructescences of few fruits. **Fruits**

FIGURE 11.100 *Bursera standleyana* L.O. Williams & Cuatrec., observed in Costa Rica: (A) leaves; (B) climbing trunk; (C) tree (photos by R. Aguilar, CC BY-NC-SA 3.0).

FIGURE 11.101 *Bursera staphyleoides* McV & Rzed., collected in Mexico (photo by Royal Botanic Gardens, Kew, CC BY 4.0).

FIGURE 11.102 *Bursera stenophylla* Sprague and Riley, observed in Sonora (photo by A. Búrquez).

0.5 to 0.7 cm long, pit completely covered by a pale pseudoaril (McVaugh and Rzedowski 1965).

This species is found only at La Huacana and its vicinity in the state of Michoacán.

Scientific Name: *Bursera stenophylla* Sprague and Riley (subgenus *Elaphrium*, Copallifera group)

Common Names: Torote blanco, to'oro chutama, to'oro sajo (Mayo)

Trees up to 12 m tall with reddish-gray to silvery gray non-exfoliating **bark**; twigs slender and delicate. **Leaves** bipinnate, 4.5 to 16 cm long, with 9 to 17 (most often 13 to 15) **leaflets**, glabrous, the margins entire. **Flowers** yellow, in small clusters. **Fruits** about 1 cm long; pit black, about two-thirds covered by an orange pseudoaril (M. Johnson 1992).

Bursera stenophylla is a handsome tree found in the region encompassing southeastern Sonora, southwestern Chihuahua, and northern Sinaloa. It grows scattered on slopes and canyons in tropical deciduous forest and lower oak woodland. Its wood is carved into household utensils.

Scientific Name: *Bursera submoniliformis* Engl. (subgenus *Elaphrium*, Copallifera group)

Common Names: Copal, copalillo blanco, copalillo, copalcahuic, tecomaca

Trees up to 12 m tall with gray to reddish-gray bark. **Leaf** blade up to 20 cm long and 7 cm wide, rachis narrowly winged, with 9 to 17 leaflets. **Leaflets** 1.3 to 5 cm long and 0.5 to 2 cm wide, velvety on upper and lower sides, margin toothed. **Flowers** arranged in inflorescences, with white petals. **Fruits** hairy, solitary or in groups, 7.5 to 12 mm long, pit almost or completely covered by the yellow or orange pseudoaril (Rzedowski, Medina Lemos, and Calderón de Rzedowski 2004).

This species inhabits tropical deciduous forests at altitudes of 500 to 1,600 m of the Balsas and Papaloapan Basins in the states of Mexico, Michoacán, Guerrero, Puebla, Morelos, and Oaxaca. The gum resin is used to alleviate pain associated with flatulence and to alleviate toothache (García Martínez 2012).

FIGURE 11.103 *Bursera submoniliformis* Engl., observed in Oaxaca: (A) leaf; (B) trunk; (C) close-up of leaf underside; (D) close-up of fruit (photos by J. Becerra and D. L. Venable); (E) female inflorescence; (F) male inflorescence (photos by E. Huerta-Ocampo).

Scientific Name: *Bursera subtrifoliolata* (Rose) Standl. (subgenus *Bursera*, Fagaroides group)

Common Name: Cuajiote

Small **shrubs** with **bark** that exfoliates in yellowish papery sheets. **Leaves** unifoliolate or trifoliolate, glabrous on both sides, 2.5 cm or less in length. **Flowers** in clusters of 2 or 3, flower stalks very short, 2 to 3 mm long (Rose 1906).

Bursera subtrifoliolata is only known from northern Jalisco and there is only one reliable herbarium specimen from the species. According to Jerzy Rzedowski, Rosalinda Medina Lemos, and Graciela Calderón de Rzedowski (2005), it may not be a valid species, instead belonging in *B. fagaroides*.

FIGURE 11.104 *Bursera subtrifoliolata* (Rose) Standl., a plant collected in Bolaños, Jalisco, now in cultivation (photo by J. Eslamieh).

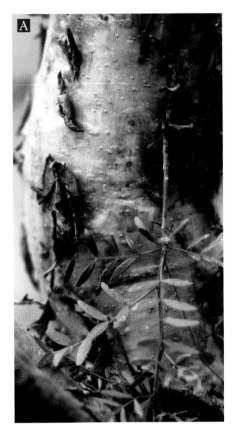

FIGURE 11.105 *Bursera suntui* Toledo, observed in Guerrero: (A) bark and leaves (photo by L. Venable); (B) male flower; (C) female flower (photos by E. Huerta-Ocampo).

Scientific Name: *Bursera suntui* Toledo (subgenus *Bursera*, Microphylla group)

Common Name: Cuajiote

Shrubs or small **trees** to 5 m tall; **bark** red or reddish brown, exfoliating in thick papery or rigid strips. **Leaves** lightly pubescent, mostly clustered on older branches or alternate on young branches, with 5 to 13 small linear **leaflets** 6.5 to 13 mm long and 2 to 4 mm wide, green, same color on both sides, largely oblong. **Flowers** yellowish green, 1.2 to 2 mm long; male and female flowers 3-merous, grouped in short inflorescences with 1 to 6 flowers. **Fruits** 5 to 13 mm long, pit completely covered by a cream-colored pseudoaril (Toledo 1982).

B. suntui is known only from the lower Balsas Basin in Guerrero, Mexico.

Scientific Name: *Bursera tecomaca* Engl. (subgenus *Elaphrium*)

Common Name: Tecomaca

Trees to 10 m tall, with rough gray bark. **Leaves** waxy, trifoliolate, 18 to 25 cm long and 15 to 23 cm wide, leaf stalk 10 to 13 cm long. **Leaflets** glabrous, 8.5 to 12 cm long, apex acuminate, toothed margin, midvein and petiole often pink or reddish. **Flowers** white in inflorescences about 13 cm long. **Fruits** 1.1 to 1.5 cm long, hanging in groups, pit black, with an orange-red pseudoaril covering only its base (Toledo 1982).

This species grows only in a few locations near Mazatlán, Guerrero, in the ecotone between tropical deciduous forest and pine-oak forests at altitudes between

1,500 and 2,100 m. It is one of the few trifoliolate species of subgenus *Elaphrium* and can easily be confused with *B. kerberi*, a common species from western Mexico, if one focuses only on its leaves. However, *B. kerberi* has red exfoliating bark, and it is absent from habitats that are home to *B. tecomaca*.

FIGURE 11.106 *Bursera tecomaca* Engl., observed in Guerrero, Mexico: (A) general aspect of plant; (B) trunk and bark; (C) close-up of a female flower; (D) branch with leaves and inflorescence; (E) typical leaf (photos by E. Huerta-Ocampo and L. Venable).

FIGURE 11.107 *Bursera toledoana* Rzed. & Calderón, observed in Michoacán: (A) branch with leaves; (B) infructescence; (C) trunk and bark; (D) tree (photos by V. W. Steinmann).

Scientific Name: *Bursera toledoana* Rzed. & Calderón (subgenus *Bursera*, Microphylla group)

   Common Names: Papelillo Amarillo, concanchire

   Shrubs or **trees** up to 8 m tall; glabrous; **bark** of trunks papyrus-like, exfoliating, dark brown, yellowish, or reddish brown. **Leaves** 3 to 7 cm long and 1.5 to 4 cm wide, with 7 to 13 largely linear **leaflets** of less than 3 cm long and 0.4 cm wide. **Flowers** solitary or in pairs with yellow petals; female flowers 3- or 4-merous; male flowers 4-, 5-, or 6-merous. **Fruits** up to 8 mm long, solitary or in small groups of up to 6, pit completely covered by a yellow pseudoaril (Rzedowski and Calderón de Rzedowski 2008).

   This species grows only in the lowlands of Michoacán and Guerrero.

FIGURE 11.108 *Bursera tomentosa* (Jacq.) Triana & Planch., observed in Oaxaca (cultivated) (photo by L. Venable).

Scientific Name: *Bursera tomentosa* (Jacq.) Triana & Planch. (subgenus *Elaphrium*, Copallifera group)

Common Names: Palu di sia slanku, takamahak, palu di sia machu, anisillo, bálsamo, caricarito, isicagua de burro

Trees 3 to 8 m tall, aromatic; **bark** smooth, entire, coppery to reddish; short branches densely pubescent at the tips. **Leaves** typically with 5 to 9 leaflets, rachis winged, pubescent. **Leaflets** highly pubescent on both sides when young, less when mature, especially on the upper side. Lateral leaflets typically 1.7 to 4.5 cm long and 1 to 2.5 cm wide; terminal leaflet 2 to 7 cm long and 1 to 2.5 cm wide. Leaflets ovate, sometimes lanceolate, with toothed margin. **Flowers** highly pubescent, in inflorescences; male and female flowers 4-merous. **Fruits** 7 to 8 mm long and 5 to 6 mm wide, reddish when mature, pit up to two-thirds covered by an orange-red pseudoaril (Castro Laportte 2013).

Bursera tomentosa is found from southern Mexico to northern Brazil, including the Lesser Antilles. One might venture a guess at its distribution from the linguistic variety in its common names.

Scientific Name: *Bursera tonkinensis* Guillaumin (not a *Bursera*)

Common Names: Rẫm bắc bộ, Búc sơ bắc bộ (Vietnamese)

This is a tree endemic to Vietnam. DNA studies indicate it is not a *Bursera* (Martínez-Habibe 2012).

Scientific Name: *Bursera trifoliolata* Bullock (subgenus *Bursera*, Fagaroides group)

Common Name: Cuajiote colorado

Trees or **shrubs** to 6 m tall; **bark** that exfoliates in red or yellow strips. **Leaves** typically trifoliolate, occasionally of 5 leaflets. **Leaflets** densely pubescent, toothed; terminal leaflet often rhomboid, 3.5 cm long and 1.5 cm wide; lateral leaflets smaller. Male **flowers** 3-merous, pubescent, arranged in short inflorescences. **Fruits** about 0.8 cm long, pit completely covered by a yellowish pseudoaril (Toledo 1982).

This species grows at altitudes between 200 and 500 m exclusively in the western portion of the Balsas Basin in the states of Michoacán, Guerrero, and Mexico.

FIGURE 11.109 *Bursera tonkinensis* Guillaumin, observed in the foothills of the Annamite Mountains, Vietnam: (A) branch with leaves; (B) leaf; (C) bark (photos by D. Daly).

FIGURE 11.110 *Bursera trifoliolata* Bullock: (A) leaves; (B) trunk and bark (photos by J. Becerra and L. Venable).

FIGURE 11.111 *Bursera trimera* Bullock: (A) leaves;
(B) male inflorescence; (C) trunk and bark (photos by
J. Becerra and L. Venable).

Scientific Name: *Bursera trimera* Bullock (subgenus *Bursera*, Fragilis group)

    Common Names: Copalchi, copal

    Trees or **shrubs** to 6 m tall, glabrous; red **bark** exfoliating in thin papery strips
or sheets. **Leaves** trifoliolate, sometimes unifoliolate; **leaflets** about 3 cm long
and 1.5 cm wide, margin toothed. Female **flowers** 3-merous; male flowers 3- or
4-merous. **Fruits** ending in a point, pit completely covered by a yellow pseudoaril
(Bullock 1936).

    This species grows in the western side of the Balsas Basin and in the canyons of
the Río Santiago at altitudes below 600 m in the states of Jalisco, Guerrero, Michoacán, and Mexico.

Scientific Name: *Bursera trinitensis* (Rose) R. O. Williams (subgenus *Bursera*, Inaguensis group)

    Common Name: Copal

    Shrubs or small **trees** to 6 m tall; **bark** gray, close. **Leaves** 1.5 to 2.5 cm long,
simple; lamina ovate; base rounded, glossy green; on both surfaces the midvein and
secondary veins prominent. Male **flowers** 5-merous, in inflorescences 12 to 16 mm
long, shorter than the leaves, 10- to 16-flowered. **Fruits** 5 to 6 mm long and 4 to
4.5 mm wide, green with reddish-purple tip or sometimes completely red, pit beige
(Martínez-Habibe and Daly 2016).

Known from Pedernales and Barahona provinces in the Dominican Republic and from a single collection in Trinidad, in dry forest or low scrub on dogtooth limestone. Flowering specimens have been collected in May to June and fruiting specimens in June to September.

Scientific Name: *Bursera vazquezyanesii* Rzed. & Calderón (subgenus *Bursera*, Fragilis group)

   Common Names: Papelillo, cuajiote

   Trees of 4 to 5 m tall with **bark** that exfoliates in large and thin orange sheets. **Leaves** less than 15 cm long and 9 cm wide, mostly grouped, forming rosettes at the end of small branches. **Leaflets** 7 to 9, lanceolate and glabrous, of no more than 6.5 cm long and 2.5 cm wide, with serrate margin. Inflorescences no more than 3 cm long grouped at the end of small branches along with leaves. **Flowers** reddish; the female ones are mostly 4-merous, while the male ones are mostly 5-merous; female flowers grouped in short inflorescences to 2 cm long, with 1 to 5 flowers, most often 3; male inflorescences to 5 cm long, with many flowers. **Fruits** 3 to 4 mm wide, pit completely covered by a whitish pseudoaril (Rzedowski and Calderón de Rzedowski 2000a).

FIGURE 11.112 *Bursera trinitensis* (Rose) R. O. Williams (photo by C. Martínez-Habibe).

This species is found only in a very restricted area of southwestern Jalisco in woodland forest at an altitude of 500 m.

Scientific Name: *Bursera vejar-vazquezii* Miranda (subgenus *Elaphrium*, Copallifera group)

   Common Name: Copal

   Trees to 12 m tall, of non-exfoliating, whitish-gray **bark**. **Leaves** large, to 41 cm long and 26 cm wide, densely pubescent, with 4 to 7 pairs of

FIGURE 11.113 *Bursera vazquezyanesii* Rzed. & Calderón: (A) leaves; (B) trunk and bark (photos by A. Frías Castro).

FIGURE 11.114 *Bursera vejar-vazquezii* Miranda, observed in Oaxaca: (A) branch with leaves; (B) smooth and nonpeeling bark (photos by J. Becerra and L. Venable).

leaflets. Lateral **leaflets** lanceolate, toothed margin, to 13.5 cm long and 4 cm wide. **Flowers** 3-merous, yellow, with a red band in the center; female flowers grouped in many-flowered inflorescences. **Fruits** 12 to 15 mm long and 5 to 6 mm wide, all but the tip of the pit covered by a yellow or red pseudoaril (Rzedowski, Medina Lemos, and Calderón de Rzedowski 2004).

This species is endemic to the easternmost drainage of the Balsas Basin, where it grows in tropical deciduous forests at altitudes of 700 to 1,450 m in the states of Guerrero, Puebla, Morelos, and Oaxaca.

Scientific Name: *Bursera velutina* Bullock (subgenus *Elaphrium*, Copallifera group)

    Common Name: Copal

    Trees or **shrubs** to 6 m tall, with nonpeeling, gray or reddish-brown **bark**. **Leaves** about 10 cm long and 3 to 4 cm wide, rachis winged, velvety on both sides, with 9 to 12 pairs of leaflets. **Leaflets** ovate, to 2 cm long and 7 mm wide, toothed, tomentose, with pronounced reticulate venation on the underside. **Flowers** grouped in inflorescences, densely haired, white. **Fruits** to 7 mm wide, glabrous, pit black, two-thirds covered by a colored pseudoaril (Toledo 1982).

    B. velutina grows at low altitudes (between 300 and 700 m) on the east side of the Balsas River, where it follows the boundary between Michoacán and Guerrero.

FIGURE 11.115 *Bursera velutina* Bullock, observed in Michoacán: (A) smooth and non-exfoliating bark; (B) leaves (photos by J. Becerra and L. Venable); (C) female flower; (D) male flower (photos by L. Venable and E. Huerta-Ocampo).

FIGURE 11.116 *Bursera xochipalensis* Rzedowski: (A) leaves (photo by J. C. Bautista CC BY-NC); (B) tree observed in Guerrero (photo by L. Venable).

Scientific Name: *Bursera xochipalensis* Rzedowski (subgenus *Elaphrium*, Glabrifolia group)

Common Names: Copal, copalillo

Trees to 10 m in height with gray **bark**. **Leaves** with 5 to 11 **leaflets** narrowly lanceolate, 3 to 8 cm long and 0.7 to 2 cm wide, margin serrated; upper side largely glabrous, underside hairy. **Fruits** 1.2 to 1.5 mm long, glabrous, pit black, partially covered by an orange pseudoaril (Toledo 1982).

Bursera xochipalensis grows on the eastern side of the Balsas River basin in the states of Guerrero, Puebla, and Oaxaca.

Scientific Name: *Bursera xolocotzii* Guevara (subgenus *Bursera*, Fagaroides group)
  Common Name: Cuajiote
  Trees up to 7 m tall; trunks with red-and-green and pale gray-green, non-exfoliating **bark**; branchlets with abundant resin of strong and malodorous smell that can sometimes be perceived from a distance. **Leaves** made up of a single **leaflet** 4.9 to 8.7 cm long, glabrous, bright on the upper side, of membranous texture, edge entire. **Flowers** pale green, solitary or in groups of up to 6; male flowers generally 4-merous, sometimes 5- or 6-merous; female flowers 3-merous, sometimes 4-merous. **Fruits** no more than 6.2 mm long, in small groups of 1 to 4, pit completely covered by a pink-red pseudoaril (Guevara-Féfer 2010).

This species has only been found around the vicinity of the Infiernillo, the torrid bottomlands of the Balsas Basin between the states of Michoacán and Guerrero.

Scientific Name: *Bursera yaterensis* M. C. Martínez, Daly & J. Pérez (subgenus *Bursera*, Inaguensis group)
  Common Names: Ayúa prieta, copal
  Subshrubs 0.5 m, rarely a shrub up to 1.8 m tall, densely branching. **Leaves** 3 to 4 cm long, simple, tip abruptly and narrowly short-acuminate, base rounded, margin entire, apex mucronate. Male **flowers** 5-merous, arranged in inflorescences to 2.6 cm long (Martínez-Habibe and Daly 2016).

FIGURE 11.117 *Bursera xolocotzii* Guevara: (A) individual observed in Infiernillo, Michoacán; (B) branch with leaves and fruits (photos by B. Vrskovy).

Bursera yaterensis is endemic to xeromorphic coastal scrub that develops in the cavities in karst (dogtooth limestone) substrates in Guantánamo and Santiago de Cuba Provinces in Cuba.

Scientific Name: *Bursera zapoteca* Rzed. & Medina (subgenus *Bursera*, Simaruba group)

Common Name: Mulato

Trees 4 to 9 m tall with reddish exfoliating **bark** and with scant resin and fragrance. **Leaves** most often unifoliolate, rarely with three leaflets. Leaf blade heart-shaped, ending in a sharp point, sometimes largely ovate; 6 to 9.5 cm long and 4 to 9 cm wide, entire margin, densely haired. **Flowers** 3-merous, red when mature, arranged

FIGURE 11.118 *Bursera yaterensis* M. C. Martínez, Daly & J. Pérez, a species endemic to Cuba (photo by C. Martínez-Habibe).

FIGURE 11.119 *Bursera zapoteca* Rzed. & Medina: (A) individual observed in the vicinities of Santiago Lachiguiri, Oaxaca; (B) leaves; (C) trunk (photos by S. Salas).

in inflorescences to 3 cm long. **Fruits** sometimes solitary or in small clusters, 6 to 7 mm long and 3 to 4 mm wide, mostly glabrous, pit completely covered by a white to pink pseudoaril (Rzedowski and Medina Lemos 2018).

This species is distinctive, growing only in subhumid forests (not in dry seasonal forest) found in the Sierra de Mixes on the west side of the Isthmus of Tehuantepec in southeast Oaxaca, at altitudes between 950 and 1,100 m. It is similar to *B. permollis* from Central America.

CHAPTER 12

Index of Plants by Major Leaf Traits and Location

The plant descriptions previously provided are organized alphabetically by species name for easy reference. This table is organized to facilitate identification by arranging species according to leaf traits and, for species found in the Caribbean or Baja California, by location. Some species are in more than one category.

Bursera angustata
Western Cuba

Bursera aromatica
Jamaica

Bursera brunea
The Bahamas

Bursera frenningae
The Bahamas and Caicos Islands

Bursera gibarensis
Hoguin Province, Cuba

Bursera glauca
Cuba

Bursera gracilipes
Dominican Republic

Bursera graveolens
Mexico to Ecuador, West Indies

Bursera hollickii
Jamaica

Bursera inaguensis
Cuba and The Bahamas

Bursera karsteniana
Curacao, Dominican Republic,
Trinidad and Tobago, Colombia

Bursera lunanii
Jamaica

Bursera shaferi
Cuba

Bursera simaruba
Florida to Northern Brazil

Bursera spinescens
Haiti, Dominican Republic

Bursera tomentosa
Mexico to Brazil, Lesser Antilles

Bursera trinitensis
Dominican Republic, Trinidad

Bursera yaterensis
Cuba

FIGURE 12.1 Plants found in the Caribbean.

Bursera cerasiifolia
Baja California Sur

Bursera epinnata
Baja California Sur

Bursera exequielii
Baja California Sur

Bursera filicifolia
Baja California Sur

Bursera hindsiana
Sonora, Baja California

Bursera laxiflora
North of Mexico, Baja California

Bursera littoralis
Baja California Sur

Bursera microphylla
Arizona, California, Sonora,
Baja California Peninsula

Bursera odorata
Baja California Sur

Bursera rupicola
Baja California Sur

FIGURE 12.2 Plants found in the Baja California Peninsula.

Bursera cerasiifolia
Baja California Sur

Bursera chemapodicta
Guerrero

Bursera crenata
Jalisco, Guerrero, Michoacán

Bursera epinnata
Baja California Sur

Bursera hindsiana
Sonora, Baja California

Bursera laurihuertae
Oaxaca

Bursera martae
Central Guerrero

Bursera rupicola
Baja California Sur

Bursera rzedowski
Northern Guerrero

Bursera schlechtendalii
Northern Mexico to Guatemala

Bursera simplex
Oaxaca

Bursera xolocotzii
Infiernillo region

Bursera zapoteca
Southeast Oaxaca

FIGURE 12.3 Plants typically unifoliolate (one leaflet).

Bursera bipinnata
Sonora to Honduras, El Salvador

Bursera diversifolia
Guerrero to Guatemala

Bursera filicifolia
Baja California Sur

Bursera laxiflora
Northern Mexico, Baja California

Bursera littoralis
Baja California Sur

Bursera ribana
Jalisco, Michoacán

Bursera stenophylla
Chihuahua, Sinaloa, Sonora

FIGURE 12.4 Plants with bipinnate leaflets.

Bursera copallifera
Guerrero, Michoacán

Bursera cuneata
Central to Southern Mexico

Bursera diversifolia
Guerrero to Guatemala

Bursera heliae
Oaxaca

Bursera asplenifolia
Oaxaca, Puebla

Bursera bicolor
Central and Southern Mexico

FIGURE 12.5 Plants of wrinkled or rugose leaves.

Bursera bicolor
Central and Southern
Mexico

FIGURE 12.6 Plants with narrow, long leaflets, dark-green above and white and tomentose (fuzzy) beneath.

Bursera attenuata
Central and Southern Mexico

Bursera grandifolia
Northern to Southern Mexico

Bursera graveolens
Southeast Mexico to Ecuador

Bursera hintonii
Mexico, Michoacán, Guerrero,
Oaxaca

Bursera jerzyi
Oaxaca

Bursera longipes
Balsas Basin

Bursera madrigalii
Michoacán

Bursera penicillata
Chihuahua, Sonora to Michoacán

Bursera roseana
Central and Southern Mexico

Bursera sarcopoda
Jalisco to Michoacán

Bursera sarukhanii
Jalisco, Michoacán, Guerrero

Bursera simaruba
Florida to Northern Brazil

Bursera standleyana
Costa Rica

Bursera vejar-vazquezii
Balsas Basin

FIGURE 12.7 Plants of large leaves, typically more than 25 cm long.

Bursera fragrantissima
Guerrero, Michoacán

Bursera infiernidialis
Guerrero, Michoacán

Bursera kerberii
Nayarit to Guerrero, Mexico

Bursera krusei
Guerrero, Oaxaca

Bursera trifoliolata
Guerrero, Mexico, Michoacán

Bursera trimera
Jalisco to Michoacán, Guerrero

Bursera tecomaca
Guerrero

FIGURE 12.8 Plants usually with 3 leaflets.

Bursera biflora
Oaxaca, Puebla

Bursera cinerea
Oaxaca, Puebla, Veracruz

Bursera denticulata
Jalisco to Michoacán

Bursera heliae
Oaxaca

Bursera heteresthes
Jalisco to Chiapas

Bursera ovalifolia
Michoacán to Costa Rica

Bursera palaciosii
Jalisco

Bursera permollis
Guatemala to Costa Rica

Bursera pontiveteris
Oaxaca, Puebla

Bursera staphyleoides
Michoacán

FIGURE 12.9 Plants typically with 3 leaflets, but with variation, sometimes 1 or 5 leaflets; sometimes variation is among individuals, sometimes within the same plant.

Bursera aptera
Guerrero, Puebla, Oaxaca

Bursera arida
Oaxaca, Puebla

Bursera exequielii
Baja California Sur

Bursera galeottiana
South-Central Mexico

Bursera microphylla
Baja California, Sonora

Bursera morelensis
South-Central Mexico

Bursera multifolia
Michoacán

Bursera paradoxa
Guerrero, Michoaán

Bursera suntui
Guerrero

FIGURE 12.10 Plants with small (short or narrow) leaflets, at least one dimension less than 4 mm.

Bursera altijuga
Puebla, Oaxaca

Bursera discolor
Colima to Oaxaca

Bursera fagaroides var.
fagaroides Mexico

Bursera fagaroides var.
purpusii Balsas Basin

Bursera glabra
Costa Rica, Colombia, Venezuela

Bursera glabrifolia
South-Central Mexico

Bursera linanoe
Puebla, Morelos, Guerrero, Oaxaca

Bursera medranoana
Hidalgo

Bursera mirandae
Oaxaca, Puebla, Guerrero

Bursera odorata
Baja California

FIGURE 12.11 Plants with leaflets usually between 2 and 3.5 cm long when mature, not linear, glabrous (no hairs).

Bursera ariensis
Nayarit to Chiapas

Bursera asplenifolia
Oaxaca, Puebla

Bursera coyucensis
Guerrero, Michoacán

Bursera velutina
Guerrero, Michoacán

FIGURE 12.12 Plants with leaflets usually between 2 and 3.5 cm long when mature, not linear, hairy.

Bursera arborea
Sonora to Chiapas

Bursera bolivarii
Guerrero and Oaxaca

Bursera bonetti
Guerrero

Bursera citronella
Jalisco to Michoacán

Bursera confusa
Jalisco, Michoacán

Bursera fagaroides var. elongata　Sonora to Nayarit

Bursera fragilis
Sonora, Chihuahua, Sinaloa

Bursera instabilis
From Jalisco to Oaxaca

Bursera lancifolia
South-central Mexico

Bursera multijuga
Southwestern Mexico

Bursera occulta
Jalisco, Michoacán

Bursera silviae
Coast of Oaxaca

Bursera vazquez-yanesii
Jalisco

FIGURE 12.13 Plants of mature leaves with distal leaflets (toward the tip) between 3.6 and 10 cm long, glabrous (no hairs).

Bursera esparzae
Oaxaca, above 1,500 m

Bursera excelsa
Sinaloa to Chiapas

Bursera isthmica
Tehuantepec, Oaxaca

Bursera macvaughiana
Limits of Jalisco and Colima

Bursera palmeri
Jalisco

Bursera pontiveteris
Oaxaca, Puebla

Bursera submoniliformis
Balsas and Papaloapan Basins

Bursera tomentosa
South of Mexico to Brazil

Bursera xochipalensis
Guerrero, Puebla, Oaxaca

FIGURE 12.14 Plants of mature leaves with distal leaflets between 3.6 and 10 cm long, hairy.

Glossary of Bursera Botanical Terms

Acuminate: Narrowing to a sharp point.

Apex: The top of something, especially one forming a point.

Bipinnate: Compound leaves in which leaflets are themselves compound.

Cataphyll: Small reduced leaves that resemble scales that antecede "true leaves" and often dry and fall within a few days of emergence. They tend to be relatively long in subgenus *Elaphrium* but very short or absent in subgenus *Bursera*.

Compound leaf: A leaf made up of a number of leaflets.

Deciduous: A plant that drops its leaves annually, usually in the fall or at the end of the rainy season.

Dioecious: Having only male or female flowers on a given tree or shrub.

Drupe: A type of fruit in which the skin surrounds the pit or pyrene that in turn contains the seed.

Elliptic: Shaped like a flattened circle.

Entire (Margin): A leaf whose edges do not have division, lobes, or teeth.

Glabrous: Smooth, without hairs or scales.

Hermaphrodite: Having both sexes in the same flower.

Imparipinnate: Compound leaves in which there is a lone terminal leaflet rather than a terminal pair of leaflets.

Inflorescence: An aggregate of flowers arranged on a stalk or peduncle.

Infructescence: A group of fruits developed from an inflorescence.

Lanceolate: Long, wider in the middle, shaped like a lance tip.

Lenticels: Cells with intercellular spaces that function as pores where exchange of gases between the bark and atmosphere can occur.

Merous: Merocity refers to the number of sepals in the calyx, the number of petals in the corolla, and the number of stamens in each of the stamina whorls.

Mucronate: Leaf or leaflet tipped with a short and abrupt point on the end of the midvein.

Oblanceolate: A lanceolate leaf with the more pointed end at the base.

Obovate: Shaped like an egg with the narrower end at the base.

Ovate: Shaped like an egg.

Petiole: The slender stem that supports the leaf blade.

Pilose: Covered with soft hair.

Polygamo-Dioecious: Mostly male or female individuals, but with either a few flowers of the opposite sex or a few bisexual flowers in the same plant.

Polyploid: A plant that has more than two paired sets of chromosomes.

Pseudoaril: An aril is a specialized structure that develops from a seed stalk and envelops it, often encouraging animal dissemination. In *Bursera*, an analogous structure, the pseudoaril, develops from the ovary stalk and covers the pit or pyrene.

Pubescent: Covered with short, soft hairs; downy.

Pit: The stone within a stone fruit.

Rachis: The axis of a leaf.

Sepal: Nonfertile parts surrounding the petals and the fertile organs in a flower, usually green.

Serrate: Saw-toothed; with asymmetrical teeth pointing forward.

Sessile: Attached without a stalk; a leaf or leaflet without a petiole.

Shrub: A small- or medium-sized woody plant that has multiple stems.

Subspherical: Not quite spherical.

Succulent: A plant that stores water over long periods.

Tomentose: A leaf covered with short matted woolly hairs.

Trifoliolate: A leaf that has three leaflets.

Unifoliolate: A leaf made of one leaflet; a simple leaf.

Untoothed: When the edge does not have pointed portions.

Valve: One of the segments into which the fruit dehisces.

Wings: Membranous expansions that protrude from the leaf rachis.

REFERENCES

Acevedo, M., P. Nuñez, L. Gónzalez-Maya, A. Cardoso-Taketa, and M. L. Villarreal. 2015. "Cytotoxic and Anti-inflammatory Activities of *Bursera* Species from Mexico." *Journal of Clinical Toxicology* 5:1–8.

Almazán-Núñez, R., L. M. Eguiarte, M. C. Arizmendi, and P. Concuera. 2015. "*Myiarchus* Flycatchers Are the Primary Seed Dispersers of *Bursera longipes* in a Mexican Dry Forest." *PeerJ* 4:e2126.

Andrés-Hernández, A. R., and D. Espinosa Organista. 2002. "Morfología de plántulas de *Bursera* Jacq. ex L. (Burseraceae) y sus implicaciones filogenéticas." *Boletín de la Sociedad Botánica de México*, no. 70, 5–12.

Andrés-Hernández, A. R., D. Espinosa, M. E. Fraile-Ortega, and T. Terrazas. 2012. "Venation Patterns of *Bursera* Species Jacq. ex L. (Burseraceae) and Systematic Significance." *Plant Systematics and Evolution* 298 (9): 1723–31.

Ávila-Lovera, E., and E. Ezcurra. 2016. "Stem-Succulent Trees from the Old and New World Tropics." *Tropical Tree Physiology* 6:45–65.

Bates, J. M. 1992. "Frugivory on *Bursera microphylla* (Burseraceae) by Wintering Gray Vireos (*Vireo vicinor*, Vireonidae) in the Coastal Deserts of Sonora, Mexico." *Southwestern Naturalist* 37 (3): 252–58.

Becerra, J. X. 1997. "Insects on Plants: Macroevolutionary Trends in Host Use." *Science* 276 (5310): 253–56.

Becerra, J. X. 2003a. "Evolution of Mexican *Bursera* (Burseraceae) Inferred from ITS, ETS, and 5S Nuclear Ribosomal DNA Sequences." *Molecular Phylogenetics and Evolution* 26 (2): 300–309.

Becerra, J. X. 2003b. "Synchronous Coadaptation in an Ancient Case of Herbivory." *Proceedings of the National Academy of Sciences* 100 (22): 12804–7.

Becerra, J. X. 2004. "Molecular Systematics of *Blepharida* Beetles (Chrysomelidae: Alticinae) and Relatives." *Molecular Phylogenetics and Evolution* 30 (1): 107–17.

Becerra, J. X. 2005. "Timing the Origin and Expansion of the Mexican Tropical Dry Forests." *Proceedings of the National Academy of Sciences* 102:10919–23.

Becerra, J. X. 2007. "The Impact of Plant-Herbivore Coevolution on Plant Community Structure." *Proceedings of the National Academy of Sciences* 104:7483–88.

Becerra, J. X., and K. Noge. 2010. "The Mexican Roots of the Indian Lavender Tree." *Acta Botánica Mexicana*, no. 91, 27–36.

Becerra, J. X., K. Noge, S. Olivier, and D. L. Venable. 2012. "The Monophyly of *Bursera* and Its Implications for Divergence Times of Burseraceae." *Taxon* 61 (2): 333–43.

Becerra, J. X., K. Noge, and D. L. Venable. 2009. "Macroevolutionary Chemical Escalation in an Ancient Plant-Insect Arms Race." *Proceedings of the National Academy of Sciences* 106 (43): 18062–66.

Becerra, J. X., and D. L. Venable. 1990. "Rapid-Terpene-Bath and Squirt-Gun Defense in *Bursera schlechtendalii* and the Counterploy of Chrysomelid Beetles." *Biotropica* 22 (3): 320–23.

Becerra, J. X., and D. L. Venable. 1999. "Nuclear Ribosomal DNA Phylogeny and Its Implications for Evolutionary Trends in Mexican *Bursera* (Burseraceae)." *American Journal of Botany* 86 (7): 1047–57.

Becerril, C. F. 2004. "Morfología y anatomía del fruto de dos especies del género *Bursera* Jacq. ex L. Sección *Bursera*." PhD diss., Universidad Nacional Autónoma de México, Mexico City.

Bercovitch, H. 2001. "In Memory of Don Pedro: Alebrije Art from a Master Artist." *Mexconnect*, January 1.

Bonfil-Sanders, C., I. Cajero-Lázaro, and R. Y. Evans. 2008. "Germinación de semillas de seis especies de *Bursera* del centro de México." *Agrociencia* 42 (7): 827–34.

Bullock, A. A. 1936. "Notes on the Mexican Species of the Genus *Bursera*." *(Kew) Bulletin of Miscellaneous Information* 1936 (6): 346–87.

Burton, R. W. 1952. "The Linaloe Tree (*Bursera delpechiana* Poisson): An Introduction into the Flora of India." *Journal of the Bombay Natural History Society* 51 (1):116–20.

Cáceres-Ferreira, W., M. Rengifo-Carrillo, L. Rojas, and C. Rosquete Porcar. 2019. "Chemical Composition of Essential Oils from *B. simaruba* (L.) Sarg. Fruits and the Resins from Three *Bursera* Species: *B. simaruba* (L.) Sarg., *B. glabra* Jack and *B. inversa* Daly." *Avances en Química* 14 (1): 25–29.

Calvillo-Canadell, L., O. J. Rodríguez-Reyes, R. Medina-Lemos, and S. R. S. Cevallos-Ferriz. 2013. "Eocene *Bursera* (Burseraceaea) [*sic*] in La Carroza Formation, Mexico: A Dry Tropical Flora Member." *Boletín de la Sociedad Geológica Mexicana* 65 (3): 631–43.

Camou-Guerrero, A. 2008. "Los recursos vegetales en una comunidad Rarámuri: Aspectos culturales, económicos y ecológicos." PhD diss., Universidad Nacional Autónoma de México, Mexico City.

Canales, M., T. Hernández, J. Caballero, A. Romo deVivar, G. Avila, A. Duran, and R. Lira. 2005. "Informant Consensus Factor and Antibacterial Activity of the Medicinal Plants Used by the People of San Rafael Coxcatlán, Puebla, México." *Journal of Ethnopharmacology* 97 (3): 429–39.

Castro Laportte, M. 2013. "Estudio taxonómico del género *Bursera* Jacq. ex L. (Burseraceae) en Venezuela." *Ernstia* 23 (2): 125–69.

Cortes-Palomec, A. C. 1998. "Biología reproductiva de *Bursera medranoana* Rzedowski & Ortiz (Burseraseae): Una especie de origen híbrido." PhD diss., Universidad Nacional Autónoma de México, Mexico City.

Cuevas, R., and J. Rzedowski. 1999. "Una nueva especie de *Bursera* (Burseraceae) del Occidente de México." *Acta Botánica Mexicana*, no. 46, 77–81.

Daly, D. C. 1993. "Studies in Neotropical Burseraceae. VII. Notes on *Bursera* in South America." *Brittonia*, no. 45, 240–46.

Dávila Aranda, P., and P. Ramos Rivera. 2017. "La flora útil de dos comunidades indígenas del Valle de Tehuacán-Cuicatlán: Coxcatlán y Zapotitlán de las Salinas, Puebla." Universidad Nacional Autónoma de México, Facultad de Estudios Superiores Iztacala, SNIB-Comisión Nacional para el Conocimiento y Uso de la Biodiversidad, Mexico City.

De-Nova, J., R. Medina, J. C. Montero, A. Weeks, J. A. Rosell, M. E. Olson, L. E. Equiarte, and S. Magallón. 2012. "Insights into the Historical Construction of Species-Rich Mesoamerican Seasonally Dry Tropical Forests: The Diversification of *Bursera* (Burseraceae, Sapindales)." *New Phytologist* 193 (1): 276–87.

De Vos, P. 2017. "Methodological Challenges Involved in Compiling the Nahua Pharmacopeia." In "Iberian Science: Reflections and Studies," special issue, *History of Science* 55 (2): 210–33.

Dickenson, W. 2002. "The Basin and Range Province as a Composite Extensional Domain." *International Geology Review* 44 (1): 1–38.

Eslamieh, J. 2013. *Cultivation of Bursera*. Fort Collins, Colo.: A Book's Mind.

Evans, P. H., and J. X. Becerra. 2006. "Non-terpenoid Essential Oils from *Bursera chemapodicta*." *Flavour and Fragrance Journal* 21:616–18.

Felger, R. S., and M. Moser. 1985. *People of the Desert and Sea: Ethnobotany of the Seri Indians*. Tucson: University of Arizona Press.

Frias Castro, A. 2008. "Revisión de *Bursera* Jacq. ex L. (sección *Bullockia*: Burseraceae) en Jalisco, México." Bachelor's thesis, Universidad de Guadalajara.

García Martínez, L. E. 2012. "Aspectos socio-ecológicos para el manejo sustentable del coal en el ejido de Acateyahualco, Gro." Bachelor's thesis, Universidad Nacional Autónoma de México, Morelia, Michoacán.

Gentry, H. S. 1942. *Rio Mayo Plants: A Study of the Flora and Vegetation of the Valley of the Rio Mayo, Sonora*. Washington, D.C.: Carnegie Institution.

Gigliarelli, G., J. X. Becerra, M. Curini, and M. C. Marcotullio. 2015. "Chemical Composition and Biological Activities of Fragrant Mexican Copal (*Bursera* spp.)." *Molecules* 20 (12): 22383–94.

Givinish, T. 1979. "On the Adaptive Significance of Leaf Form." In *Topics in Plant Population Biology*, edited by O. T. Solbrig, S. Jain, G. B. Johnson, and P. H. Raven, 375–407. New York: Columbia University Press.

Gorgua Jiménez, G., O. Nieto Yañez, P. A. Ruiz Hurtado, N. Rivera Yáñez, M. A. Rodríguez Monroy, and M. M. Canales Martínez. 2015. "*Bursera arida*: Evaluación de su actividad antiparasitaria y caracterización fitoquímica del extracto metanolico." In *11 Reunión Internacional de Investigación en Productos Naturales*, edited by A. Navarrete, 104–5. San Carlos, Sonora, Mexico: Revista Latinoamericana de Química.

Greenberg, R., M. S. Foster, and L. Márquez-Valdelamar. 1995. "The Role of the White-Eyed Vireo in the Dispersal of *Bursera* Fruit on the Yucatan Peninsula." *Journal of Tropical Ecology* 11 (4): 619–39.

Greenberg, R., D. K. Niven, S. Hopp, and C. Boone. 1993. "Frugivory and Coexistence in a Resident and a Migratory Vireo on the Yucatan Peninsula." *Condor* 95 (4): 990–99.

Guevara-Féfer, F. 2010. "Una nueva especie de *Bursera* (Burseraceae) endémica de la cuenca baja del río Balsas en los estados de Michoacán y Guerrero, México." *Acta Botánica Mexicana*, no. 92, 119–28.

Guevara-Féfer, F., and J. Rzedowski. 1980. "Notas sobre el género *Bursera* (Burseraceae) en Michoacán (México). I. Tres especies nuevas de los alrededores de la presa del Infienrnillo, con algunos datos relativos a la región." *Boletín de la Sociedad Botánica de México* 39:63–81.

Hernández-Apolinar, M., T. Valverde, and S. Purata. 2006. "Demography of *Bursera glabrifolia*, a Tropical Tree Used for Folk Woodcrafting in Southern Mexico: An Evaluation of Its Management Plan." *Forest Ecology and Management* 223 (1–3): 139–51.

Hernández de Toledo, F. 1615. *Quatro libros: De la naturaleza y virtudes de las plantas y animales.* n.p.: n.p.

Ionescu, F. 1974. "Phytochemical Investigation of *Bursera arida* Family Burseraceae." PhD diss., University of Arizona, Tucson.

Ionescu, F., S. D. Jolad, J. R. Cole, S. K. Arora, and B. Bates. 1977. "The Structure of Benulin, a New Pentacyclic Triterpene Hemiketal Isolated from *Bursera arida* (Burseraceae)." *Journal of Organic Chemistry* 42 (9): 1627–29.

Jiménez Ramírez, J., and R. Cruz Durán. 2001. "Una especie nueva de *Bursera* (Burseraceae) del estado de Guerrero, México." *Acta Botánica Mexicana*, no. 55, 7–12.

Johnson, M. B. 1992. "The Genus *Bursera* (Burseraceae) in Sonora, Mexico and Arizona, USA." *Desert Plants* 10 (3): 126–43.

Johnson, R. A., M. F. Willson, J. N. Thompson, and R. I. Berin. 1985. "Nutritional Values of Wild Fruits and Consumption by Migrant Frugivorous Birds." *Ecology* 66 (3): 819–27.

Junor, G.-A. O., R. B. R. Porter, T. H. Yee, and L. A. D. Williams. 2008. "Chemical Composition and Insecticidal Activity of the Essential Oils from *Bursera hollickii* (Britton) Found in Jamaica." *Journal of Essential Oil Research* 20 (6): 550–65.

Junor, G.-A. O., R. B. R. Porter, T. H. Yee, and T. Waugh. 2010. "The Volatile Constituents from the Leaves, Bark and Fruits of *Bursera aromatica* (Proctor) Found in Jamaica." *Journal of Essential Oil Research* 22 (1): 19–22.

Kuijt, J. 2009. "Monograph of *Psittacanthus* (Loranthaceae)." *Systematic Botany Monographs* 86:1–361.

León de la Luz, J. L., A. Medel Narváes, and R. Domínguez Cadena. 2017. "A New Species of *Bursera* (Burseraceae) from the East Cape Region in Baja California Sur, Mexico." *Acta Botánica Mexicana*, no. 118, 97–103.

León de la Luz, J. L., and J. J. Pérez-Navarro. 2010. "Dos nuevos taxa de *Bursera* (Burseraceae) de Baja California Sur, México." *Acta Botánica Mexicana*, no. 91, 37–49.

Lona, N. V. 2012. "Objects Made of Copal Resin: A Radiological Analysis." *Boletín de la Sociedad Geológica Mexicana* 64 (2): 207–13.

López-Villalobos, A., A. Flores-Palacios, and R. Ortiz-Pulido. 2008. "The Relationship between Bark Peeling Rate and the Distribution and Mortality of Two Epiphyte Species." *Plant Ecology* 198:265–74.

Marcotullio, M. C., M. Curini, and J. X. Becerra. 2018. "An Ethnopharmacological, Phytochemical and Pharmacological Review on Lignans from Mexican *Bursera* spp." *Molecules* 23 (8): 1976.

Martínez-Habibe, M. C. 2012. "Systematics, Biogeography and Leaf Anatomy and Architecture of *Bursera* subgen. *Bursera* (Burseraceae) in the Greater Antilles and the Bahamas." PhD diss., Claremont Graduate University.

Martínez-Habibe, M. C., and D. C. Daly. 2016. "A Taxonomic Revision of *Bursera* subgen. *Bursera* in the Greater Antilles and the Bahamas, Including a New Species from Cuba." *Brittonia* 68:455–71.

McVaugh, R., and J. Rzedowski. 1965. "Synopsis of the Genus *Bursera* L. in Western Mexico, with Notes on the Material of *Bursera* Collected by Sessé & Mociño." *Kew Bulletin* 18 (2): 317–82.

Medina Lemos, R. 2013. "Una nueva especie de *Bursera* (Burseraceae) del Sur de México." *Acta Botánica Mexicana*, no. 103, 19–25.

Meurgey, F. 2016. "Bee Species and Their Associated Flowers in the French West Indies (Guadeloupe, Les Saintes, La Désirade, Marie Galante, St Barthelemy and Martinique) (Hymenoptera: Anthophila: Apoidea)." *Annales de la Société entomologique de France (N.S.)* 52 (4): 209–32.

Monardes, N. B. 1565. *Historia medicinal de las cosas que se traen de nuestras Indias Occidentales.* Seville: n.p.

Montano-Arias, G. 2004. "Morfología y anatomía del fruto de dos especies del género *Bursera* Jacq. ex L. Sección *Bullockia*." Bachelor's thesis, Universidad Nacional Autónoma de México, Mexico City.

Nakanishi, T., Y. Inatomi, H. Murata, K. Shigeta, N. Iida, A. Inada, J. Murata, M. A. P. Farrera, M. Iinuma, T. Tanaka, S. Tajima, and N. Oku. 2005. "A New and Known Cytotoxic Aryltetralin-Type Lignans from Stems of *Bursera graveolens*." *Chemical and Pharmaceutical Bulletin* 53 (2): 229–31.

Nilsen, E. T., M. R. Sharifi, P. W. Rundel, I. N. Forseth, and J. R. Ehleringer. 1990. "Water Relations of Stem Succulent Trees in North-Central Baja California." *Oecologia* 82 (3): 299–303.

Noge, K., and J. X. Becerra. 2010. "(*R*)-(–)-Linalyl Acetate and (*S*)-(–)-Germacrene D from the Leaves of Mexican *Bursera linanoe*." *Natural Product Communications* 5 (3).

Okeowo, A. 2017. "A Mexican Town Wages Its Own War on Drugs." *New Yorker*, November 27.

Olavarrieta Marenco, M. 1977. *Magia en los Tuxtlas.* Mexico City: Instituto Nacional Indigenista.

Ornelas, J. F. 2019. "Los muérdagos *Psittacanthus* en México: Ecología, evolución, manejo y consevación." *Biodiversitas* 146:12–16.

Ortiz-Rodríguez, E., E. Y. Guerrero, and J. F. Ornelas. 2018. "Phylogenetic Position of Neotropical *Bursera*-Specialist Mistletoes: The Evolution of Deciduousness and Succulent Leaves in *Psittacanthus* (Lorantaceae)." *Botanical Sciences* 96 (3): 443–61.

Pérez Navarro, J. J. 2001. "El género *Bursera* Jacq. ex L. (Burseraceae) en la península de Baja California." Master's thesis, Centro de Investigaciones Biológicas del Noroeste, S.C., La Paz, Mexico.

Peraza-Sánchez, S. R., and L. M. Peña-Rodríguez. 1992. "Isolation of Picropoligamain from the Resin of *Bursera simaruba*." *Journal of Natural Products* 55 (12): 1768–71.

Porter, D. M., and A. Pool. 2001. "Burseraceae." In *Flora de Nicaragua: Introducción Gimnospermas y Angiospermas ("Acanthaceae-Euphorbiaceae")*, edited by W. D. Stevens, C. Ulloa

Ulloa, A. Pool, and O. M. Montiel, 500–507. Monographs in Systematic Botany from the Missouri Botanical Garden 85. St. Louis: Missouri Botanical Garden Press.

Purata Velarde, S. E. 2008. "Algunos usos del copal." In *Uso y manejo de copales arómaticos*, edited by S. E. Purata Velarde, 14–16. Mexico City: Comisión Nacional para el Conocimiento y Uso de la Biodiversidad.

Ramos-Ordoñez, M. F. 2009. "Dispersión biótica de semillas y caracterización de frutos de *Bursera morelensis* en el Valle de Tehuacán, Puebla." PhD diss., Universidad Nacional Autónoma de México, Mexico City.

Ramos-Ordoñez, M. F., J. Márquez-Guzmán, and M. C. Arizmendi. 2012. "The Fruit of *Bursera*: Structure, Maturation and Parthenocarpy." *AoB PLANTS* 2012: pls027.

Rivas-Arancibia, S. P., E. Bello-Cervantes, H. Carrillo-Ruiz, A. R. Andrés-Hernández, D. M. Figueroa-Castro, and S. Guzmán-Jiménez. 2015. "Variaciones de la comunidad de visitadores florales de *Bursera copallifera* (Burseraceae) a lo largo de un gradiente de perturbación antropogénica." *Revista Mexicana de Biodiversidad* 86 (1): 178–87.

Rodríguez-Godínez, R., L. Sánchez-González, M. C. Arizmendi, and R. C. Almazán-Núñez. 2022. "*Bursera* Fruit Traits as Drivers of Fruit Removal by Flycatchers." *Acta Oecologica* 114 (May): 103811.

Rose, J. N. 1906. *Studies of Mexican and Central American Plants No. 5*. Contributions from the United States National Herbarium. Washington, D.C.: Government Printing Office.

Rose, J. N. 1911. "Burseraceae." *North American Flora* 25 (3): 241–61.

Rosell, J. A., and D. M. Olson. 2014. "The Evolution of Bark Mechanics and Storage Across Habitats in a Clade of Tropical Trees." *American Journal of Botany* 101 (5): 764–77.

Rosell, J. A., M. E. Olson, A. Weeks, J. A. De-Nova, R. Medina Lemos, J. Pérez-Camacho, T. P. Feria, R. Gómez-Bermejo, J. C. Montero, and L. E. Eguiarte. 2010. "Diversification in Species Complexes: Tests of Species Origin and Delimitation in the *Bursera simaruba* Clade of Tropical Trees (Burseraceae)." *Molecular Phylogenetics and Evolution* 57 (2): 798–811.

Rzedowski, J. 1968. "Notas sobre el genero *Bursera* (Burseraceae) en el Estado de Guerrero (Mexico)." *Anales de la Escuela Nacional de Ciencias Biológicas, México* 17:17–36.

Rzedowski, J. 1978. *Vegetación de México*. Mexico City: Limusa.

Rzedowski, J., and G. Calderón de Rzedowski. 1996. "Nota sobre *Bursera Cinerea* Engl. (Burseraceae) en el estado de Veracruz." *Acta Botánica Mexicana*, no. 37, 33–38.

Rzedowski, J., and G. Calderón de Rzedowski. 2000a. "Tres nuevas especies de *Bursera* (Burseraceae) de la región costera del occidente de México." *Acta Botánica Mexicana*, no. 50, 47–59.

Rzedowski, J., and G. Calderón de Rzedowski. 2000b. "Una especie nueva de *Bursera* (Burseraceae del estado de Oaxaca, México)." *Acta Botánica Mexicana*, no. 52, 75–81.

Rzedowski, J., and G. Calderón de Rzedowski. 2002. "Dos especies nuevas de *Bursera* (Burseraceae) del estado de Oaxaca (México)." *Acta Botánica Mexicana*, no. 59, 81–90.

Rzedowski, J., and G. Calderón de Rzedowski. 2008. "Dos especies nuevas de *Bursera* (Burseraceae) de los estados de Guerrero, Michoacán, and Oaxaca (México)." *Acta Botánica Mexicana*, no. 82, 75–85.

Rzedowski, J., and G. Calderón de Rzedowski. 2009. "Nota sobre *Bursera heteresthes* (Burseraceae)." *Acta Botánica Mexicana*, no. 88, 81–93.

Rzedowski, J., and F. Guevara-Féfer 1992. *Familia Burseraceae*. Vol. 3 of *Flora del Bajío y de regiones adyacentes*. Pátzcuaro, Michoacán, Mexico: Instituto de Ecología.

Rzedowski, J., and R. Medina Lemos. 2021. "Clave para la identificación de las especies de *Bursera* Jacq. ex L. (Burseraceae) del Estado de Oaxaca (México)." *PALIBOTANICA*, no. 52, 11–23.

Rzedowski, J., R. Medina Lemos, and G. Calderón de Rzedowski. 2004. "Las especies de *Bursera* (Burseraceae) en la cuenca superior del Río Papaloapan (México)." *Acta Botánica Mexicana*, no. 66, 23–151.

Rzedowski, J., R. Medina Lemos, and G. Calderón de Rzedowski. 2005. "Inventario del conocimiento taxonómico, así como de la diversidad y del endemismo regionales de las especies mexicanas de *Bursera* (Burseraceae)." *Acta Botánica Mexicana*, no. 70, 85–111.

Rzedowski, J., R. Medina Lemos, and G. Calderón de Rzedowski. 2007. "Segunda restauración de *Bursera ovalifolia* y nombre nuevo para otro componente del complejo de *B. simaruba* (Burseraceae)." *Acta Botánica Mexicana*, no. 81, 45–70.

Rzedowski, J., and R. Medina Lemos. 2018. "*Bursera zapoteca* (Burseraceae), New Arboreous Species from the Southeast of Oaxaca, Mexico." *Polibotánica*, no. 45, 1–6.

Rzedowski, J., and E. Ortiz. 1988. "Estudios quimiotaxonomicos de *Bursera* (Burseraceae). II. Una especie nueva de origen híbrido de la Barranca de Tolantongo, estado de Hidalgo." *Acta Botánica Mexicana*, no. 1, 11–19.

Sahagún, B. de. 1577. *Historia general de las cosas de Nueva España: The Florentine Codex.* n.p.: n.p.

Sandoval Ortega, H., I. Martínez, and M. Arellano-Delgado. 2022. "Flower-Visiting Hummingbirds and Avian Fruit Consumers in Two *Psittacanthus* Species from Aguascalientes, Mexico." *Árido-Ciencia* 7 (1): 7–13.

Scott, P. E., and R. F. Martin. 1984. "Avian Consumers of *Bursera*, *Ficus*, and *Ehretia* Fruit in Yucatan." *Biotropica* 16 (4): 319–23.

Smith-Pardo, A. 2005. "The Bees of the Genus *Neocorynura* of Mexico (Hymenoptera: Halictidae: Augochlorini)." *Folia Entomológica Mexicana* 44 (2): 165–93.

Stevens, G. C. 1983. "*Bursera simaruba* (Indio Desnudo, Jinocuave, Gumbo Limbo)." In *Costa Rican Natural History*, edited by D. H. Janzen, 201–2. Chicago: University of Chicago Press.

Stevenson, P. R., A. Link, and B. H. Ramírez. 2005. "Frugivory and Seed Fate in *Bursera inversa* (Burseraceae) at Tinigua Park, Colombia: Implications for Primate Conservation." *Biotropica* 37 (3): 431–38.

Toledo, C. A. 1982. "El género *Bursera* en el estado de Guerrero." PhD diss., Universidad Nacional Autónoma de México, Mexico City.

Toledo, C. A. 1984. "Contribuciones a la flora de Guerrero: Tres especies nuevas del genero *Bursera* (Burseraceae)." *Biótica* 9 (4): 441–49.

Trainer, J. M., and T. C. Will. 1984. "Avian Methods of Feeding on *Bursera simaruba* (Burseraceae) Fruits in Panama." *The Auk* 101 (1): 193–95.

Tripplett, K. J. 1999. "The Ethnobotany of Plant Resins in the Maya Cultural Region of Southern Mexico and Central America." PhD diss., University of Texas at Austin.

Unitt, P. 2000. "Gray Vireos Wintering in California Elephant Trees." *Western Birds* 31:258–62.

Van Devender, T. R. 2002. "Environmental History of the Sonoran Desert." In *Columnar Cacti and Their Mutualists: Evolution, Ecology and Conservation*, edited by T. Fleming and A. Valiente-Banuet, 3–24. Tucson: University of Arizona Press.

Velázquez-Herrera, J. 2011. "Biología reproductiva de dos especies del género *Bursera*." PhD diss., Universidad Nacional Autónoma de México, Mexico City.

Vergara-Torres, C. A., M. C. Pacheco-Álvarez, and A. Flores-Palacios. 2010. "Host Preference and Host Limitation of Vascular Epiphytes in a Tropical Dry Forest of Central Mexico." *Journal of Tropical Ecology* 26 (6): 563–70.

Vidal-Gutiérrez, M., R. E. Robles-Zepeda, W. Vilegas, G. A. Gonzalez-Aguilar, H. Torres-Moreno, and J. C. López-Moreno. 2020. "Phenolic Composition and Antioxidant Activity of *Bursera microphylla* A. Gray." *Industrial Crops and Products* 152 (September): 112412.

Wang, H. C., M. J. Moore, P. S. Soltis, C. D. Bell, S. F. Brockington, R. Alexandre, C. C. Davis, M. Latvis, S. R. Manchester, and D. E. Soltis. 2009. "Rosid Radiation and the Rapid Rise of Angiosperm-Dominated Forests." *Proceedings of the National Academy of Sciences* 106 (10): 3853–58.

INDEX

Please note: Page number in bold type indicates location in photograph caption. In the species list, the final page number usually refers to the location of the individual species description. Geographical locations outside Mexico included in plant descriptions have an entry in the index. Otherwise, the descriptions stand alone.

ABOUT THE AUTHORS

Judith Becerra is an associate professor in evolutionary ecology and entomology at the University of Arizona. Her research interests include the evolution of the genus *Bursera* and its interaction with herbivores, with special interest in the chemical adaptation of plants and the behavioral counteradaptations of insects. She has published more than thirty articles on the phylogeny, ecology, chemistry, and ethnobotany of *Bursera* in scientific journals that include *Science* and PNAS.

David Yetman is a distinguished outreach faculty and research social scientist at the Southwest Center of the University of Arizona, where he has worked since 1992, specializing in peoples and ecology of northwest Mexico and the southwestern United States. Yetman has a PhD in philosophy from the University of Arizona and is the author of numerous books and articles, including *Sonora, an Intimate Geography* (University of New Mexico Press), *Colonial Conflict: Indians, Priests and Settlers in Colonial Sonora* (University of New Mexico Press), *The Great Cacti: Ethnobotany and Biogeography of Columnar Cacti* (University of Arizona Press), *Natural Landmarks of Arizona* (University of Arizona Press), and *The Saguaro Cactus: A Natural History* (University of Arizona Press), of which he is the first author. Yetman was host for ten years of the PBS series *The Desert Speaks* and now is host and co-producer of the PBS travel/adventure series *In the Americas with David Yetman*. He is a frequent lecturer on the history and ecology of northwest Mexico.